PRAISE

'Few people can have thought as deeply on Wittgenstein's reflections on 'other minds' and on understanding people as Constantine Sandis. His essays exhibit wide knowledge of the confusions of philosophers, psychologists and cognitive neuroscientists, as well as exemplary sensitivity to the complexity, cultural relativity and context dependence of human relations.'

—*Peter Hacker, St. John's College, Oxford*

'A rich and readable collection of essays that is concerned not with the traditional problem of other minds, but with the ordinary obstacles to understanding others, and how we should understand the failures to connect which characterise the human condition. Although Wittgenstein is the dominant influence in the essays, Sandis also draws on a wide range of Wittgenstein interpreters, philosophical, literary and historical sources, which he uses in developing his own distinctive view of what is involved in understanding, and failing to understand, others.'

—*Marie McGinn, Professor Emerita, University of York*

'Among the many eminent commentators that have shed light on Wittgenstein's thought, Constantine Sandis stands out by dint of the extraordinary range of his interests and his ability to think and write "outside the box". The title of this collection nicely captures both this open-mindedness and a unifying theme – namely the challenges involved in trying to understand subjects which are or at least seem to be remote from our own parochial perspective. These subjects range from human individuals and communities through non-human animals – Wittgenstein's famous "speaking lion" – to works of art and artificial systems. In all of these cases, Sandis sheds invaluable light, in a prose that is both lucid and precise, and often displays a puckish sense of humour. Essential reading for anyone interested in the importance of Wittgenstein's work in contemporary hermeneutic themes.'

—*Professor Hans-Johann Glock, Department of Philosophy, University of Zurich*

'With an impressive command of the literature on understanding others, Sandis explores the later Wittgenstein's enigmatic remarks, providing a multi-layered context in which to appreciate them. From a lion who can talk, to conversations with machines, to the songs of Bob Dylan, this revised compilation of Sandis's essays presents an excellent contribution to Wittgenstein Studies.'

—*Julia Tanney, Independent Researcher*

'In this collection of essays, Constantine Sandis reminds us that there is a lot more to the philosophical issue of other minds than the sceptical question of their existence. He expertly explores some of Wittgenstein's fascinating remarks on the difficulties of understanding other people. The essays are lucidly written, well-informed and insightful.'

—*Severin Schroeder, the University of Reading, UK*

'Constantine Sandis is a leading expert on the philosophy of Wittgenstein and also a serious and original philosopher in his own right. These engaging and persuasive essays address the question of how we can understand those alien to us, be they humans, animals or artworks. An invaluable contribution in an age of conflict and dissent.'

—*Edward Kanterian, Emeritus Reader in Philosophy, University of Kent, UK*

'Constantine Sandis's remarkable new book offers a fascinating journey, and a true testament to the transformational power of Wittgenstein's philosophy. Sophisticated yet accessible, these seductively curious essays scrutinise Wittgenstein's views on the so-called problem of other minds. It is a truly important book we can all learn from.'

—*Lambros Malafouris, the University of Oxford, UK*

'In this enthralling collection of essays, Constantine Sandis presents us with a highly original, multifaceted discussion of Wittgenstein's approach to understanding others. By subtly departing from mainstream themes, Sandis succeeds in illuminating a most urgent, personal and philosophical Wittgensteinian concern: what it is to understand (rather than know) one another.'

—*Chon Tejedor, Profesora de Filosofía, Universitat de València, Spain*

'This volume by Constantine Sandis is, on the one hand, accessible and funny, with frequent pop-cultural and historical references, and humorous, reflective storytelling. On the other hand, it provides much-needed critical engagement with dominant understandings of some of the later Wittgenstein's key contributions, and with the misunderstandings about what it means to know other minds that permeate popular and philosophical thought.'

—*Ruby Main, Durham University, Durham, UK*

Wittgenstein on Other Minds

ANTHEM STUDIES IN WITTGENSTEIN

Anthem Studies in Wittgenstein publishes new and classic works on Wittgenstein and Wittgensteinian philosophy. This book series aims to bring Wittgenstein's thought into the mainstream by highlighting its relevance to 21st century concerns. Titles include original monographs, themed edited volumes, forgotten classics, biographical works and books intended to introduce Wittgenstein to the general public. The series is published in association with the British Wittgenstein Society.

Anthem Studies in Wittgenstein sets out to put in place whatever measures may emerge as necessary in order to carry out the editorial selection process purely on merit and to counter bias on the basis of gender, race, ethnicity, religion, sexual "orientation and other characteristics protected by law. These measures include subscribing to the British Philosophical Association/ Society for Women in Philosophy (UK) Good Practice Scheme.

Series Editor

Constantine Sandis – Lex Academic and University of Hertfordshire, UK

Forthcoming Titles in the Series

Sense and Value in Wittgenstein's Tractatus

Iron Pyrite - Reflections on Kripkean Themes

Nightmariners And Wideawakes - The Philosophy Of Dreams

The Existential Dimension of Doubt - Sceptical Themes in Kierkegaard, Wittgenstein and Cavell

Freud's Paradoxical Achievement - A Wittgensteinian Perspective

Wittgenstein on Other Minds: Strangers in a Strange Land

Constantine Sandis

ANTHEM PRESS

Anthem Press
An imprint of Wimbledon Publishing Company
www.anthempress.com

This edition first published in UK and USA 2026
by ANTHEM PRESS
75–76 Blackfriars Road, London SE1 8HA, UK
or PO Box 9779, London SW19 7ZG, UK
and
244 Madison Ave #116, New York, NY 10016, USA

First published in the UK and USA by Anthem Press in 2025

British Library Cataloguing-in-Publication Data
A catalogue record for this book is available from the British Library.

Library of Congress Control Number: 2026942494

ISBN-13: 978-1-80136-053-1 (Pbk)
ISBN-10: 1-80136-053-7 (Pbk)

Cover credit: Wittgenstein, Acrylic on Canvas,
Louise Rebecca Chapman (2017)

This title is also available as an eBook.

For Peter Hacker
(who first introduced me to Wittgenstein)
and for Danièle Moyal-Sharrock
(for welcoming this prodigal son back to the fold).

CONTENTS

PREFACE

As a prospective undergraduate, I had wanted to apply for Oxford's now defunct Psychology, Philosophy, and Physiology (PPP) degree, but lacking the maths A Level required for the statistics component, I came to St Anne's College to read Philosophy and Theology instead (apparently no maths is required to contemplate the infinite). In late 1996, I began my final year somewhat disillusioned with the direction that contemporary analytic philosophy had taken, never mind analytic theology. My wonderful tutor, Alison Denham, sent me to Peter Hacker at St John's College for the Philosophy of Mind paper, with the words 'he won't be as forgiving as me if you write a poor essay'. Peter's weekly tutorials introduced me to the philosophy of Wittgenstein, as well as that of G. E. M. Anscombe, Norman Malcolm, Gilbert Ryle, P. F. Strawson, G. H. von Wright, Alan R. White and many other greats of that bygone era.

At the end of the eight-week term, Peter generously asked whether instead of parting ways, I should like to return for four additional tutorials in the philosophy of action to supplement the topics we had covered in the philosophy of mind. Intrigued by the sound of a subject that seemed to resemble PPP in its interests and scope, I accepted and returned the following term to discuss such things as the nature of action, intention, reasons and causes, voluntariness, and the will. So not only did he introduce me to Wittgenstein, Peter also introduced me to the philosophy of action. For better or worse, he is the reason I did not give up philosophy.

The philosophy of action was to largely preoccupy me during my graduate studies at the University of Reading and subsequent decade lecturing at Oxford Brookes University. While Wittgenstein's later philosophy has deeply influenced me, I did not explicitly engage with his work during this period. By the time I left Brookes for the University of Hertfordshire, I had become interested in the fact that there is much more to understanding a person than knowing the reasons for which they acted. My philosophical interests accordingly shifted from classic issues in action explanation to the philosophy of understanding, particularly as it applies to sentient beings.

The essays in this volume draw on material previously published between 2012 and 2024. I spent the greater part of this period at the University of Hertfordshire, under whose auspices I wrote most of the work that comprises this book. But institutions largely stand or fall with the people who comprise them, and I owe particular thanks to my friend, colleague and collaborator Danièle Moyal-Sharrock, as well as to the *British Wittgenstein Society*, which she founded in 2008 and first joined there as Treasurer and then as Secretary. This book is dedicated to both Peter and Danièle, whose friendship and Wittgenstein scholarship continue to sustain me intellectually.

CS
Maidenhead, September 2024

ACKNOWLEDGMENTS

I'm incredibly chuffed that the cover of this book features Louise Chapman's amazing artwork, as photographed by Glenn Chapman. When Glenn was photographing it, a fly came in through the window and landed on the top right corner of the canvas. I asked Anthem Press if they could use one of the shots in which it appears, explaining that Wittgenstein described his way of doing philosophy as showing the fly the way out of the fly bottle. To my pleasant surprise, they agreed, despite the fact that I had failed to get the fly itself to sign a release form.

This book, and much more besides, would not have been possible without the editorial help and support of everyone at Lex Academic, who also prepared the index. Lex are my family and tribe and I thank them all for their high levels of conscientiousness. I should also like to thank Jebaslin Hephzibah, Gomathy Ilammathe, Tej Sood, and Mario Rosair at Anthem, as well as the wonderful editorial board of my *Anthem Studies in Wittgenstein* series.

There is not enough space to mention here the various conferences and other events at which earlier versions of the essays here were presented, nor to list every participant whose questions and comments contributed to the improvement of the material. I would be remiss, however, not to mention the help I have received with various parts of this book from Hanne Appelqvist, Maria Balaska, Katja Behrens, David Cockburn, Rémi Clot-Goudard, Giuseppina D'Oro, Max de Gaynesford, David Dolby, Richard Gipps, Hanjo Glock, Ian Ground, Peter Hacker, Garry Hagberg, Lars Hertzberg, Sandra Laugier, Andreas Lind, Andrew Lugg, Katherine Morris, Danièle Moyal-Sharrock, Luke Mulhall, Sami Philström, Catherine Rowett, Severin Schroeder, Ralf Stoecker, Yudai Suzuki, Roger Teichmann, Chon Tejedor, Sophia Vasalou, Robert Vinten, Leora Weitzman, and Istvan Zardai, as well as from all of the members of the Welsh Philosophical Society and the Oxford Wittgenstein Reading Group, whose regular meetings have been invaluable to me over the years. Special thanks is due to Richard Harper, for allowing me to include the conversation between us, which concludes the book.

All of the essays collected here have been completely revised and updated since their original publication, which I hereby acknowledge in chronological order, with kind thanks to the relevant publishers for any permissions due:

'Understanding the Lion For Real' in (eds.) A. Marques & N. Venturinha, *Knowledge, Language and Mind: Wittgenstein's Thought in Progress* (de Gruyter), 2012, 138-61.

'One Fell Swoop: Small Red Book Historicism Before and After Davidson', *Journal of the Philosophy of History* (9), 2015, 372-92.

"If Some People Looked Like Elephants and Others Like Cats": Wittgenstein on Understanding Others and Forms of Life', *Nordic Wittgenstein Review*, Vol. 4, 2015, 131-153.

'Period and Place: Collingwood and Wittgenstein on Understanding Others', *Collingwood and British Idealism Studies*, 22:1, 2016, 171-98

'If an Artwork Could Speak: Aesthetic Understanding After Wittgenstein', in (ed.) G. Hagberg, *Wittgenstein on Aesthetic* Understanding (Palgrave Macmillan), 2017, 355-382.

'Wittgenstein and Communication Technology - A conversation between Constantine Sandis and Richard Harper', *Philosophical Investigations*, 2018, 241-262.

'Making Ourselves Understood: Wittgenstein and Moral Epistemology', *Wittgenstein-Studien*, Vol. 10, No. 1, 2019, 241-259.

'Wo Are "We" for Wittgenstein?', in (ed. H. Appelqvist), *Wittgenstein and the Limits of Language* (Routledge), 2019, 172-196.

'Understanding Other Cultures (Without Mind-reading)', in (ed. C Tejedor), *Intercultural Understanding* (Anthem Press), 2023, 3-19.

'On Safari with Glock', in (eds.) C. Pfisterer, N. Rathgeb, & E. Schmidt, *Wittgenstein and Beyond: Essays in Honour of Hans-Johann Glock* (Routledge), 2024, 67-80.

ABBREVIATIONS OF WITTGENSTEIN'S WORKS

BEE	*Nachlass: The Bergen Electronic Edition*
BT	*Big Typescript:* TS 213
CV	*Culture and Value*
LW	*Last Writings on the Philosophy of Psychology*, vol. 1
MS	manuscript from BEE (identified by number)
NB	*Notebooks 1914–1916*
OC	*On Certainty*
PI	*Philosophical Investigations*
PPF	*Philosophy of Psychology: A Fragment* (in Hacker and Schulte revised 4th edition of PI)
RFGB	*Remarks on Frazer's Golden Bough*
ROC	*Remarks on Colour*
RPP II	*Remarks on the Philosophy of Psychology*, vol. 2
TLP	*Tractatus Logico-Philosophicus* (TLP-R indicates the revised translation)
TS	typescript from BEE (identified by number)
WC	*Wittgenstein in Cambridge: Letters and Documents 1911–1951* (edited by B. McGuinness)
Z	*Zettel*

INTRODUCTION: THE MENTAL LIVES OF OTHERS

This book is called *Wittgenstein on Other Minds*, but it could have also been called *Wittgenstein on Understanding* or perhaps *Wittgenstein on Understanding Others*. In philosophy, the so-called problem of other minds is often understood as a problem in epistemology about how we can know what anybody else is thinking or feeling, although as Anita Avramides states, 'there is little agreement either about the problem or the solution to it' (Avramides 2019, § 1).[1]

At its solipsistic extreme, the alleged problem is that of knowing that other minds exist at all. How can I know that other 'people' are not actually automata or even mere figments of my imagination, perhaps the work of some Cartesian demon who can deceive me about anything except for the fact that I, myself, exist? While the young Wittgenstein may have fallen prey to such doubt, in his later work, Wittgenstein showed all of these worries to be spurious, not because we can *know* that other minds exist but because it ordinarily makes no sense to doubt such things. 'Other people have minds' is neither true nor false but, rather, a rule of grammar or 'hinge' that enables us to make truth-apt statements about the mental lives of others, claims that need to proceed by way of interpretation.[2]

So, while there is no genuine philosophical problem of other minds, for the later Wittgenstein, this does not entail that there are no real-life difficulties in understanding others and, indeed, even ourselves (for self-understanding is not a matter of introspecting an inner theatre of the mind to which we have

1 See also the essays in Avramides and Parrott 2019.

2 Cf. Addis 1999; Avramides 2000, Chapter 8; Morrick 1967, Part II. The later Wittgenstein is arguably also interested in what Thomas Nagel refers to as the 'conceptual problem' of how to understand the attribution of psychological predicates to others (Nagel 1986, 19–20; cf. Avramides 2000, Part III), but this question is peripheral to the real-life difficulties of understanding others.

privileged access).[3] In his private life, Wittgenstein's pessimism regarding the possibility of understanding others was unmatched. This was not on the grounds of its being *in principle* impossible to understand anybody but because it is *in practice* very difficult to do so, arguably even in our own case. The difficulty is not an abstract metaphysical or even epistemological one but rather an everyday psychological and sociological one. This is what Marie McGinn refers to as 'the real problem of others' (McGinn 2022, 19–48). As McGinn puts it, 'Wittgenstein is deeply opposed to the idea that our everyday doubts about others amount to a way of "living scepticism" or reveal a truth in the sceptic's image of our metaphysical separation' (McGinn 2022, viii).[4]

The book's opening chapter, 'If Some People Looked Like Elephants and Others Like Cats', introduces this tension between the public Wittgenstein's optimism about knowledge of other minds and the private Wittgenstein's pessimism about understanding others. There are three related considerations that ultimately render the tension unproblematic. We have already seen that the barriers to other minds that Wittgenstein sought to expose as illusory were philosophical, whereas those he struggled to overcome in real life were personal. In addition, Wittgenstein's official view is chiefly about *knowledge*, while his unofficial one is about *understanding*. Last, Wittgenstein's official remarks on understanding themselves fall into two distinct categories that do not match the focus of his unofficial ones. One comprises those remarks in the *Investigations* that challenge the thought that understanding is an inner mental process. The other consists primarily of those passages in his later philosophy that are concerned with the difficulty of understanding others without immersing oneself in their form of life. In the unofficial counterparts to these remarks, Wittgenstein focuses on *individuals* rather than collectives. The official and the unofficial sets of remarks are united in assuming a distinction between understanding a *person* and understanding the meaning of their *words*. If to understand a language is to understand a *form* of life, then to understand a person is to understand a *whole* life (arguably including one's own).

In the second chapter, 'Making Ourselves Understood', I contrast Wittgenstein's approach to understanding others with various philosophical and scientific trends according to which this understanding is to be achieved through some kind of emotional tool, popularly believed to be empathy, which

3 For Wittgenstein's thoughts on the asymmetries between understanding others and self-understanding, see Avramides 2000, esp. 193, and McGinn 2022, 19 ff.

4 McGinn's discussion is equally informed by Merleau-Ponty's discussions of uncertainties that are rooted in the lived experience of our coexistence with others.

provides an access pass to otherwise hidden 'mental contents'. This trend is founded upon John Locke's assumption that understanding another is a matter of obtaining and decoding the thoughts that are hidden inside the minds of others. The contrasting Wittgensteinian insight I explore here goes against the popular grain of empathy as a form of informational 'mind-reading'. I argue that the Locke-inspired account of what it takes to understand others is radically distorted, and that we would do best to replace it with a stance that places priority on shared aspects of our lives. Only then can we even begin to tackle our moral, cultural, religious and sociopolitical differences.

But who are 'we', anyway? In the early Wittgenstein, it is the 'I' that is mysterious; in the later work, it is the 'we'. How ought we to understand Wittgenstein's frequent references to 'us'? Who are 'we' who practise philosophy, who could not understand a lion if it spoke and whose form of life finds expression in language? Chapter 3, 'Who Are "We" for Wittgenstein?', addresses such questions by examining Wittgenstein's later usages of 'we' and its cognates. As I read Wittgenstein, the term 'we' sometimes refers to the community of philosophers, while at other times it is intended to point to language users, to average people or to a specific cultural community. Such groups ought to be contrasted both with the collection of all humans in general and with the transcendental 'we' invoked by interpretations that read the later Wittgenstein as a linguistic idealist.

With this 'we' now in place, Chapter 4, 'Understanding the Lion For Real', asks how we can be confident that we have correctly understood someone – or that they, in turn, have understood us. Wittgenstein cryptically claimed that 'if a lion could speak, we could not understand him'. But what did Wittgenstein really mean by this? Rejecting a number of misinterpretations and objections along the way, I argue that the remark does not concern lions *per se* or even non-human animals in general but, rather, that it probes a limiting case that might shed some light on what it takes to understand another. 'Lion' is not Wittgenstein's shorthand for 'non-human animals' any more than 'we' is his shorthand for 'humans'. Chapter 5, 'On Safari with Glock', continues the theme of Chapter 4 but with a focus on the views of Hans-Johann Glock, from whom I have learnt much over the years, but from whom I also diverge on certain small but important points regarding the lion remark. In particular, I maintain that we would do best to conceive of Wittgenstein's lion as speaking in words, not roars or growls.

Chapter 6, 'Understanding Other Cultures (Without Mind-Reading)' deploys an analogy with historical understanding to argue that understanding contemporary cultures that may appear alien to us involves a form of *thinking with* that requires, not any agreement in opinion, but a sharing of parallel thought processes. This idea is explored in relation to recent attempts to make sense of the ghost narratives that emerged in the aftermath of the 2011 Tōhoku earthquake and tsunami. Building on the previous chapters while additionally drawing from Clifford Geertz, I conclude that understanding the thoughts of another culture is not a question of mind-reading but rather of conceptual immersion.

In Chapter 7, 'Period and Place', I compare Wittgenstein's thoughts on understanding radically different others with those developed by R. G. Collingwood during roughly the same time. Their approaches differ in focus along three *prima facie* significant axes: (i) period vs. place, (ii) individual vs. collective and (iii) re-enactment vs. forms of life. I demonstrate that these contrasts amount to little more than a divergence in emphasis and that we must view their approaches as complementary rather than opposed. This is not a simple case of reaching the same conclusions by different routes, let alone incompatible ones. Far from it; the two philosophers use similar methods and reason in similar ways when considering the relation of thought to action and that of both to explanation and understanding. This is particularly remarkable in light of the fact that the two thinkers are often thought to stand at opposite ends of the methodological spectrum with respect to the value of metaphysics.

Continuing with the historical theme, Chapter 8, 'One Fell Swoop', revisits some anti-causalist accounts of action explanation put forth in the late 1950s and early '60s in what Davidson (1976, 261) dismissively described as a 'neo-Wittgensteinian current of small red books'. Although chiefly remembered for subscribing to what has come to be called the 'logical connection' argument, the positions defended across these volumes are in fact as diverse as they are subtle, loosely united by an anti-scientistic spirit that may reasonably be described as historicist. Davidson's attack was motivated by an important explanatory insight borrowed from Hempel but it caused serious damage to the philosophy of action by effectively bulldozing over a number of subtle distinctions. In seeking to revive these, I propose an approach that rescues the anti-causalist baby from the historicist bathwater. This chapter also serves as a link between this book and my work on action explanation (see Sandis 2012a and 2024).

The book's penultimate chapter, 'If an Artwork Could Speak', asks what it is to understand a work of art. According to Rush Rhees, this boils down to understanding the ideas that it contains. I argue against such cognitive approaches, which risk transforming all art (and downgrading some of it) into conceptual art. Aesthetic cognitivism systematically neglects crucial aspects of aesthetic experience and *pari passu* distorts various art forms, such as jazz and rock n' roll improv. The argument here builds on Chapter 2's criticism of Lockean notions of understanding as a matter of accessing the 'mental contents' of others. Like Mary, who (in Frank Jackson's (1982, 130) famous thought experiment) is in possession of all of the physical facts about colour but has never perceived it, one can be told all there is to know about a particular musical performance and still not get it. But this is not because understanding an artwork is a matter of attuning oneself to some ineffable phenomenological experience. Indeed, direct experience of art may leave one none the wiser, more akin to Mr Jones in Bob Dylan's 'Ballad of a Thin Man' than to Mary when she is released from her black and white room.

The tenth and final chapter, 'Wittgenstein and Communication Technology', documents a conversation I had with Richard Harper under the auspices of the British Wittgenstein Society's 10th anniversary conference in 2017. I am very much the interviewer and Richard the interviewee. But I wanted to include it in this volume, because Richard and I have been thinking and working together for over a decade, and this conversation captures the common spirit in which we approach questions of human–computer interaction and what, if anything, it might mean to understand artificial intelligence (AI) and be understood by it in turn. We discuss not only how communication technology can enable us to understand one another but also how the uses we put it to can (intentionally or otherwise) impede understanding. The first chapter in this book began with an exploration of Wittgenstein's struggles to communicate his thoughts and feelings via postal mail and even telephone. It is perhaps fitting that the volume should conclude with a Wittgenstein-inspired discussion of AI-mediated communication.

As is to be expected in a book of collected essays, there is some repetition and overlap among the chapters that constitute it. While this has been reduced as much as possible, each chapter has been designed to be read in its own right, without the reader needing to flick back and forth each time a cross-reference appears.

Chapter 1

'IF SOME PEOPLE LOOKED LIKE ELEPHANTS AND OTHERS LIKE CATS': WITTGENSTEIN ON UNDERSTANDING OTHERS AND FORMS OF LIFE

> The older I get the more I realize how terribly difficult it is for people to understand each other, and I think that what misleads one is the fact that they all look so much like each other. If some people looked like elephants and others like cats, or fish, one wouldn't *expect* them to understand each other and things would look much more like what they really are.
>
> Wittgenstein, Letter to P. Sraffa, 23 August 1949

> Here is a tin of ground white pepper and with no such thing as a pepper mill in the house I wonder how we could ever have hoped to understand one another when we even use different kinds of pepper.
>
> Alan Bennett, 'Cocktail Sticks', 80

Prologue

Interpreters of different spots and stripes all agree that the later Wittgenstein is an enemy of the idea that the thoughts and feelings of other people – and by extension of animals – are hidden from us in any sense that might raise a serious philosophical problem of other minds. Whatever the precise details of his view, it seems clear that Wittgenstein doesn't think that there is any general epistemic worry to be had about others:

> If we are using the word 'to know' as it is normally used (and how else are we to use it?), then other people very often know when I am in pain. (PI, § 246)

On this view, there is no metaphysical barrier to knowledge of others, the overcoming of which would require some kind of argument from analogy à la Russell (PI, § 420 ff. – which forms a bridge to the remarks on seeing-as in PPF, xi). In the *Philosophical Investigations*, this stance is primarily expressed in relation to knowledge of sensations, inner speech, beliefs and intentions. Following Norman Malcolm (1986), we may see it as part of a much wider attack on the traditional philosophical assumption that all sorts of interesting things are systematically hidden from us (i.e. necessarily 'private'), be they the essences of things, the functions of words or the minds of people (PI, §§ 92, 133, 155, 293, 301, 307, 323–4, 435, 559).

It would be natural therefore to expect Wittgenstein's remarks on *understanding* to follow the same general train of thought as those on *knowledge*, not least because the verbs 'to know' and 'to understand' may be used interchangeably in various contexts.[1] Such expectations are met to the extent that Wittgenstein sees no metaphysical obstacle to everyday cases of understanding other people. Nonetheless, his writings create two distinct moments for pause here.

First, we have the famous pair of passages – and their various cousins across the *Nachlass* – in which Wittgenstein speaks of the tribe with which we *cannot* find our feet and the lion whom we *could not* understand even if it spoke English (PPF, § 327). Second, there is an extensive range of biographical material demonstrating that in his personal life, Wittgenstein not only found it almost impossible either to understand *many* other people or to be understood by them but also maintained that this is typical of the human condition. I shall refer to the first idea as his *official view* and the second as the *unofficial* one, in which I include remarks from *Culture and Value* as these 'do not belong directly with his philosophical texts' (von Wright, preface to CV). In the case of the latter, I give particular focus to two letters from Wittgenstein to his friend (the Italian economist) Piero Sraffa as a case study of a wider phenomenon in his life.

I aim to show that although Wittgenstein is indeed marking some valuable distinctions between knowledge and understanding that analytic philosophers have neglected at their peril, we should favour interpretations of his *official* view according to which our understanding of others is as commonplace as our knowledge of their thoughts and feelings. While this is in some *prima facie* tension with his *unofficial* view, it is ultimately not only compatible with it but also a significant supplement to it. Or so I shall be arguing by suggesting that his official remarks on the role played by forms of life in our understanding of certain *groups* of people are mirrored by a concern with the relation of entire lives to our understanding of specific *individuals*.

1 For different uses of the word 'understanding' and their relation to both knowledge and explanation, see Hertzberg 2005.

The Official View: Lions and Tribes

The later Wittgenstein's official remarks on understanding largely occur in four contexts: (a) PI, §§ 138–182; (b) PPF, §§ 326 ff.; (c) LW, §§ 190–8; and (d) remarks in *On Certainty* about what to make of certain peculiar – often philosophical – utterances (§§ 32, 157, 526, 563).[2] The stance found across these occasions is sufficiently unified to render switching back and forth between them seamless. It is nonetheless worth considering the first set of these remarks in relative isolation, as their primary focus is not on understanding others but on the relation of meaning to use. Wittgenstein is here combatting the view that understanding the meaning of a word is an inner mental process of some kind. Here is a typical passage:

> What really comes before our mind when we *understand* a word? Isn't it something like a picture? Can't it *be* a picture? Well, suppose that a picture does come before your mind when you hear the word 'cube', say the drawing of a cube. In what way can this picture fit or fail to fit a use of the word 'cube'? Perhaps you say: 'It's quite simple; if that picture occurs to me and I point to a triangular prism for instance, and say it is a cube, then this use of the word doesn't fit the picture'. But doesn't it fit? I have purposely so chosen the example that it is quite easy to imagine *a method of projection* according to which the picture does fit after all. The picture of the cube did indeed *suggest* a certain use to us, but it was also possible for me to use it differently. (PI, § 139, emphasis in the original)

These thoughts slowly morph into his discussion of rule-following (§§ 140 ff.), the connecting thread being that the ability to follow a rule is an ability to *understand* or *grasp* how one is meant to carry on. I do not propose to defend a particular exegetical account here but merely to note the obvious connection between understanding a rule and knowing how to go on:

> Suppose I now ask: 'Has he understood the system if he continues the series to the hundredth place?' [...] Perhaps you will say here: I have got the system (or again, to understand it) can't consist in continuing the series up to *this* or *that* number: *that* is only applying one's understanding. Understanding itself is a state which is the *source* of the correct use. [...] 'When *I* say I understand the rule of a series, I'm surely not saying

2 *On Certainty* also continues, in the context of giving grounds and persuading, the theme of understanding other cultures, which Wittgenstein first explored in his *Remarks on Frazer's Golden Bough* (e.g. OC, § 609–12). Danièle Moyal-Sharrock (2004, 136) helpfully distinguishes here between 'localized' forms of life and the single 'human' form of life.

> so on the basis of the *experience* of having applied the algebraic formula in such-and-such a way! In my own case at any rate, I surely know that I mean such-and-such a series, no matter how far I've actually developed it.' [...] So you mean that you know the application of the rule of the series quite apart from remembering actual applications to particular numbers. And you'll perhaps say: 'Of course! For the series is infinite, and the bit of it that I could develop finite.' [...] But what does this knowledge consist in? Let me ask: *When* do you know that application? Always? Day and night? Or only while you are actually thinking of the rule of the series? Do you know it, that is, in the same way as you know the alphabet and the multiplication table? Or is what you call 'knowledge' a state of consciousness or a process say a thinking-of-something, or the like? (PI, §§ 146–8, emphasis in the original)

Wittgenstein's reservations about the kind of knowledge that his imagined interlocutor has in mind do not preclude him from identifying the understanding of rules with a form of knowledge, namely that which Ryle baptized as 'know-how'.[3] But we should not conclude from this that Wittgenstein takes the words 'knowledge' and 'understanding' to be interchangeable. Far from it:

> The criteria which we accept for 'fitting', 'being able to', 'understanding', are much more complicated than might appear at first sight. That is, the game with these words, their use in the linguistic intercourse that is carried on by their means, is more involved; the role of these words in our language is other than we are tempted to think. (PI, § 182)

Before returning to the distinction between knowledge and understanding, I wish to first look first at Wittgenstein's more private remarks on understanding certain people and then explore how these relate to his official remarks on the role played by forms of life in understanding collectives.

The Unofficial View: Endless Misunderstandings

What we might reasonably refer to as Wittgenstein's pessimism regarding the possibility of understanding others manifests itself in his private correspondence, culminating in the second of two consecutive letters that he writes to

3 I remain neutral here on whether knowledge-how (or, indeed, understanding-how) is, in actual fact, always reducible to knowledge-that (or understanding-that). What interests me is Wittgenstein's own conception of the relation between different forms of understanding and knowledge.

Sraffa in 1948. Sraffa's mother had died on 25 June 1948, and upon hearing that Wittgenstein hadn't sent Sraffa his condolences, G. H. von Wright urged him to call Sraffa immediately. Wittgenstein did so, but von Wright overheard him telling Sraffa, 'I did not write because what happened didn't mean anything to me'. We know this because, in the letter that von Wright may have subsequently advised him to write, Wittgenstein tells Sraffa that what he had 'very clumsily' tried to say was: 'I did not not write because what happened didn't mean anything to me'. In this first letter, dated 11 July 1949 (WC, § 409, 449), Wittgenstein optimistically tells Sraffa, 'you knew exactly how I felt'. This adds poignancy to the deep pessimism of the second letter, dated 23 August 1949, a reply to a letter by Sraffa that Wittgenstein characterizes as not really calling for a reply. I quote it at some length, though not in full:

> I have *very slowly* in my life come to the conviction that some people *cannot make themselves understood to each other*, or at least only in a very narrowly circumscribed field. If this happens each is inclined to think that the other doesn't want to understand, and there are ENDLESS misunderstandings. This of course doesn't improve the friendliness of the intercourse. I could go into details about *us*, but I don't want to. The general situation however is often this that one man thinks that the other could understand if he only wanted to, hence he gets rude, or nasty (according to the temperament) and thinks that he is only kicking back, and so it starts. –
>
> In order to understand why it's impossible, or almost impossible, for certain people to understand each other, one has to think *not* of the few occasions on which they meet, but of the differences of their *whole lives*; and there can be nothing more different than your interests and mine, and your movements of thought and mine. Only by a real tour de force was it possible for us to talk to each other years ago when we were younger. And if I were to compare you to a mine in which I worked to get some precious ore, I must say that my labour was *extremely* hard; though also that what I got out of it was well worth the labour. But later, when we no longer could give each other anything (which does *not* mean that each of us had got all the other had), it was natural that only an almost complete lack of understanding should remain; and, at least on my part, for a long time a wish that an understanding should again be possible. (WC, § 410, 450, emphasis in the original)

The letter is followed by a striking postscript, quoted in its entirety at the outset of this essay. In both the letter's main body and his postscript to it,

Wittgenstein is not making a general claim about understanding others but rather a qualified one about understanding *certain* others. The word 'certain' here is itself ambiguous as it could refer to either certain *types* of individuals or to *specific* individuals, be they considered as *sui generis* or *qua* falling under a recognizable type.[4] This resembles the commonplace idea that people with different backgrounds have greater difficulty in understanding one another than those who share a certain culture, mindset and range of experiences. What is odd is the incongruity of the remark with Wittgenstein's philosophies of mind and knowledge as expressed, for instance, in PI, §§ 138–82, discussed earlier in this chapter. In particular, the feeling that one might never understand what is *going on inside* (viz. the inner life of) another person is one naturally attributed to Wittgenstein's interlocutor. Of course, Wittgenstein is not here endorsing such feelings, merely reporting their occurrence.

It is of utmost importance that the lives of others are not metaphysically hidden from us. In his *Last Writings on the Philosophy of Psychology*, Wittgenstein warns against the error of thinking that people we find mysterious would become crystal clear to us if only we could see their hidden thoughts:

> Even if someone were to express everything that is 'within him', we wouldn't necessarily understand him [...] Think of how puzzling a dream is. Such a riddle doesn't *have* to have a solution. It intrigues us. It is *as if* there were a riddle here. This could be a primitive reaction. It is as if there were a riddle here; but it doesn't have to be a riddle [...] He behaves like a man in whom complicated thought processes are taking place; and if only I understand them I would understand him. – Let us *imagine* this case; and now he is reciting his thoughts to himself, and in a certain sense I understand his actions. That is, I see the trains of thought and I know how they lead to his actions. In this way he would cease being a riddle to me. (LW, §§ 191 ff., emphasis in the original)

As with philosophical problems, we must accept that there need not be a hidden truth waiting to be discovered. And when there is, it is not to be gotten by peering inside another person's mind (or soul), for this really wouldn't get one far at all:

> If God had looked into our minds he would not have been able to see there whom we were speaking of. (PPF, § 284)

4 In Chapter 3, I try to show how all this sheds an interesting light on the 'we' in the lion remark. Could this 'we' refer to a collective of people who would be better represented by different kinds of heads?

The connection Wittgenstein is in fact interested in is that between the near-impossibility of understanding certain others and significant differences between entire lives. His realization that this is true not only of 'other others' but also equally so of those closest to us did not fall out of any philosophical picture; it was a personal truth that Wittgenstein reluctantly came to accept over the years. This could explain why he eventually trusted his philosophical ideas to those friends and lovers with whom he shared his *life* much more than to his academic peers.

Part of Wittgenstein's disappointment with Sraffa and others could be that he took himself to share a great number of things (e.g. a certain intellectual disposition) with them, only to discover that it wasn't enough. It is not too far-fetched to think that his friendships with Sraffa and Russell ended, from Wittgenstein's point of view at least, not because of intellectual differences of opinion but rather because of the complete inability of each of the two parties to understand the other.

So we might take the message of his postscript to be something like this: if only members of each different group of like-minded people who could understand each other (be they 'Catholics', 'Europeans' or a considerably more complex grouping akin to the hybrid creatures of Greek mythology) resembled one another while looking strikingly different from the members of other groups (so some would look like elephants and others like fish) then we would have a better idea of who is more likely to understand us and vice versa. Thus understood, it is not that each and every one of us would look substantially different but that certain *sorts* of people would. Of course, this may already be true to some extent (e.g. Mediterraneans are as a rule of thumb much shorter and darker than Scandinavians), but Wittgenstein has far more radical physical differences and spiritual similarities in mind. 'Don't judge a book by its cover', warns the cliché. 'People need better covers', Wittgenstein effectively retorts.

In correspondence with the 10th century litterateur and philosopher Abū Ḥayyān al-Tawḥīdī, the Persian philosopher and historian Abū ʿAlī Miskawayh states that '[i]f the physiognomist finds that a person's features and physical structure bear a resemblance to one of the two animals [lions and hares] and judges that he possesses a closely related mixture and its ensuing character, he will not be far from the truth [...] The reasoning [...] can be applied to every mixture specific to a given animal [...] slyness and deceitfulness in foxes, malice and duplicity in wolves, fawning and geniality in cats [...] If a person's mixture and physical structure have an affinity to a lion, we judge that he possesses a lion's character, along with all its other indicants' (al-Tawhidi and Miskawayh 2021, 63.6, 158-9). This may seem silly to us, and perhaps it is, but it is worth recalling here the instructive parallels Alasdair

MacIntyre (1972) has set out between the methodology and findings of the far more ludicrous pseudoscience of phrenology and those of certain forms of contemporary neuroscience.

At an arguably more intuitive level, many Southern Africans traditionally use totems to identify the various clans that make up the historical dynasties of their civilization. The Shona people of Zimbabwe, for example, use animal and body-part 'mitupo' such as of those of Monkey (Soko), Antelope (Mhara), Lion (Shumba), Zebra (Mbizi/Tembo), Leopard (Nhewa/Ingwe), Fish (Hove), Eagle (Shiri/Hungwe), Hippo (Dziva), Buffalo (Nyati), Python (Shyto), Elephant (Nzou), Heart (Moyo), Lung (Bepe), Male Genitalia (Tsiwo), and Eland (Mhofu).[5] Importantly for our purposes, totems are also meant to serve as indications of character traits associated with each clan, such as bravery or kindness. This may still seem very 'primitive' because clearly one can exhibit character traits that are not prevalent in one's social group. But it is no more primitive than talking of British politeness and stiff upper lip, German efficiency, French elegance and so on. And let us also not forget that people who live together – share lives – for long periods of time end up looking like each other, if only because they adopt one another's mannerisms and facial gestures.

There is some truth in such generalizations, even if it cannot be extracted to fit each particular example. Given that one's character is very much influenced by that of the society one is brought up in, it's no wonder that we may not understand others well without some wider understanding of their whole life. Here, it is prudent to note that not only does understanding come in degrees, but one can also understand another fully in one respect, yet not at all in some other. I may, for example, fully get your politics but be left completely cold by your appreciation of a certain musical artist. (There is a difference between not understanding something specific about a person and not understanding them, *period.*)

Wittgenstein seems uninterested in such subtleties here, but we should not infer from this that he would not be open to them. He implies, for instance, that someone can be an enigma only if there are others that I can understand:

5 These are often further broken down into gendered names that may also serve as family names; people of the same totem are descendants of one common ancestor and as such are forbidden to have any intimate relationship, thereby preventing clanism (but creating serious difficulties for orphans of unknown origin).

> He is incomprehensible to me means that I cannot relate to him as to others. (LW, § 198)[6]

Moreover, Wittgenstein's general stance on mutual understanding is in keeping with our practice of finding the lowest common denominator (hunger, thirst, bus timetables, the weather) when conversing with people who are completely unlike us in other respects.[7] And even then, approaches to food and so on can be so different from our own that the gulf is much larger than the common ground. This brings us to the concept of a shared form of life. Wittgenstein adopted the term 'form of life' (which occurs only six times in his published output) to refer to 'the intertwining of culture, world-view, and language', including 'patterns of behavior' (Glock 1996a, 124–5).[8] Failure to understand another, it might therefore seem, results from the lack of a shared form of life.

Individual and Collective Forms of Life

As Peter Hacker notes, widespread use of the phrase 'form of life' in nineteenth- and early twentieth-century literature had become 'humdrum' by the time of the *Investigations*.[9] One early use noted by Wittgenstein scholars is found in Eduard Spranger's book *Lebensformen*, the title of which refers to types of individual characters; indeed, the book is translated as *Types of Men* and not *Forms of Life*. These types are very crudely defined in ways that wouldn't help members of different groups understand each other at all,[10] but I nonetheless

6 I spare the reader the usual rehearsal of possible isolation scenarios, from Mowgli to Robinson Crusoe.

7 With non-human animals we share such things as birth, death, sexual relations, hunger and thirst, but not marriage, religion and so on (cf. Berlin 1974, 344; Vico 1725, 77; Winch 1964, 43, 47). Whether animals have language is a moot point, but Wittgenstein's lion remark demonstrates that it is not a crucial one. Rhees claims that between animals 'there is no question of understanding here, any more than there is a question of discussion' (2006, 148). This seems to me to be utterly wrong.

8 The full list, considered in detail by Hacker 2015, is PI, §§ 19, 23, 241; MS 160, 51; PPF, §§ 1, 345.

9 Hacker 2015.

10 They are: (i) the Theoretical (who most values truth); (ii) the Economic (who most values pragmatism); (iii) the Aesthetic (who most values harmony); (iv) the Social (who most values people); (v) the Political (who most values power); (vi) the Religious (who most values unity).

wish to suggest that there is a connection between Spranger's use of 'form of life' and Wittgenstein's private writings on understanding *certain people*.[11]

While Wittgenstein's official remarks about forms of life are about understanding entire *communities* of people, his personal remarks on understanding are about *individuals*. Wittgenstein uses 'forms of life' to refer to *regular* forms of living (Hacker 2015, § 3), but we may wish to extend the concept to cover a particular individual's unique – perhaps even *irregular* – way of living. So conceived, a form of life may be not the way an entire community lives, but simply the way an individual does. Inquiries into what makes another person tick are often highly personal. This is not to deny a continuum between certain difficulties we have in understanding individuals who are reasonably close to us and those we have in understanding people in other cultures (thus, I may have difficulty understanding the humour of a particular colleague or an entire community).[12]

I am not as concerned here with whether Wittgenstein ever used the expression this way as with introducing a new – but not unrelated – use of the phrase to indicate connections between (a) his thoughts on understanding others in relation to their communities and (b) his thoughts on understanding others in relation to their personal biographies. Understanding what Sraffa says, for example, is not just a matter of understanding how the words he speaks are used by other Italians. If 'to imagine a language is to imagine a form of life' (PI, § 19), does this not also apply to the language of a particular person? Here I mean, not a *private* language in Wittgenstein's technical sense, but the language of a particular person nonetheless.[13]

Wittgenstein's more personal remarks seem to suggest that different forms of life lead to different types of people to the point where it would be helpful if each type had a different animal head assigned to it.[14] The much less plausible alternative understanding of Wittgenstein's forms of life as 'part of our inflexible biological human nature'[15] sits uneasily with all the evidence

11 Worth noting here is that it is primarily forms of life that lead to types of character and not the other way round.

12 See also Winch 1997.

13 Do Wittgenstein and Sraffa share a 'localized' form of life? Only to some extent. This highlights the limitations of the concept, which needs considerable stretching before it can do any real philosophical work. At this point we may wonder whether the expression is more of a hindrance than a help, if explaining it requires us to appeal to things we already understand.

14 Wittgenstein refers to 'human types' in CV (84e), remarking that Shakespeare doesn't portray them '*true to life*' (emphasis in the original).

15 The phrase – but not the interpretation – is from Glock 1996, 124–5. For Glock's views on these issues, see Chapter 5.

we have been discussing so far. This is not to say that biological differences cannot underlie or enable cultural ones, but only that the everyday difficulty of understanding others is not based on biology any more than the lack of a philosophical problem of knowing other minds is attributable to biological sameness.

It is wrong to think that we are forced to choose between a difference between forms of life that is *purely* biological and one that is *merely* cultural or ethnological. The criteria for the possibility of understanding are behavioural:

> [...] [H]e [the explorer in the foreign land] can come to understand it [the foreign language] only through its connections with the rest of the life of the natives. What we call 'instructions', for example, or 'orders', 'questions', 'answers', 'describing', etc. is all bound up with very specific human actions and an order is only distinguishable as an order by means of the circumstances preceding or following // accompanying it //. (MS 165, 97 ff., in Baker and Hacker 1985, 191; 2009, 177)

> Suppose you came as an explorer to an unknown country with a language quite unknown to you. In what circumstances would you say that the people there gave orders, understood them, obeyed them, rebelled against them, and so on? Shared human behaviour [*Die gemeinsame menschliche Handlungsweise*[16]] is the system of reference by means of which we interpret an unknown language. (PI, § 206)

All this includes both natural and nurtured behaviour. Moreover, as Glock holds along with Baker and Hacker, even the culture-specific is ultimately rooted in biology:

> [...] [U]nderstanding an alien language presupposes convergence not of beliefs, but of patterns of behaviour, which presuppose common perceptual capacities, needs and emotions [...] [W]e 'could not find our feet' with a community of human beings who give no expression or feeling of any kind, and we would presumably be at a loss with spherical Martians. (Glock 1996a, 128)

> Shared human behaviour provides the essential leverage for understanding humankind. This 'shared behaviour' is not only the common behaviour of humankind which manifests our animal nature, our

16 See Hintikka and Hintikka 1986, 209; Mạ and van Brakel 2016, Chapter 6; von Savigny 1991, 113–14, for an account of why Anscombe's rendition of this phrase as 'the common behaviour of mankind' is deeply problematic.

> natural needs for food, drink, warmth, our sexual drives, our physical vulnerability, etc. It also includes the culturally specific forms of behaviour shared by members of a tribe – their specific forms of social behaviour – observation of which and interaction with which enables us to interpret their language [...] [A]ny 'form of life' accessible to lions, given their natural repertoire of behaviour and their behavioural dispositions, is too far removed from ours for any noises they might emit to count as speech. (Baker and Hacker 2009, 173, inc. n. 1; see also 218 ff.)[17]

In PI § 241, Wittgenstein writes:

> [I]t is in their *language* that human beings agree. This is agreement not in opinions but in forms of life. (emphasis in the original)

There is an instructive parallel between what Wittgenstein is saying here and what Rush Rhees writes about understanding in his notes on Wittgenstein:

> The misunderstandings of human beings are not simply fights or antipathies, and falling out in that sense. (2006, 148–9)

Just as to share a language is not to agree on the thoughts one expresses in it, so to have a shared understanding is not to agree on matters of fact. A friendship or professional relationship might end because the parties involved understand one another *only too well*. By the same token, two people may completely fail to understand each other despite a deep agreement in opinions, as in Jane Austen's *Pride and Prejudice*, which nicely illustrates that one's failure to understand is not always free from ethical judgement.[18] Understanding cannot be achieved through the mere acquisition of information. Rhees continues:

> If they were, there would be no problem. Criticisms and questions and objections [...] that is not the sort of bewilderment that comes into misunderstandings between friends. As though there were something which somebody could tell you, although he has not. Or as though the

17 In this revised version of Baker and Hacker (1985, 186–7), 'shared behaviour' has replaced what was previously 'common behaviour' throughout, thereby making it clearer that the common behaviour of humanity does not completely exhaust our shared behaviour, which also includes behaviour that is 'culturally specific' (the term helpfully replaces what was previously described as 'the diverse species-specific forms which such behaviour may naturally take for human beings').

18 See Hertzberg (2005, 8 ff.) for cases in which '[m]y not understanding is bound up with my finding the activity abhorrent'. Hertzberg concludes that '[i]n saying that I find someone's behaviour incomprehensible, what I am saying, roughly, is that an appropriate attitude towards it is impossible to find' (ibid., 14).

> want of understanding came from a want of intelligence [...] They cannot understand what is being said: they cannot understand one another. Those two are pretty well equivalent here. (ibid.)[19]

The 'what is said' at issue here is not the 'what is said' of expression (or even of utterance) meaning but that of speaker meaning. I may understand your words perfectly well but completely fail to get what you are saying. This need not be a (mere) failure to grasp the intended conversational implicatures, as opposed to the conventional meaning.[20] Deeper failures to understand occur when the very spirit of what one is saying is missed. Whether or not this can be explained with additional information depends on how much else in life is already shared.[21]

Pari passu, one cannot fully understand what someone has said if one does not understand *why* she has said it (cf. Collingwood 1946, 177; Anscombe 1957, § 46) – and not in the sense that can be easily addressed with a statement about one's reasons or with causal generalizations that might enable future predictions:

> So he gets angry, when we see no reason for it; what excites us leaves him unmoved. – Is the essential difference that we can't foresee his reactions? Couldn't it be that after some experience we might know them, but still not be able to follow him? (LW, § 192)

Hence the idea, common in relationship breakdowns such as that between Wittgenstein and Sraffa, that if it turns out that the other person never understood something that mattered deeply to oneself, all other communication must have ultimately been illusory or at best skin-deep. This can be true of even the most mundane things, such as the example Alan Bennett gives of his father's not caring about good pepper.

The understanding we have of another person's life cannot be reduced to propositional knowledge that can be possessed by someone who doesn't already have enough in common with the person in question. My 'getting' you may enable me to pass on knowledge about you in propositional form, but the

19 For more on the distinction between understanding and agreement, see Klagge 2011, 41 ff.

20 Jennifer Saul helpfully distinguishes between 'constrained' (overt) and 'unconstrained' (contextualist) understandings of what is said (2012, 27 ff.).

21 The *tone* in which one says something is important here: try telling a dog 'good doggie' in a harsh voice or 'bad doggie' in a pleasant one and see the confusion that ensues. This is why the philosophical enterprise of reducing meaning to 'propositional content' is doomed to fail.

information I pass on will not on its own lead others to also understand you.[22] Our understanding of another cannot be fully captured in propositional form (see Beardsmore 1996, 54) any more than our understanding of jazz could.[23] The failure to understand another is not a failure to reach consensus on some factual or moral matter any more than understanding is a matter of agreement. What is missing, it would seem, is forms of life. (Wittgenstein's lion remark provides a limiting case of a more general difficulty.) The barrier to sharing forms of life is not metaphysical or even biological but *biographical*.[24] It is tempting to conclude from all this that communication is made possible by – perhaps even results from – the prior existence of shared forms of life. Rhees denies this outright:

> [...] [Y]ou cannot say that it is because they have a common life that they are able to engage in conversation [...] It is because of its connexion with the rest of the language that any of their utterances is connected with what they are doing. (Rhees 2006, 130)

Rhees' point is that forms of life do not function as part of a linear explanation of how conversation and understanding (of what is said) are possible. By the same token, a failure to understand cannot simply be attributed (as it seems to be by Wittgenstein in his letter to Sraffa) to a lack of shared lives. For the two-way act of attempting to understand and be understood by another is an attempt to bring the other into one's life and/or to enter into the other's life. This is no more than to make a start, of course, and some starts can be false. But it would be most bizarre if one couldn't even *begin* to understand another unless there already existed a shared form of life in the strong cultural sense (Wittgenstein is hardly denying that he and Sraffa shared certain biological needs). There must surely exist points of entrance.[25]

In his book *Radical Hope: Ethics in the Face of Cultural Devastation*, Jonathan Lear describes the reluctance of Frank B. Linderman to say that he knows much about 'the Indian' despite the fact that he had 'studied him' for more

22 It would be a mistake to think that if understanding is some kind of non-propositional knowledge then it is a form of *know-how* à la Ryle. In many cases it is a form of know-*who*, know-*what or* know-*why*.

23 Tilghman (1983) makes a similar point. I explore what it might mean to understand a work of art in Chapter 9.

24 Of course biographical knowledge in no way guarantees understanding. If it were otherwise, self-understanding would be relatively easy to achieve, and autobiographies would be a testament to this.

25 Hence the following remark by Rhees: '"Learning to speak" and "learning to understand people" – those seem to go together' (ibid., 139).

than forty years and had been told by his own subject that he had 'felt his heart' (Lear 2006, 2). Lear's book centres around the possibility that when Indian chief Plenty Coups stated that 'nothing happened' after the buffalo went away, he meant this in a literal way that we (non-Indians) cannot begin to comprehend. Lear writes:

> I cannot pretend to say with confidence what Plenty Coups really meant. His remark is enigmatic in part because it is compatible with so many different interpretations. Some of them are superficial; others delve to the heart of the human condition. (ibid., 5)

An even more radical example may be found in Matt Groening's *Futurama*. Two aliens from the planet Omicron Persei 8 watch an episode of the human television series *Friends*, laughing at all the jokes. When it is over, one of them says to the other, in English: 'Why does Ross, the largest friend, not simply eat the other five?' This particular joke focuses on a species as a whole, but it also holds true of both sub-species collectives and individuals whose bodily and speech acts we may – up to a point – understand while possessing only limited knowledge of how these fit into their wider lives. Understanding a creature is not just a matter of being able to translate individual sentences it utters. This is why, jokes aside, talking animals in books and films typically possess a full gamut of human concepts that cannot be acquired independently of knowledge about a range of habits, values, feelings and motivations.

Given their reaction to television comedy, we can barely imagine what these aliens would make of something like the Eucharist. They have obviously not understood the first thing about humans, despite the stipulation that they nonetheless (*per impossibile*) understand one or more human languages. One cannot understand a language while lacking any clear notion of the practices in which it is embedded (see Chapter 4).

Epilogue

Writing about her friendship with Wittgenstein, Elizabeth Anscombe draws the following contrast between knowledge and understanding:

> I must confess that I feel deeply suspicious of anyone's claim to have understood Wittgenstein. That is perhaps because, although I had a very strong and deep affection for him, and, I suppose, knew him well, I am very sure that I did not understand him. (Anscombe, in Engelmann 1967, xiv)

This might have been what the young Wittgenstein had in mind, for example, when at the end of his 1929 PhD viva in Cambridge he allegedly told Bertrand Russell and G. E. Moore, 'I know you'll *never* understand it', a suspicion that strengthened as his work became more popular. This led him to announce in the Preface to the *Investigations* that he 'could not help noticing that the results of [his own] work [...] were [...] frequently misunderstood',[26] and he has also been quoted as having maintained that Ryle was one of just two philosophers who understood his work (Monk 1991, 436). In a similar vein, he told Russell that Frege 'doesn't understand a single word of my work' (letter dated 6 October 1919; WC, § 67, 103), and a few years later he wrote:

> I must confess that the number of people to whom I can talk is constantly diminishing. (letter c. April 1922; WC, § 94, 132–3)

It is a mistake to think of these as instances of arrogance, for Wittgenstein's insistence that others cannot understand him is accompanied by a similar pessimism about his ability to understand others. This manifests itself in the fear that it only *seems* to him that he understands things and people precisely because he doesn't in fact understand much at all:

> Is my understanding [*Verständnis*] only blindness to my own lack of understanding [*Unverständnis*]? It often seems so to me. (OC, 418)

James C. Klagge (2011) explains this phenomenon by arguing that Wittgenstein was simply out of place in the twentieth century (and in some sense exiled from an earlier era). In what way might the inability to understand a speaking lion differ from the inability to understand Wittgenstein when he speaks? '[I]t is very unlikely that we will understand and appreciate Wittgenstein's work', Klagge writes, 'unless we have the right temperament and sensibility' (2011, 39).

Understanding comes in degrees, but we have already seen that the private Wittgenstein is working with a relatively demanding notion of understanding. This is further evidenced by his incredibly high personal standards for every aspect of life (see Monk 1991). Of course feeling that we will never understand some people is compatible with in principle being able to do so (even if we never come to manage it). A well-known philosopher once confessed to me that Russell does not *speak* to him. By this he did not mean that he could not understand any individual sentence or paragraph but, rather, that he does

26 If understanding the expression meaning of what anybody says were always sufficient for understanding the person there would be minimal need for exegesis.

not share the sort of interests required to find his feet with what Russell was generally trying to get at. Such reactions need not be negative (see Chapter 9).

I have tried to show that the tension between the public Wittgenstein's optimism about knowledge of other minds and the private Wittgenstein's pessimism about understanding (and being understood by) others, including those closest to him, is not a problematic one. There are three related reasons for this. First, the barriers he sought to destroy were metaphysical (allegedly necessary) ones, whereas those he struggled to overcome were psychological (presumably contingent). Second, Wittgenstein's official 'nothing is hidden' view is chiefly about *knowledge*, while his unofficial view is about *understanding*, and it is part of his larger project to demonstrate that the latter cannot be reduced to the former. Last, Wittgenstein's official remarks on understanding themselves fall into two distinct categories that do not neatly match the focus of his unofficial ones. One set comprises those remarks near the beginning of the *Investigations* that challenge the thought that understanding is an inner mental process accompanying behaviour such as speaking and reading. The other consists primarily of the famous 'tribes and lions' passages in PPF and *On Certainty* concerned with the difficulty of understanding others without immersing oneself in their respective forms of life. Here the problem is cultural or sociological, and Wittgenstein strikes a balance between optimism and pessimism. Meanwhile, unofficially, Wittgenstein focuses on *individual* people rather than collectives and is much less optimistic about success, not least because he sets the bar for understanding those closest to him so high that he may appear not to acknowledge that understanding is a matter of degree rather than kind (although, in fact, he writes of an 'almost complete lack of understanding'). The official and unofficial sets of remarks are here united in assuming a distinction between understanding a *person* and understanding the (expression or utterance) meaning of their *words*. If to understand a language is to understand a *form* of life, then to understand a person is to understand a whole life.

Chapter 2

MAKING OURSELVES UNDERSTOOD: WITTGENSTEIN AND MORAL EPISTEMOLOGY

> In today's human society, more and more people are less and less in agreement and that is the reason they fight among themselves. But why can't they understand each other? Why can't they get themselves out of this situation?
>
> Luis Buñuel (in de la Colina and Turrent 1986, 160)

> No one should be astonished that men are so far removed from one another that they cannot understand one another, that they wage war and kill one another. One should be much more surprised that men believe they are close, understand one another, and love one another.
>
> C. G. Jung (2009, 317–18)

Prologue

In his book of interviews with the documentary maker Nick Broomfield, Jason Wood describes the following scene from Broomfield's 1975 film *Juvenile Liaison*, a case study of the questionable 'no-nonsense' methods employed by the officers of a police unit in Blackburn, Lancashire (UK) focused on young offenders from 'impoverished working-class backgrounds':

> There's a sequence with a young Asian girl who is accused of stealing pencils, and what becomes all too apparent from the reaction of her teachers and from the female police officer who visits the girl's parents is that there is *absolutely no understanding of this culture*. The police officer is *unable to even understand what the father of the girl is saying*. (Wood 2005, 47; emphasis added)

Broomfield responds as follows:

> One of the troubles, for all of us really, is that we grow up and are taught in a very particular moment of history, but history does not continue in

> that moment, so somebody who is trained at that moment will be out of date twenty years later – which was certainly the case with these teachers, who certainly needed to be retrained. They weren't bad people with a sadistic side to them; they were largely well-meaning people who just happened to be a little out of their depth. (Ibid.)

Broomfield isn't offering a general answer to the perennial question of why good people do bad things, let alone an account of how our evaluations of them relate to our evaluations of their deeds (see Sandis 2017a). But he does try to explain why a specific set of 'largely well-meaning' people acted as they did. This involves a threefold layer of understanding. Most immediately, we have (i) the viewer's understanding of how the subjects of the documentary saw things. But this involves understanding why and how the subjects themselves lacked (ii) an understanding of the people who they, in turn, were dealing with. Finally, we have (iii) the world as understood by the latter.

It would not be amiss to label Broomfield an 'empathetic' filmmaker, owing to his natural inclination to feel for the subjects he is filming and his related attempts to portray things to the viewer from their point of view, without letting this affect his ultimate judgement of the situation (in the example above, he is adamant that the teachers in question need retraining). But what exactly is the role played by empathy in all of this?

It is currently the fashion to speak of understanding others as an activity of the imagination, to be achieved through the simulative employment of empathy and/or rational sympathy as some kind of tool providing one with an all-access pass to the so-called mental contents of others. This is to conceive of understanding others as a form of mind reading by which we obtain and decode information stored in other minds. But is this what really goes on in situations such as the one that Broomfield brings us into? Broomfield and Wood themselves prefer to point to an understanding of cultural, historical and socioeconomic conditions without which we cannot even understand *what* people are saying, let alone why. Empathy is not so much the cause of such understanding as its effect.[1]

We would do well, I think, to reject all 'mind-reading' accounts of what it takes to understand others, replacing them with an approach that leaves more space for the role played by shared outlooks and the behavioural practices that embody them. Only then can we begin to properly tackle our moral, cultural, religious and sociopolitical differences. Somewhat surprisingly, the

1 The error of 'confusing cause and effect' is, of course, the first of the Four Great Errors that Nietzsche warns against in *Twilight of the Idols* (1889, 176).

philosopher best equipped to help us with both the negative and the positive parts of this task is one who constantly professed that he had real trouble understanding – and making himself understood by – others, including most of his closest friends. In the essay that follows, I try to show what exactly it is that Wittgenstein can teach us about the moral epistemology of understanding others, and why his own struggles with this ultimately count in favour of the position he holds.

Locke and Key

How can we come to better understand another person's moral point of view? It is popular nowadays to conceive of understanding others as a matter of accessing information that is in some sense stored within the mind of the person (or other being) in question. This outlook may be traced back to John Locke's semiotics of communication, according to which shared language is a kind of key we use to unlock the thoughts of others (which he conceives of as the contents of their minds) and, by the same token, to communicate our own hidden thoughts to them. On the very last page of *An Essay Concerning Human Understanding*, Locke writes:

> [B]ecause the Scene of *Ideas* that makes one Man's Thoughts, cannot be laid open to the immediate view of another, nor laid up any where but in the Memory, a no[t] very sure Repository: Therefore to communicate our Thoughts to one another, as well as record them for our own use, Signs of our *Ideas* are also necessary. Those which Men have found most convenient, and therefore generally make use of, are articulate Sounds. (Locke 1975, Book IV, Chapter XXI, § 4, 5–10, 721; emphasis in the original)

This is an alluring statement, precisely because it appears so innocuous at first sight that we cannot imagine why anyone would want to deny it. But is it really true that the thoughts of others are hidden from direct view, accessible only via linguistic acts of coding and decoding?

Wittgenstein's fight against this popular picture of communication as a 'relation between minds' (Burns 1923, v) was encapsulated in the slogan 'nothing is hidden' (PI, §§ 43, 559; PPF, §§ 301 ff.), employed by his sympathizers to combat twentieth-century modifications of both the Lockean theory of communication and the Cartesian epistemology it had failed to overcome, as popularized by Chomsky, Fodor, Pinker and Steiner.[2] The particular picture these thinkers are all in the grip of is one that Timothy Potts dismisses as 'the communication of meaning as a branch of transport studies' in which 'meanings are like passengers, which embark in sentences in order to travel from one person to the another, alighting when they reach their destination' (Potts 1977, 920; see also Chapter 2 in Peters 1999). As Stanley Cavell puts it:

> Talking together is acting together, not making mistakes and noises at one another, not transferring unspeakable messages or essences from the inside of one closed chamber to the inside of another. (Cavell 1958, 33–4)

The mistake of thinking otherwise deepens once we compound it with the additionally misguided thought that to understand another person *just is* to have the meaning of their thoughts reach our own minds. This confused cocktail has recently been given a new life within empathy studies, which basically contributes an additional layer (or latch) to the Lockean account by insisting that we cannot understand others unless we are able to *feel* what others are feeling. We are thus frequently told that empathy is the key to understanding others, to being moral and, ultimately, to making the world a better place. However, neither its proponents nor its detractors seem able to agree on what empathy is, other than that it has something to do with mirror neurons, which are not only form the foundation of empathy but have also been said to solve the problem of other minds.[3] The publisher's blurb for Marco Iacoboni's book *Mirroring People: The New Science of How We Connect with Others*, for example, reads as follows:

> What accounts for the remarkable ability to get inside another person's head—to know what they're thinking and feeling? [...] until recently, scientists didn't understand what in the brain makes it possible.This has all changed in the last decade. Marco Iacoboni [...] explains the groundbreaking research into mirror neurons, the "smart cells" in our brain that allow us to understand others.[4]

2 See Malcolm 1986 and the essays in Vesey 1977, particularly those by G. H. R. Parkinson, M. A. Stewart and Timothy C. Potts; cf. Sandis 2017a, 368–73.

3 Iacoboni (2008). See also Baron-Cohen 2011, 25–6; Gallese 2001; Haidt 2012, 244; Krznaric 2014, 21–6; Rizzolatti and Craighero 2004; Segal 2018, 10–11; Stueber 2006, 132–52; Zahavi 2014, 154 ff.

4 https://us.macmillan.com/books/9781429990752/mirroringpeople; last accessed 30 September, 2024.

Researchers have identified empathy with a feeling, a skill, an ability, a disposition, an activity, a process, a capacity, a mechanism, a method and an art. Which, if any, of these is it? One of the most prevailing conceptions of empathy sees it as a kind of emotional process which enables us 'to gain a grasp of the content of other people's minds', which most philosophers take to double as their motivating reasons (Coplan and Goldie 2011, ix). According to many who share this informationalist outlook, there seems to be no limit to what empathy can unlock. In the slogans of clinical psychologist Simon Baron-Cohen:

> Being able to empathize means being able to understand accurately the other person's position [...] Empathy avoids *any* risk of misunderstandings or miscommunication [...] Empathy allows you to make a close friend. (Baron-Cohen 2011, 12; emphasis added)

So construed, empathy is a magic access pass not only to the minds of others but also indeed to a world in which we all understand one another's positions with no risk of miscommunication. Unsurprisingly, its defenders take it to have huge sociopolitical and moral ramifications. Thus, for example, Baron-Cohen attempts 'to redefine "evil" in terms of empathy' (ibid., ix), by which he means that evil is identical to zero degrees of empathy, with good on the other side of the spectrum. Such claims are not only misguided – given how some of the cruellest acts require the perpetrator to understand all too well what the victim is feeling – but morally dangerous when accompanied by further suppositions, such as the claim that people with autism are seriously lacking in empathy (Haidt 2012, 116–7, citing Baron-Cohen).[5]

The introduction of empathy transforms the question of understanding 'other minds' from a critique of pure transport to one of a moral epistemology that goes well beyond David Hume's dictum that 'sympathy is the chief source of moral distinctions' (2000, 3.3.6.1–2, 618–9), by which he simply meant that we do not reach moral conclusions through pure reason alone (as might a certain kind of robot) but with the help of sentiments.

Empathy has its detractors, most notably the cognitive psychologist Paul Bloom, whose picture is that mirror-opposite of Baron-Cohen's:

> Empathy [...] grounds foolish judgments and often motivates indifference and cruelty. It can lead to irrational and unfair political decisions, it can corrode certain important relationships [...] and make us worse

5 For a much more helpful approach to understanding people with autism, see Chapman (2023:1-8, 114ff.)

> at being friends, parents, husbands, and wives. I am against empathy. (Bloom 2016, 3)

Yet such rejections of empathy (and the 'simulation' theories of understanding that naturally go hand in hand with it[6]) typically hang onto the idea that understanding is a matter of acquiring information stored in 'other minds', replacing simulation with the 'theory-theory' that we understand others by applying a folk-psychological theory to their behaviour and drawing inferences from analogies to our own.[7] This opposition retains the Lockean assumption that understanding others is a matter of accessing the 'contents' of their 'mental states', which in turn double as their reasons for action.

In what follows, I hope to show how Wittgenstein's alternative approach reveals that all such accounts of understanding as a form of informational 'mind reading'[8] are misguided, regardless of how they balance empathy with reason. More positively, it replaces their focus on uncovering 'mental contents' with one in which understanding is to be achieved through shared practices and the behaviour they enable.

Eyes Wide Shut

In his later work, Wittgenstein attempts to dismantle a solipsistic picture of human relations that had once appealed to him and that to this day remains attractive to philosophers and non-philosophers alike. His arguments and the controversies surrounding them are well known, so I shan't attempt to rehearse or evaluate them here. As I hope will become clear in due course, it is sufficient for my purposes to highlight a very specific anti-sceptical feature of his view. This is exemplified in those remarks in which Wittgenstein states that we frequently *know* – and can even be *certain* of – what another is thinking or feeling:

> If we are using the word 'know' as it is normally used (and how else are we to use it?), then other people very often know if I'm in pain. (PI, § 246)
>
> I can know what someone else is thinking. (Ibid., § 315)
>
> I can be as certain of someone else's feelings as of any fact. (PPF, § 330)

6 Naturally, but not necessarily (see Stueber 2006, 146–7).

7 See Carruthers and Smith 1996.

8 See, for example, Carruthers 2011, Chapter Eight; Nichols and Stich 2003; Spaulding 2018.

> 'But if you are certain, isn't it that you are shutting your eyes in face of doubt?' They've been shut. (PPF, § 331)

The last of these statements shows the psychological element of Wittgenstein's anti-scepticism about 'other minds'.[9] While his arguments centre around the language game of certainty (PPF, § 332) and our ordinary uses of phrases such as 'to know' and 'to doubt' (PPF, §§ 315, 328; OC, §§ 175, 504), they are intended to cure the reader of any actual doubt that philosophizing may have produced in them, viz. the only kind of *philosophical* doubt worth worrying about.[10] Wittgenstein insists that he is making a logical (as opposed to psychological) distinction between different kinds of certainty (PPF, § 330), but this does not guarantee that his anti-sceptical reasoning leaves no one with a psychological residue. Indeed, Pritchard has recently argued that the *inevitable* effect of any Wittgensteinian dissolving of sceptical problems is a kind of vertigo:

> The problem of radical scepticism has always been a very real existential issue for me, and so I do not use this terminology lightly. Discovering that the sceptical problem has no real answer is something that should unsettle any responsible inquirer [...] [W]hile I believe the solution I offer to the sceptical problem genuinely is a remedy for epistemic *angst*, this is not to say that the anxiety in question will be entirely removed. This is because I think there is an inevitable psychological vestige of doubt that remains even once the solution has been embraced [...] I call this psychological state epistemic *vertigo* (or epistemic *acrophobia* if

9 The later Wittgenstein's solipsistic targets include those who claim that understanding others is a matter of having (inevitably) indirect knowledge of their minds and those who reduce it to knowledge of mere external behaviour. For a drawn-out attack on such philosophies, see Wisdom 1952.

10 To this extent, Wittgenstein is following in the Pyrrhonist tradition, which avoids the insulation problem of academic sceptics (cf. Pritchard 2011; Sandis 2019a, Chapter Three; Tor 2014). Duncan Pritchard highlights the fact that hinge anti-scepticism shares with radical scepticism (against G. E. Moore) the claim that 'the structure of rational evaluation is ultimately grounded in arational commitments' (Pritchard 2017, 567). The difference between Wittgenstein and the radical sceptic is that the former's case for the 'groundlessness of our believing' (OC, § 166) involves the claim that our animal commitments are 'beyond being justified or unjustified' (ibid., § 359) and are therefore *not* ones 'that could be rationally supported' (Pritchard 2017, 567). Commitments *qua* hinges are ungrounded, but they don't *lack* grounds. Pritchard's vertigo is arguably the result of his additional desire to reconcile certainty with closure (he is here inspired by what I take to be the interlocutor in OC, § 183). For a critique of Pritchard's closure argument see Moyal-Sharrock 2016a.

> one wants to be pedantic), in order to capture the idea that it is essentially a kind of phobic reaction to one's epistemic predicament [...] We have, as it were, epistemically 'ascended' and adopted a vantage point that we would not normally adopt. From this unnatural vantage point, epistemic vertigo is a natural response. (Pritchard 2016, 6–7; emphasis in the original)

Wittgenstein's early work (e.g. TB, 82, 85; TLP, 5.62, 5.64, 6.45–6.521) suggests that the more solipsistic aspects motivating a certain kind of radical scepticism were a real-life concern that often tortured him. As Brian McGuinness puts it:

> [H]is solipsism [...] was not an intellectual exercise but a moral and mystical attitude. Everything that he was involved in was seen as part of what passed before, what constituted the world for, a mind or soul, and the task of that mind or soul was to accept and thereby harmonize that multiplicity. (McGuinness 1988, 228; see also 78, 106, 225; cf. Lange 2017)[11]

But the PPF § 331 exclamation that his eyes have 'been shut' makes it clear that Wittgenstein feels no residual vertigo – not even a shadow of a doubt (OC, § 414). Indeed, his use of the past perfect suggests that our eyes are *ordinarily* shut. Philosophy sees its role as that of opening our eyes, but this is not always a good thing. Not because illusion is preferable to truth, but because shutting one's eyes in the face of the mere logical possibility that one is wrong is the appropriate response, not least when that logical possibility is part of the very conditions of knowledge (PPF, § 315). Once the cloud of sceptical philosophy has been condensed to grammar, it is no longer capable of opening our eyes to its promise of rainfall. The real difficulty is to *realize* the groundlessness of our believing (OC, § 166), not to *live* with it once it has been properly understood. For there is nothing to be afraid of once we understand that our most basic certainties do not lack grounds that they might have had but, rather, are in no need of them.[12] The vertigo that Pritchard speaks of arises only when we fail to keep our eyes wide shut.

---

11 Solipsism and scepticism are typically treated as different topics within the secondary literature on Wittgenstein (see, e.g., Glock and Hyman 2017; Kuusela and McGinn 2011). Whatever the taxonomical benefits of this may be, the approach to other minds that the later Wittgenstein combats is clearly a solipsistic one (see Glendinning 1998, 8–9).

12 See Moyal-Sharrock 2004, esp. 75 ff.; Sandis 2022; Sandis and Tejedor 2017, 581 ff. It is not just that our hinge commitments do not require grounding but that there

The PPF remarks against other-minds scepticism are located within a larger narrative about the concept of hiddenness and its relation to the inner/outer dichotomy (PPF, §§ 301–32).[13] These remarks focus on two distinct ways in which we can fail to understand one another. The first way makes clear Wittgenstein's view that accessing the 'hidden contents' of another's mind wouldn't help us to understand them one bit:

> If God had looked into our minds [*Seelen*] he would not have been able to see there whom we were speaking of. (PPF, § 284)

The reasons that make this true are legion. Indeed, the remark could even be defended by a Davidsonian supporter of mental holism.[14] But Wittgenstein's primary contention here is that anything found in our mind, brain or soul would be a meaningless 'dead' mark (ibid., §§ 454–5). Our behaviour, by contrast, is saturated with significance:

> [I]f one sees the behaviour of a living thing, one sees its mind. (Ibid., § 357)[15]

To see another's mind in this sense – which precludes 'looking into' it – is not yet to understand them, for we may well find the behaviour in question baffling. But it is a prerequisite for something that could never be achieved by accessing any information 'stored' in their mind, regardless of whether this is attempted via empathetic or rationalistic means.[16]

---

could be no such thing as the very practice of grounding without them (PI, §§ 324–6 and 477–85).

13 See Schroeder 2019, 75–8.

14 See Davidson 1970, 221–3.

15 The original Anscombe translation has 'soul'. This may be literally more accurate, but 'mind' coheres better with Anscombe's own translation of PPF § 284, which remains unchanged in the revised fourth edition. Translators must make a choice on the basis of the topic of the remark and Wittgenstein's own uses of 'mind' and 'soul' in his English dictations and notes for lectures. Peter Hacker suggested to me that if the mind is the capacity for thinking and reasoning, and the soul is associated with emotions and a sensitivity to good and evil, then §§ 284 *and* 357 are obviously concerned with the former. Joachim Schulte reminded me that there were resonant debates on the 'true' meanings of words such as 'Geist' and 'Seele' within Wittgenstein's lifetime (see Klages 1929–32). Finally, it is true that Wittgenstein had the German word 'Psyche' at his disposal (see Schulte 2018, 328, n. 6), but it is worth asking whether he would have used it for a dog.

16 This has radical implications for the intelligibility of artificial intelligence (AI), particularly the mistaken assumption that the problem of AI can be solved by converting black boxes to transparent ones. See Sandis 2017c and 2018.

The second way in which attempts to understand others can fail contrasts with the above because it involves public ('outer') verbal behaviour as opposed to ostensibly private ('inner') thoughts. Wittgenstein writes, for example:

> Even if someone were to express everything that is 'within him', we wouldn't necessarily understand him. (LW, § 191)[17]

> If I were to talk to myself out loud in a language not understood by those present, my thoughts would be hidden from them. (PPF, § 317)

One needn't keep one's thoughts or reasons to oneself to not be understood by others and, *mutatis mutandis*, we can understand another perfectly well even when (and, at times, precisely because) they hide such things from us. Let me illustrate this with a real-life anecdote shared with me by Mark Lance:

> I'm at the Hamilton[18] at a table with a 60-something couple and two Japanese women. The latter are speaking Japanese. The former are using English words and I hear all those words. Yet somehow I understand the Japanese women better than the couple. It is a very strange circumstance. (Personal correspondence to author, October 2014)[19]

Lance explained to me that the former pair were saying utterly bizarre things to one another such as 'some people pronounce it *guill*otine and others guillo*tine*, and that is what we mean by context', completely out of the blue, along with other extremely weird emphases such as 'I am going to cut this burger in *half!!!!!*', uttered as if the speaker had just discovered the source of the Nile. Not only did recognizing grammaticality and truth conditions not guarantee that the conversation made any sense, but sharing a language with the speakers only served to make them appear all the more alien.

The Japanese women, by contrast, were clearly discussing what to order, how beautiful a scarf was and how much they liked the singer. This was all very easy to pick up from their behaviour without knowing a single word of Japanese (indeed, Lance wasn't even one hundred per cent certain it was Japanese).

It is worth highlighting, in this context, that the penultimate remark of the *Tractatus* hangs on a distinction between understanding its propositions and understanding their author: 'My propositions serve as elucidations in the following way: anyone who understands *me* eventually recognizes them as

17 This line is placed immediately after the lion remark (cf. RPP, §§ 566–9).

18 A restaurant in Washington, D.C.

19 The first pair could perhaps also be understood as engaging in surrealist discourse.

nonsensical [...]'.[20] Understanding *what* Wittgenstein is doing in the work (and why) does not entail that the nonsensical propositions are themselves there in order to be understood.[21]

Reading Wittgenstein, it can sometimes seem as if understanding another person is an all-or nothing affair. But we may understand another perfectly in some respects and not others. Moreover, we are all on a continuum of comprehensibility, ranging from transparency to complete enigma. On this spectrum we find people who are colour-blind (RC, I.13), 'mental defectives' (ibid., I.75, III.118–9),[22] people with 'perfect pitch' (ibid., III.28, III.292; Z, § 328),[23] people who have been 'brought up from early youth to give no expression of feeling *of any kind*' (ibid., § 383, emphasis in the original; cf. RPP, § 568), dogs (Z, §§ 384–90)[24] and, of course, the hypothetical speaking lion (PPF, § 327).[25]

The above are thought to be incomprehensible to 'us' to the extent that 'we'[26] cannot *relate* to them (LW, § 198). In the next section, I explore what Wittgenstein has in mind here. In so doing, I try to show that he really did feel epistemic angst, but not the angst described by Pritchard. *That* angst comes across as highly academic, despite Pritchard's (no doubt genuine) assurance that it has a real existential pull for him.

Together Through Life

Wittgenstein's anti-scepticism about other minds contrasts sharply with his remarks about the (often insuperable) obstacles to understanding others. It is tempting to think that Wittgenstein must be drawing a rigid distinction between knowledge and understanding, but this is not the case:

20 TLP-R, 6.54, my emphasis.

21 Cf. Tejedor (2014, 4, 12, n.18, 156–63).

22 Cf. Glover 2014.

23 See Lugg 2017.

24 Cf. Bekoff 2018.

25 Simon Glendinning (1998, 70–2) argues that Wittgenstein's modalities stress a 'difference of *order*' between (i) the opacities that human beings encounter in relation to other humans and (ii) those that they encounter in relation to other animals. I challenge this reading in Chapter 4, but remain in general agreement with the main thrust of Glendinning's argument regarding how significance is manifested in behaviour while simultaneously transcending the body.

26 I explore who 'we' are for Wittgenstein in Chapter 3.

> The grammar of the word 'know' is evidently closely related to the grammar of the words 'can', 'is able to'. But also closely related to that of the word 'understand'. (PI, § 150)

> The criteria which we accept for 'fitting', 'being able to', 'understanding', are much more complicated than might appear at first sight. [...] [T]hat's why definitions usually aren't enough [...] (Ibid., § 182)

Although Wittgenstein does not always use 'knowledge' and 'understanding' as synonyms, he is not making a philosophically pertinent distinction between the two terms. The real distinction is between (i) abstract *philosophical* questions about the possible acquisition of either knowledge or understanding and (ii) *real-life* obstacles to the actual achievement of either. We saw a sample of each set in the section titled 'Eyes Wide Shut' above, but it is in his more personal remarks on understanding others that the difference between (i) and (ii) is heightened. The tension between Wittgenstein's (largely philosophical) remarks about how nothing is hidden and his (much more personal) comments on how impossible it is to understand others is a resolvable one. This is because his argument against the academic sceptic's principled reasons why we can never be certain what anybody else is thinking is perfectly compatible with his real-life scepticism concerning the extent to which we are ever capable of understanding (and being understood by) those around us (see Sandis 2015a).

Obstacles to the latter – we have already seen – may come in (combinations of) linguistic, conceptual, cultural, historical, educational, biological and other forms. But none of these are ordinarily overcome by obtaining information stored in another person's mind. Hence Wittgenstein's remark, quoted above, about the possibility of other people's being completely transparent to us. Such transparency is *not* a matter of being able to look directly into another's mind but of her thoughts' and feelings' being all too apparent and her behaviour's being all too recognizable. We saw in Chapter One how Wittgenstein could become deeply distressed by the collapse of understanding between himself and a close friend. But here I wish to focus on Wittgenstein's suggestion that the key to making ourselves understood by one another – a collective enterprise – lies in the differences and similarities across our lives. We have already seen that grasping these differences and similarities does not provide a key with which one may unlock another person's 'inner contents'. Rather, it is a necessary condition of understanding what others mean by the words they use, why they employ them as they do and the things they do with them.

In his essay 'Talk and Talkers', Robert Louis Stevenson nicely brings out the difference between merely linguistic understanding and the far deeper understanding that requires a wealth of common knowledge and/or experience:

> Natural talk, like ploughing, should turn up a large surface of life, rather than dig mines into geological strata. Masses of experience, anecdote, incident, cross-lights, quotation, historical instances, the whole flotsam and jetsam of two minds forced in and in upon the matter in hand from every point of the compass, and from every degree of mental elevation and abasement – these are the material with which talk is fortified [...] (Stevenson 1887, 106)

Stevenson proceeds to describe the kind of communication between friends that Wittgenstein wished he could have had with Sraffa:

> Communication is no longer by words but by the instancing of whole biographies, epics, systems of philosophy, and epochs of history in bulk. That which is understood excels that which is spoken in quantity and quality alike; ideas thus figured and personified, change hands, as we may say, like coin; and the speakers imply without effort the most obscure and intricate thoughts. (Ibid., 107)

Note how Wittgenstein's references to (i) understanding within a 'narrowly circumscribed field' and (ii) 'whole lives' more or less mirror those of Stevenson to (i) 'mines into geographical strata' (ii) and 'instancing of whole biographies', respectively. Sharing part of one's actual life with someone, while frequently helpful in the latter respect, is neither necessary nor sufficient for understanding. Thus, Stevenson offers the nice example of '[s]trangers who have a large common ground of reading' and who 'will, for this reason, come the sooner to the grapple of genuine converse' (ibid.).

The contrasting inability to fathom why anybody would speak or act as they do is not normally overcome by simulation or analogy from one's own behaviour.[27] Indeed, as Hutto notes, '[m]any of our routine encounters with others take place in situations in which the social roles and rules are well established, so much so that unless we behave in a deviant manner we typically have no need to understand one another in terms of their unique beliefs and desires at all' (Hutto 2007, 45). And yet accounts such as the following by Jaegwon Kim remain prevalent in contemporary philosophical literature:

27 This sort of unfathomability would require beings far more alien to us than even lions, such as the octopus (see Godfrey-Smith 2014).

> A third-person understanding of action results from an empathetic projection of the first-person point of view [...] One corollary of the proposed account is that we can understand the actions of only those agents who are 'like ourselves' [...] in that they share with us similar principles of rational action. (Kim 2010, 23–4; cf. Schroeder 2019, 83–6)

A more promising approach would be to figure out where the other person is coming from – what her interests, presuppositions and principles of rationality are. Wittgenstein elaborates:

> An education quite different from ours might also be the foundation for quite different concepts [...] What interests us would not interest *them.* [...] We could not possibly make ourselves understood to them. [...] (Z, §§ 387–90; emphasis in the original)

As in his letter to Sraffa, the emphasis – and responsibility – has shifted from understanding *others* to making *ourselves* understood. There is no quick and easy way for two or more people to come to understand one another. This is even more the case with actions and events long since past there is little anyone can do (on an individual or collective basis) to initiate oneself into past forms of life, long evolved into something else. For people from the past to succeed in having made themselves understood to us, we would have to find some non-spiritualist way of enabling them to *speak* to us. Historiography is a particularly difficult case in point here (see Chapter 7).

Understanding one another is not a matter of any empathetic 'mind-reading' skill, rational inference or other form of information acquisition, but rather involves lives that are (in one way or another) shared. A more poetic expression of this outlook is found in the belief of the Ojibwe that they understand animals better than the Anglo-European settlers because their ancestors married the animals and learned their ways.

Epilogue

In *The Righteous Mind*, Jonathan Haidt makes a number of remarks that on their surface seem amenable to the sort of picture sketched above. Like Nick Broomfield, Haidt places considerable emphasis on the general goodness of people with whom we disagree (e.g. 2012, 313), whose point of view is worth apprehending if we are to avoid living in a state of dysfunctional polarization:

> [M]oral diversity can so easily divide good people into hostile groups that do not want to understand each other. (Haidt 2012, xvii; see also 274 ff.)

> Can partisans even *understand* the story told by the other side? (Ibid., 286; emphasis in the original)

> So the next time you find yourself seated beside someone from another matrix [...] [d]on't bring up morality until you've found a few points of commonality or in some other way established a bit of trust. (Ibid., 318)

Haidt's approach has much to recommend it (see Sandis 2012b) – but, as already hinted at in 'Locke and Key' above, his account of what it takes for partisans to understand one another's 'stories' is steeped in the language of empathy to the point of stating that only those with a *brain* that is good at empathizing (!) are capable of the understanding in question (2012, 116 ff.; see also 46). He even assesses his own capacity for empathy as far more helpful in this respect than someone's being an anthropologist (ibid., 102).

This chapter should be read as a plea to let philosophical anthropology do its work, in the hope that empathy will result from it. It is undeniable, of course, that people will vary in the degree of empathy and compassion they tend to feel for others as they get to understand them better, but such feelings are not themselves the magic key to understanding others.

Chapter 3

WHO ARE 'WE' FOR WITTGENSTEIN?

> 'Why can't Panama invest in Panama?' she complained [...] 'Why do we have to have *Asians* do it? We're rich enough. We've got one hundred and seven banks in this town *alone*, don't we? Why can't we use our own drug money to build our own factories and schools and hospitals?' The 'we' was not literal. Louisa was a Zonian, raised in the Canal Zone in the days when by extortionate treaty it was American territory for ever, even if the territory was only ten miles wide and fifty miles long and surrounded by despised Panamanians.
>
> John Le Carré, The Tailor of Panama, 3

Prologue

We might, as I am doing now, employ the first-person plural 'we' to invite our readers to join us in a collective form of self-consciousness, thereby narrowing, or at least concealing, the distance between author and reader. But one may equally widen the distance by using impersonal pronouns instead.[1] Wittgenstein does both in his writings, but the former approach predominates.

'If a lion could speak', Wittgenstein famously states, 'we [*wir*] could not understand him'. But who are 'we' for Wittgenstein? It is commonplace to assume that he is referring to 'us humans' and, by the same token, that 'a lion' stands for all non-human animals.[2] This assumption is often found in defences of Wittgenstein's remark such as those by Nancy E. Baker (2012, 63), John Dupré (2002, 232), Rami Gudovitch (2012, 147–48) and Vicki Hearne (1994, 160). Dupré, for example, writes that the thought behind Wittgenstein's remark is that

1 I discuss the relation of 'one' to 'we' in Chapter 2, 'Eyes Wide Shut'.

2 For instance, Kipling 1894, 33 and Epstein 2005, 158. Nietzsche describes this as 'the denial of the individual ("all lions are at the bottom only one lion")' (GS, § 99). Cf. Tyler n.d.

> since lions, and other animals, lead wholly different lives, **their** hypothetical language could make no sense to **us**.[3]

Numerous anti-Wittgensteinians share this thought that Wittgenstein's 'we' refers to all humans, in contrast to all lions or perhaps even all (other) animals:

> Wittgenstein once claimed, 'If a lion could talk, we would not understand him.' He seemed to assume that because the **lion's** consciousness is so different from **ours**, even if there were a spoken lion language, it would be too alien for **us** to understand. However, lions and many other animals do indeed communicate in their own ways, and if **we** make an effort to understand their communications, **we** can learn much about *what **they** are saying*. (Bekoff 2007, 38)

> Wittgenstein said that if a lion could speak, **we** couldn't understand a word it was saying, since the form of a **lion's** world is so massively different from **our own**. He was wrong. I know he was wrong. (Foster 2016, 21)[4]

But while Wittgenstein's invitations to his readers are typically issued in virtue of varying assumed shared features, he never uses 'us', 'we', 'them' (or related possessive adjectives and pronouns such as 'our' and 'theirs') to mark a neat division between 'us' humans and 'them' animals. Instead, he refers to human beings in the third person (e.g. RPP, II: § 33; cf. RPP, II: §§ 29–30) and groups 'them' together with other animals (NB, 82, 84; PI, § 224). Invitations need not be taken up, of course. The reader may find that she can only go so far before realizing or deciding that the author's 'we' does not speak for her.[5] Indeed, the question of who we are is not always separable from the questions of who we want to be and who we want 'we' to be.[6] No amount of precision on the part of the author can settle these things in advance. Nor should it. Every audience is, to a certain extent, self-selecting.

---

3 Dupré 2002, 232. All quotations retain *italics* for original emphasis, with my own additional emphasis in **bold**.

4 Despite Foster's explicit dismissal of Wittgenstein, his book is an excellent illustration of Wittgenstein's ideas about what one needs to share with a foreign being in order to understand it better – and where the limits of such understanding lie.

5 See Barnes (1987, 176), who distinguishes between a royal, an editorial and a conspiratorial 'we'.

6 Incidentally: https://whodowewanttobe.weebly.com.

We Philosophers

There are numerous remarks in which the later Wittgenstein uses the pronoun 'we' to refer to people engaged in philosophical activity:

> Of course, what confuses **us** is the uniform appearance of words when **we** hear **them** in speech, or
>
> them written [...] For **their** use is not that obvious. Especially when **we** are doing philosophy! (PI, § 11)

The 'other' that contrasts with 'us' here is not a creature but the words we hear or read. Their appearance confuses 'us' especially *qua* philosophers, for to be confused by them in the relevant way is part and parcel of what Wittgenstein refers to as '[t]he dogmatism into which **we** fall so easily in doing philosophy' (PI, § 131):

> When **we** do philosophy, **we** are like savages, primitive people, who hear the way in which civilized people talk, put a false interpretation on it, and then draw the oddest conclusions from this. (PI, § 194)

However, it is also *qua* philosophers (of a diametrically different kind) that 'we' are to escape such confusions:

> The work of **the philosopher** consists in marshalling recollections for a particular purpose. (PI, §127; cf. §§ 52, 110)
>
> **Learning philosophy** is *really* recollecting. **We** remember that **we** really did use words that way. (BT, § 89)

Wittgenstein uses 'philosophy' to refer to both a kind of malady *and* its cure – that is, to both bad (unhealthy) and good (healthy) ways of philosophizing. When referring to the former, he sometimes distances himself and 'us' from philosophers:

> When **philosophers** use a word – 'knowledge', 'being', 'object', 'I', 'proposition/sentence', 'name' – and try to grasp the essence of the thing, **one** must always ask oneself: is the word ever actually used in this way in the language in which it is at home? –
>
> What ***we*** do is to bring words back from their metaphysical to their everyday use. (PI, § 116; cf. PI, §§ 124–8)[7]

7 The extent to which 'the author of the *Tractatus*' (PI, § 23; cf. 4e, § 46) is one of 'us' is a moot point, as is about to become evident.

> **We** are, indeed, also interested in the correspondence between concepts and very general facts of nature [...] **we** are not doing natural science [...] **we** can also invent a fictitious natural history for our purposes. (PPF, § 365)

There are echoes here of Nietzsche's more bombastic, esoteric appeals to 'We scholars' (BGE, VI); 'We artists' (GS, § 59; BGE, § 250[8]); 'we (last; good) Europeans' (GS, § 352; BGE, §§ 214, 241, 267); 'we incomprehensible ones' (GS, § 371); 'we philosophers of the present and the future' (GS, § 372); 'we modern men' (GS, § 375); 'we northerners' (BGE, § 48); 'we new philosophers' (WTP, § 988); 'we few or many [...] pagans in faith' (WTP, § 1034); 'we free spirits' (BGE, § 61); 'we first born of the twentieth century' (BGE, § 214).[9] These pick out the kind of philosopher that Nietzsche thought he was, often via an (implicit or explicit) reference to his gender[10] or the time and place in which he is writing.

Both philosophers hover between speaking as if they are *alone* in opposing the old guard and implying that they are part of a wider 'we' who practise this new method. Nietzsche thus advertises his *Human, All Too Human* as 'a book for free spirits' and his *Thus Spoke Zarathustra* as a 'Book for All and None'. Wittgenstein likewise writes with very few specific individuals in mind, making references to the few possible readers who might understand what he was up to.[11] In his 1918 Preface to the *Tractatus*, Wittgenstein states that '[p]erhaps this book will be understood only by someone who has oneself already had the thoughts that are expressed in it – or at least similar thoughts' (TLP-R, 3/26).[12] Little had changed by the time of his 1945 Preface to the *Investigations*:

---

8 The 2001 translation has 'artists like us'.

9 The contrast between these pluralities and the 'I' that dominates the section titles of *Ecce Homo* is striking (see Sandis 2019b).

10 For the problem of privileged maleness within the philosophical 'we', see Naomi Scheman, who writes that '[p]art of what is distressing to many women in reading philosophical texts is the experience of taking oneself to be included in the 'we' and coming up short against the realisation that one really wasn't' (Scheman 1990, 27).

11 For Wittgenstein's personal difficulties in understanding others and being understood by them, see Chapter 1.

12 The original Ogden translation reads 'those who have themselves' (TLP, 3), and the revised Pears and McGuinness one reads 'someone who has himself'. Katja Behrens pointed out to me that while Wittgenstein starts with the masculine '*der*', he ends with the neutral '*selbst*', which is closer to 'oneself' than 'himself', but that the revised translation is right to emphasize that Wittgenstein is writing in the singular. So, while this does not exclude the possibility of more than one reader who understands Wittgenstein, the expectations of a plurality's doing so are very low indeed.

> It is not impossible that it should fall to the lot of this work [...] to bring light into one brain or another – but, of course, it is not likely. (PI, 4)

Wittgenstein differs from Nietzsche in not contrasting the 'we' of those philosophizing in the right way with a 'they' of completely distinct *others* who have gone wrong. Indeed, the 'they' who contrasts with Wittgenstein's 'us' is arguably his own past self:

> A picture held **us** captive. And **we** couldn't get outside it, for it lay in **our** language, and language seemed only to repeat it to **us** inexorably. (PI, § 115)

If this is the case, then PI §§ 115–16 is contrasting a present-tense royal 'we' (referring to the author of the *Investigations*) with a past-tense royal 'us' (referring to the author of the *Tractatus*). Certain remarks in the *Investigations* offer some support to this autobiographical reading:

> The real discovery is the one that enables me to break off philosophizing when **I** want to. – The one that gives philosophy peace, so that it is no longer tormented by questions which bring itself in question. (PI, § 133; cf. § 255)

> What is **your** aim in philosophy? – To show the fly the way out of the fly-bottle. (PI, § 310)

Wittgenstein's uses of 'we' and 'us' thus serve to both unite him to and separate him from his earlier self. We should not exclude the possibility, however, that the scope of each indexical extends more widely to include kindred spirits:

> Philosophy is a struggle against the bewitchment of **our** understanding by the resources of **our** language. (PI, § 109)

So understood, Wittgenstein uses 'we' to talk of philosophers both when in the grip of a misleading picture of language (PI, §§ 11, 131, 194, 295, 303, 520, 598) and when dissolving the pseudo-problems presented by the picture (PI, §§ 109, 127, 393; BT § 89). While he sometimes refers to philosophers in the third person (PI, §§ 309, 514), it is never in the pejorative sense in which some of his followers talk of certain kinds of philosophers as the misguided enemy whose confusions they are too enlightened to share. Wittgenstein includes himself among those who, tricked by language, are on the verge of lapsing into philosophy:

> What **we** are 'tempted to say' [...] is, of course, not philosophy; but it is its raw material. (PI, § 244; cf. PI, § 38)

But 'we' are also they who *rise* to a better way of doing philosophy, one that proceeds by way of observing how it is that the use of words tempts us so.

We Language Users

Wittgenstein writes that for 'a large class of cases – though not for all – in which **we** employ the word "meaning" it can be defined thus: the meaning of a word is its use in the language' (PI, § 43; cf. LW, II, 38e–39e). Applied to the word 'we' itself, this introduces a potential problem of circularity: must 'we' already know how the word 'we' is being used to know who the 'we' who are using the word in the first place are? But the difficulty, such as it is, is not insuperable. For the question to be settled is only how Wittgenstein himself is using the word 'we' in various philosophical contexts. One obvious answer is that he uses it to refer to users of language. If so, then the 'we' here picks out competent users of a lexical language who are not misapplying a rule (for mere competency does not render one immune to error), with the presumption that this set includes both author and reader. His later work is replete with such uses of 'we':

> **We** can put it like this: This sample is an instrument of the language, by means of which **we** make colour statements. (PI, § 50)
>
> Consider, for example, the activities that **we** call 'games'. (PI, § 66)
>
> If **we** are using the word 'know' as it is normally used (and how else are **we** to use it!), then other people very often know when I am in pain. (PI, § 246)
>
> But would **we** really say that he feels pity? Wouldn't **we** say 'It really isn't pity because he isn't acquainted with any pain of his own' –? (RPP, II, §28)
>
> **We** would say, perhaps, of a green pane: it colours the things behind it green, above all the white behind it. (ROC, I: § 26; see also ROC, I: §§ 24, 25, 33, 40)
>
> **We** speak of the 'colour of gold' and do not mean yellow.
>
> (ROC, I, § 33; see also ROC, I, §§ 47–8)

It is tempting to think that 'we' shifts from German speakers to the speakers of all the languages into which the text has been translated, even in cases in which Wittgenstein could not anticipate – let alone authorize – the translation. But, in contrast to phrases such as '*wir deutsch sprechen*' (see below), none of these examples seems to exclude the typical reader of the phrase in translation. It would be far more sensible to assume that in the passages 'we' includes anyone who shares the concept expressed by any German word(s) he discusses. Wittgenstein contrasts such people (viz. 'us') with *other* people, whose language games are different from ours:

> Now it is conceivable that **some people** might have a verb whose third person would be *exactly* equivalent to **our** 'He is afraid'; but whose first person is not equivalent to **our** 'I am afraid'. (RPP, II, § 169)

This assumes the existence of a 'we' that includes Wittgenstein himself, alongside others who all share certain concepts and grammatical training, including the concept expressed by the German word 'wir' and the English word 'we'. These words are no different from others in being used in a variety of interrelated ways across contexts, including the following by his near contemporaries:

> 'Good' [...] if **we** mean by it that quality which we assert to belong to a thing, when **we say** that the thing is good, is incapable of any definition. (Moore 1903, §§ 6–10)

> Where **we** are tempted to speak of 'different senses' of a word which is clearly not equivocal, **we** may infer that **we** are in fact pretty much in the dark about the character of the concept which it represents. (Anscombe 1957, § 1)

> To maintain that good is indefinable is not to maintain that **we** cannot know what it is like or that **we** cannot say anything about it but only that it is not reducible to anything else. (Ewing 1953, 89)

> **[W]e** might observe what words have actually been used by commentators on real incidents, or by narrators of fictitious incidents. However, **we** do not have the time or space to do that here. **We** must instead imagine some cases [...] and try to reach agreement upon what **we** should in fact say concerning them. If **we** can reach this agreement, **we** shall have some data [...] which **we** can then go on to explain [...] Of course, **we** shall then have arrived at nothing more than an account of certain ordinary 'concepts' employed by English speakers: but also at no less a thing. (Austin 1966, 429)

Prima facie, Austin's 'we' may seem to refer to English speakers. But his works have been translated into numerous languages. One can imagine translating 'by English speakers' in the last sense both literally as '*wir englischsprachige*' and more liberally as '*wir deutschsprachige*'. But the latter 'translation' would be viable only in cases (such as Austin's) in which the remainder of the phrase, as well as its wider context, made no allusion to any non-transferable peculiarities of English speakers.

The question of the relationship between how words are used in a particular language and how concepts function across languages is undoubtedly important.[13] But we need not agree on the answer to allow that when Austin describes how 'we' use a certain word in English, the remark need not be read either as inviting only English-speaking readers to join him in a shared consciousness or as explicitly speaking to a wider circle.

When someone (*even* a philosopher) uses the word 'we', they need not have in mind any precise parameters of its referent. As Wittgenstein himself maintains in his discussions of meaning and intention, what we have in mind when we use a certain word or phrase might make itself manifest only as and when the need for precision arises (often enough, there is no need for precision at all; see PI, § 70). Suppose you ask me to clean your room, and I tidy the inside of your desk. Upon finding out, you tell me that you did not mean for me to do that but only to empty the bin, hoover the floor and the like. Must the precise range of what you did and did not mean for me to do have flashed before your mind when you originally asked me to clean your room? Wittgenstein asks a similar rhetorical question in the notes accompanying PI, § 70:

> Someone says to me, 'Show the children a game.' I teach them gambling with dice, and the other says, 'I didn't mean that sort of game'. In that case, must he have had the exclusion of the game with dice before his mind when he gave me the order? (PI, 33n.; cf. RPP, II, § 244)

One need no more have such an idea in mind than entertain a precise definition of a novel when entering a bookshop and coming out with a copy of Anthony Powell's *A Question of Upbringing*.

Appeals to what 'we' say and do of the sort found in the work of Wittgenstein and others have in recent years become the target of experimental philosophy and related forms of scepticism regarding so-called 'ordinary language philosophy'. Thus, for example, Kwame Anthony Appiah asserts:

> If conceptual analysis is the analysis of **'our'** concepts, then shouldn't **one** see how **'we'** – or representative samples of **us** – actually mobilize

13 Cf. Cassin 2014, Crane 2015, Das 2006, Deutscher 2011, Harrison 1832, Soames 2005, 323–30.

> concepts in **our** talk? So one strain of this work seeks to elicit and tabulate intuitions people have about various scenarios. (Appiah 2008b, § VI)[14]

He elaborates, elsewhere:

> For Austin, what a person knows in knowing English, say, is what every competent speaker *should* say in a certain situation; and so, being competent myself, I know what everyone else *would* say if they were competent. That is why it wouldn't matter if **we** found individuals who *didn't* say it: it would just show that they weren't competent. In section 21 of the *Philosophical Investigations* Wittgenstein wrote: '**We** do in fact call "Isn't the weather glorious today?" a question, although it is used as a statement.' Until recently, philosophers in my tradition would have thought it impertinent to ask who the '**we**' is here, and pointless to go out and inquire of people in the street whether someone who said these words was really asking a question. (Appiah 2008a, 19–20; see also Appiah 2008b, 12)

The old-fashioned (armchair) philosophers that Appiah berates are to be contrasted with the new (street) philosophers conducting surveys. Here is how some of the latter conceive of what *they* do, and why they consider their approach superior:

> [T]he conceptual analyst might write 'in this case, one would surely say...,' while the experimental philosopher would write, 'in this case, 79% of subjects said...' and back her claims with statistical data. (Knobe and Nichols 2008, 4)
>
> [A]reas of philosophy that rely on (i) intuition-pumps and thought experiments, (ii) appeals to commonsense and pre-philosophical intuition or (iii) conceptual analysis based in part on ordinary usage [...]

14 Appiah adds the following cute anecdote: 'In the empirical spirit, I should report that, when I typed the phrase "it would be natural to say" into Google's Book Search, it happily returned, as its top search results, passages by Gilbert Ryle, Peter Strawson, Max Black, and Bertrand Russell' (Appiah 2008b, § VII). But my own empirical research via search engines accessed from the proverbial armchair reveals that Russell (who hated anything vaguely resembling appeal to ordinary language philosophy) is not the utterer of the phrase appearing in connection with him and that high up in the search results for the phrase are situationist Gilbert Harman (1973), biosemanticist Ruth Garrett Millikan (1994), Kantian logician Charles Parsons (1974) and evolutionary psychologist Steven Pinker (2007), who speaks of certain sentences sounding 'odd to an English-speaker's ears' (33).

> are ripe for investigation by experimental philosophers [...] examining these things in a controlled and systematic way [...] [T]here is a **shared** distrust of philosophers' (common) claims of the general form [...] 'The ordinary use of "X" is Y,' [...] based upon armchair reflection on their own intuitions and (perhaps selective) consideration of their conversations with friends, family, and especially students [...] [using] methods [...] highly susceptible to well-known biases. (Naddelhoffer and Nahmias 2007, 125)

Leaving aside obvious questions about who 'we' and 'one' are for Appiah, or who is sharing the distrust of Naddelhoffer and Nahmias, these passages collectively incorporate a jumble of confusions, including the mistaken assumptions that (i) Wittgenstein and Austin were in the business of offering *analyses* of concepts, (ii) such 'conceptual analysts' rely on nothing more than *intuitions* under the guise of 'common sense' (see Appiah 2008a, 73) and (iii) remarks about 'what we say' are to be verified by statistical facts about actual usage. I unravel these elsewhere in more detail (Sandis 2010a), so I shall here focus solely on their relation to how we should view uses of 'we' in philosophy.

At times, it would appear that experimental philosophers take the 'we' of Wittgenstein, Austin and others to be referring to *all* speakers of a language, regardless of whether or not they use language correctly. But it is perhaps fairer to ascribe to these critics the view that there is no distinction to be made here at all: meaning really just *is* collective use. Either way, the claims of Wittgenstein and others about 'what *we* ordinarily say' are not expressions of their intuitions about what a statistical survey would reveal about the usage of native speakers (RPP, II, § 28) but rather claims describing the norms of linguistic use. To be sure, the norms grow *out of* actual linguistic and non-linguistic behaviour (see ROC, I, § 3), but they live a life of their own. As we have already seen, the 'we' in question often picks out an idealization of *competent* speakers at their best.[15] One could distinguish here, as Hume does, between what *philosophers* say and what 'the *vulgar*' say (noting that members of both groups misuse terms to the extent that they fail to grasp the proper significance of any given idea).[16] By contrast, we have seen that Wittgenstein

15 In a critique of experimental philosophy, Neil Levy uses the word 'we' to refer to a small, clearly defined community: 'By "we" I mean the geographically and temporally extended philosophical community, engaged in an open-ended debate. Everyone is invited to participate in this debate, but the price of entry is hard work: only when you expose your intuitions to the best arguments and the full range of relevant cases will they count as (defeasible) evidence for and against philosophical theories' (Levy n.d.).

16 Hume 1739, I.3.14, I.4.2.30. For exegesis, see Chapter 4 in Sandis 2019a.

uses 'we' to refer sometimes to philosophers and other times to competent speakers ('We Language Users', the current section). The latter group, a linguistic analogue of the proverbial 'man on the Clapham omnibus',[17] should not be confused with the 'vulgar' in Hume, and neither is identical to the class of all humans.

We shall below that, like Hume before him, Wittgenstein sometimes uses 'we' to talk of the 'average' or 'normal' human being. This elusive construct may overlap with that of the competent speaker, but Wittgenstein is not interested in hypothesizing precisely how such a person might use language but rather in how her concepts might differ from those of people who are altogether more unusual. To speak of the latter, he could equally have used the pronoun 'one' or perhaps even the more direct 'you'. Indeed, the famous final sentence of the *Tractatus*[18] has been translated both as 'whereof **one** cannot speak, thereof **one** must be silent' (Ogden) and as 'what **we** cannot speak about **we** must pass over in silence' (Pears and McGuiness). It is, however, more literally translated as reaching right up to the reader in terms of what '*you*' cannot speak of and should thus remain silent about. The use of 'we' to mean 'one' is also present in Nietzsche:

> *What* **others** *know about* **us**, – What we know about **ourselves** and remember is not so decisive for the happiness of our life as **people** suppose. One day that which *others* know about us (or think they know) assaults us – and then we realize that this is more powerful. (GS, 52; cf. D, 292; HATH, 428; GM, Preface)

Here, the 'us' refers to all individuals *qua* themselves, while 'others' refers to all individuals *qua* others.[19]

17 A legal fiction, the origins of which may be traced back to Walter Bagehot's *The English Constitution*: '[p]ublic opinion' nowadays 'is the opinion of the bald-headed man at the back of the omnibus', representing 'the ordinary mass of educated, but still commonplace mankind' (Bagehot 1867, 325–6).

18 '*Wovon man nicht sprechen kann, darüber muss* **man** *schweigen*' (TLP, § 7).

19 In a recent study, Orvell et al. (2018) discovered that children (ages 2–10) tend to interpret the second person pronoun 'you' as generic (viz. referring to people in general) in normative contexts and canonical (viz. referring to the addressee) in descriptive ones. When asked, for example, 'What do you do with books?' or 'What should you do with books?' they generally responded, 'You read them'. By contrast, when asked, 'What do you *like* to do with books?' they tended to answer, 'I read them'. The generic 'you', but not the canonical one, is replaceable with the third-person singular pronoun 'one'. The research team informally noticed that *parents* seemed to use 'we' frequently in normative contexts. It is not as easy to distinguish generic from canonical uses

We 'Normal' People

Jonathan Lear puts forth the following worry about Wittgenstein's use of 'we' in the sorts of passages discussed so far. He writes:

> 'We must do away with all explanation.' To whom is this injunction addressed? Who are the 'we' who must do away with all explanation: we philosophers? we anthropologists? On the split-level interpretation, the injunction would be restricted to philosophers. But philosophy is not so divorced from the rest of **our** lives. Wittgenstein should have distinguished between the 'We' and a form of life in much the same way that Kant should have distinguished the 'I' from the 'I think'. 'Form of life' is a predicate which may be predicated of various objects. **We** may use the term narrowly and label disparate social groups alternative 'forms of life'; or **we** may use the term widely to mark the form of life which we all constitute. Switching to the first person plural, *form of life* is a reflective concept, used by philosophers and anthropologists when they try to construct a representation of us. It is 'We' as 'We' appear to ourselves. Even if **we** represent ourselves as reflective thinkers trying to understand who **we** are, by the very nature of the anthropological stance **we** will end up with a form of life, not with what I have gestured at calling 'We'. Who are we?! If, on the one hand, we are one group among others, then Wittgenstein's remarks about forms of life lacking justification would seem to encourage a slide toward relativism. If, on the other hand, the 'We' encompasses us all, encompasses any being who might in the widest of senses count as one of us, then doesn't the first person plural lose its force? [...] In this instance at least, I believe there is a middle course. (Lear 1998, 263–76)

It is striking that in a passage questioning who 'we' must be for Wittgenstein, Lear refers to the relation of philosophy to 'our' lives without specifying what he means by 'our'.[20] His own 'middle course' is that of the 'we' that picks out the very mindedness that is a 'constitutive condition' of what occurs in any human form of life (in Wittgenstein's sense of the term). But there is nothing

---

here, because 'we' could refer to either people in general (generic) or parent and child (canonical). Once again, only the former is replaceable with 'one'.

20 Striking, but not uncommon (see also, e.g., Despret 2008, 123). Despite his officially transcendental position, Lear gives away that he actually thinks of 'we' as all humans: 'Perhaps there are Martians who speak a language which because of some kinks in our hardwiring we will never be able to recognize as such' (Lear 1998, 279–80; cf. Sagan et al. 1978, 5–6, 14).

to rule out philosophizing by alien language users.[21] Moreover, philosophy is not yet possible for toddlers and other human beings who are not competent speakers of any language. It is tempting to think that we might do better and try to think of philosophy as part and parcel of the life of the average human being. But this cannot be right either, and not just because of the possibility of alien philosophers. The problem is that we cannot answer the 'we' question without looking at why Wittgenstein claims that 'we' should do away with explanation.

Wittgenstein is not claiming that the average human being, let alone humans as a species, must cease explaining things. Good science, after all, is often explanatory. Nor could Wittgenstein be thinking that everyone within the academy must do away with explanation, not least because he does not think of philosophy as being limited to (or even primarily connected with) activities conducted within the academy.

Philosophy is part and parcel of the lives of those linguistic beings who are ordinary users of words. But it does not follow that such beings should never attempt to explain anything. In fact, it is not clear that Wittgenstein can really think that we are not sometimes, even *qua* philosophers, in the business of explaining why certain things follow from other things. Indeed, he often speaks of explaining this or that himself. What Wittgenstein really has in mind is the philosopher's tendency to seek logical or metaphysical explanations of phenomena when a mere description of how we use words will do. Whether or not the shoe fits anthropological and other investigations is an open question to be judged on a case-by-case basis.

Lear talks as if there is a general problem. But there is no philosophically difficult question of where 'we' are meant to draw the line. 'We' must do away with all explanation when engaging in a certain kind of philosophical activity, and for this to be true 'we' had better be the sort of creatures able to engage in such activity. For Wittgenstein, this means that 'we' often picks out creatures that can use human language and be puzzled about the philosophical questions it tempts us into. This excludes those who either are unable to say anything or would be tempted to say very different things because they are in some way not like 'us':

> What would a society of all deaf men be like? Or a society of the 'feeble-minded'? *An important question!* What then of a society that never played any of **our** customary language games? (Z, § 371)

21 The point is made by Bernard Williams (Williams 1974, 160), though I reject his transcendental framing of it at the end of this chaper.

Wittgenstein raises such questions time and time again, contrasting 'us' with certain non-human animals, alien tribes, young infants, people who are blind or colour-blind, people with differing abilities and impediments, and 'mental defectives'.[22] For his purposes, the lion is in many respects no different from the colour-blind person, the extraterrestrial, or the member of some foreign tribe. The other side of this coin is that by focusing on 'normal people', Wittgenstein allows that those with special abilities (whether acquired or innate) that the rest of 'us' lack – be they horse whisperers or those with perfect pitch – are capable of understanding things and creatures (including one another) that 'we' normal people cannot.[23] In *Remarks on Colour*, our normality is often fixed in relation to something specific, particularly sight. While possibly relevant to certain empirical investigations, it is of little interest to his conceptual exploration of colour whether the set of normally sighted people includes those of 'us'[24] who are horse whisperers, bad at hearing or spelling, left-handed, autistic, musical prodigies, mathematical geniuses or moral monsters (ROC, I, § 40). What is required and assumed is that the people in this set are otherwise capable of employing and sharing concepts with us:

> **We** say: 'Let's imagine people who do not know this language-game.' But in doing so **we** still have no conception of the life of **these people** in so far as it differs from **our** own. **We** do not yet know what we are supposed to imagine; for the life of **these people** is in all other ways to correspond with **ours**, and it still must be determined what **we** would call a life corresponding to **ours** under these new conditions. (LW, II, 71e)

> Lichtenberg says that **very few people** have ever seen pure white. So do **most people** use the word wrong, then? And how did *he* learn the correct use? – He constructed an ideal use from the ordinary one [...] And of course such a construct may in turn teach **us** something about the way **we** in fact use the word. (ROC, I, §§ 3-4)

> And to whom can I describe all the things ***we* normal people** can learn? (ROC, III, § 121).

22 Related examples can be found in passages such as ROC, I, § 81 and ROC, III, §§ 28, 31. As we shall see, he sometimes shifts the reference of 'them' to particular subsets of 'normal people' such as 'the Chinese'.

23 Hence my earlier claim (n. 4) that Foster's book is more aligned with Wittgenstein's own views than he thinks.

24 Note how easily the context allows 'us' to contrast with who 'we' were in the previous paragraph.

These are to be contrasted with the following:

> People might have the concept of intermediary colours or mixed colours even if **they** never produced colours by mixing (in whatever sense). **Their** language games might only have to do with looking for or selecting already existing intermediary or blended colours. (ROC, I, § 8)

> **The colour-blind** not merely cannot learn to use **our** colour words, **they** can't learn to use the word 'colour-blind' as **a normal person** does. They cannot, for examplw, establish colour-blindness in the same way as **the normal** do. (ROC, I, § 77; see also ROC, III, §§ 97 and 112)

> Imagine a *tribe* of colour-blind people, and there could easily be one. **They** would not have the same colour concepts as **we** do. For even assuming **they** speak, e.g. English, and thus have all the English colour words, **they** would still use them differently than **we** do and would *learn* **their** use differently. Or if **they** have a foreign language, it would be difficult for **us** to translate **their** colour words into **ours.** (ROC, I, § 13; cf. ROC, III, §§ 128–9 and PPF, § 325)

Wittgenstein continues:

> But even if there were also people for whom it was natural to use the expressions 'reddish-green' or 'yellowish-blue' in a consistent manner and who perhaps also exhibit abilities which **we** lack, **we** would still not be forced to recognise that **they** see *colours* which **we** do not see. There is, after all, no *commonly accepted* criterion for what is a colour, unless it is one of **our** colours. (ROC, I, § 14)

Here, 'we' are being contrasted with both those who lack an ability 'we' have and those who have an ability 'we' lack. In the context of *Remarks on Colour*, Wittgenstein's examples of such abilities are understandably ones relating to perception (usually of colour, although he sometimes employs analogies with sound). But his thoughts on the relation of language use to concepts and, in turn, the relation of concepts to abilities should not be limited to such examples.

Wittgenstein sometimes talks of 'mental defectives'[25] and, again, he could have also added those with extraordinary mental abilities that 'we' lack. 'We', then, often means 'most of us'. Who is counting? Wittgenstein is not in the business of providing statistical data. Rather, the 'most' is indicative of a

25 ROC, I, § 75; ROC, III, § 118; RPP, I, §§ 179, 198, 216, 957.

typical norm that could easily change across very long periods of time (e.g. the norm that most of us are not colour-blind). In this he resembles David Hume, who despite being labelled a kind of 'sceptic' always begins with a 'we' and not an 'I' (see Sandis 2019a, 50).

The passages from *Remarks in Colour* quoted here (written in 1950 and revised March 1951) revisit the issues raised in Chapter XI of the second part of the *Investigations* (written 1948–49; hereinafter PPF).[26] Indeed, we can imagine them fitting between PPF § 325 and § 326 (just before the lion remark in § 327):

> **We** also say of a person that he is transparent to **us**. It is, however, important as regards **our** considerations that one **human being** can be a complete enigma to another. **One** [*man*] learns this when **one** comes into a strange country with entirely strange traditions; and what is more, even given a mastery of the country's language. **One** does not *understand* the **people**. (**And not because of not knowing what they are saying to themselves**). **We** can't find **our** feet with **them** [*Wir können uns nicht in sie finden*]. (PPF, § 325)

> "I can't know what is going on in him" is, above all, a *picture*'. It is the convincing expression of a conviction. It does not give reasons for the conviction. *They* are not obvious. (PPF, § 325; emphasis in original)

Wittgenstein's foreign tribes and peoples may be fictional, but their inspiration is not always very far away from home:

> It is important for **our** approach, that someone may feel concerning **certain people** that he will never know what goes on inside **them** [*was in inhnen vorgeht*]. He will never understand **them** (**Englishwomen** for **Europeans**). (CV, 74e)

> 'Which **foreigner** doesn't feel that way when **he** comes to England?' (TS 232 and MS 135–7)

> **We** tend to take the speech of a Chinese for inarticulate gurgling. Someone who understands Chinese will recognize *language* in what **he** hears. Similarly **I** often cannot discern the *humanity* in **a man**. (CV, 1e)

26 In her Editor's Preface to ROC, Anscombe writes that she has, *inter alia*, 'left out material on "inner-outer"' because it was 'both marked as discontinuous with the text and also will appear elsewhere', namely LW II. These remarks form a natural continuation of the themes of PPF §§ 301–32, sections that are primarily concerned with the concept of hiddenness in relation to inner/outer.

> **We** don't understand Chinese gestures any more than Chinese sentences. (Z, 219; see also LW, II, 89)

This problematic othering once again betrays traces of Nietzsche, who contrasts his 'we' (see Section 1) with groups such as 'the Greeks' (GS, §§ 155, 356; D, §§ 15, 72; BGE, § 260), 'savage tribes' (GS, § 147), 'the Englishman' (BGE, § 252), 'the Celts' (BGE, § 48), 'the Chinese' (BGE, § 267), 'the Jesuits' (BGE, § 48), 'the Brahmins' (BGE, § 61), 'the Jews'[27] (D, § 72; BGE, §§ 61, 250) and 'the first Christians'[28] (D, § 72), 'German middle-class Protestants' (BGE, § 58) and, indeed, 'the German(s)' (BGE, §§ 11, 28, 246).[29]

Wittgenstein might not *always* tell the reader who 'we' and 'they' are quite as explicitly as Nietzsche but, *pace* Lear, he paints a reasonably clear picture across different contexts and contrasts – for better or worse. Both are far removed from the collective of *all* humans. In contrast to Nietzsche's superhuman 'we', Wittgenstein's 'we' typically represents people who are as normal as possible in some relevant respect.[30] This use is easy to follow without entering into metaphysical debates regarding the ontology of we-groups.[31]

Epilogue

One might find it odd that Wittgenstein seems philosophically uninterested in the first-person plural, despite his fascination with the singular first-person pronoun, from his early pronouncement that 'the I is what is deeply mysterious!' (NB, 80) to his later scepticism about 'I' referring to a 'self' (PI, §§ 404–13). Of course, 'we' is not the plural of 'I' (Lyons 1968, 277) but, rather,

---

27 While Wittgenstein's problematic remarks about 'Jews' are in the third person, they are not intended to exclude him: 'Amongst Jews "genius" is found only in the holy man. Even the greatest of Jewish thinkers is no more than talented. (Myself for instance.)' (CV, 18e; see also CV, 13e, 16e). Wittgenstein also offers a rather elaborate example (written between 1946 and 1947) of a 'tribe that we want to enslave' (RPP I, § 96; cf. Z, § 528) that is much too close to home. For explorations of Wittgenstein's remarks concerning Jewishness, see McGuiness 2001 and Stern 2001, esp. 254–62.

28 Nietzsche also refers to 'Christians' across his works, but the locution is relatively rare by comparison to 'Christianity' and 'the Christian X'.

29 Nietzsche reminds us that the names of peoples are usually terms of abuse. 'The Tartars, for example, are literally "the dogs"; that is what the Chinese called them. The "Germans": this originally meant "heathen"; that is what the Goths after their conversion named the great mass of their unbaptized kindred tribes' (GS, § 146).

30 This is not to dismiss the fact that Wittgenstein, who was no normie, nevertheless uses phrases such as 'we normal people' in ways which would now be rightly deemed to be problematic.

31 Cf. Stekeler-Weithofer 2019, § 1.

'a plural term lacking first-person form' (de Gaynesford 2006, 41).[32] For 'we' does not amount to 'I and I' (Bierce 1911/2000, 116), which finds meaning only in Rastafari vocabulary (Iyaric) signifying the oneness of two people, one of whom may, but need not, be God (said to be within all humans).[33] And what, if anything, would a chorus uttering 'we think, therefore we are' prove?[34]

Bernard Williams ingeniously suggests that Wittgenstein's 'well-chartered moves in the later work from "I" to "We"' take place '*within the transcendental ideas themselves*' and that the 'important element of idealism' that the later work retains helps to explain the 'pervasive vagueness and indefiniteness evident in the use Wittgenstein makes of "we"' (Williams 1974, 147). Curiously, Williams' own article begins with a quotation from TLP-R § 5.61 in which Wittgenstein talks of what '**we** [***Wir***] cannot say in logic' and states that '**we** cannot think what **we** cannot think; so **we** cannot think what **we** cannot *say* either'.[35] The fact that this is being quoted as evidence of Wittgenstein's 'me' stance in the *Tractatus* betrays a peculiar downplaying of an important linguistic thread that runs throughout Wittgenstein's early and later work.

On Williams' view 'one finds oneself with a *we* which is not one group rather than another in the world at all, but rather the plural descendent of that idealist *I* who was not one item rather than another in the world' (Williams 1974, 160). This reading is motivated by the thought that 'we' in Wittgenstein refers neither to 'our group as contrasted with other human groups' nor to 'humanity' (ibid., 160). I have tried to show that while it indeed does not refer to humanity, we would be wrong to think that Wittgenstein's 'we' never refers to our group in contrast to others. While there is no doubt that Wittgenstein

32 De Gaynesford adds: '*I* is crucially unlike the so-called "first person plural" if, as some argue, *We* "leaves room for anaphora and binding" [Vallée 1996, 230]' (de Gaynesford 2006, 92); for free and bound variable pronouns see Higginbotham 1980 and Franz 2018.

33 Similarly, 'Me ne me' in the Twi language of Ghana can be used instead of 'you and I' or 'we'. For recent observations of 'I' metamorphosing into 'we', see Sullivan 2018, 4 and P. Williams 2019, 11; cf. Vallée 1996, 220 ff.

34 Cf. Stekeler-Weithofer (2019, §1). Brendan Larvor has pointed out to me a peculiar use of 'we' that effectively means 'the others' in contemporary journalism when the journalists are bemoaning something about 'us'. The journalist exclaims, for example, that 'we' have forgotten the meaning of Christmas. Unless the article is self-flagellatory, the 'we' cannot include the author, who is the one pointing out what has been forgotten. If the similar-minded reader is to be flattered, it does not refer to him or her either. It is *they* – the *other*s – who have forgotten the true meaning of Christmas, but 'we' (you and I: reader and author in unison) know better than that.

35 The Ogden translation is the same in all crucial respects.

transitions to a more practice-based philosophy in his later work,[36] we have seen that he often uses 'we' to mark specific in-groups, be they united by culture, ability, philosophical disposition or mere averageness. Not only do such groupings not require a transcendental 'we', they positively forbid it. As Ilham Dilman puts it, Wittgenstein's 'speakers are themselves *in* the world of the language they speak' (Dilman 2002, 86). The social worldview that this is embedded in Section 2 is incompatible with a linguistic idealism in which the solipsistic suggestion that 'the limits of *my* language mean the limits of *my* world' is simply replaced with the mass idealism that 'the limits of *our* language mean the limits of *our* world' (Williams 1974, 150).[37]

Part of the explanation of Wittgenstein's apparent lack of puzzlement with 'we' is that, *pace* Williams and Lear, he takes the context of each remark to render the intended referent of the term reasonably obvious. Accordingly, 'we' functions as a linguistic shifter whose meaning depends on the message, who is delivering it and the context in which it is being delivered.[38] Indeed, as Julia Kursell notes, 'the pronoun "we" opens up the possibility to include or exclude the participants of a communicative situation' (Kursell 2010, 218). She illustrates this by reference to Bertolt Brecht's '*Wer aber ist die Partei?*', a song highlighting features that render 'we' an important rhetorical tool in politics.[39] The shifter's political power is also captured by George Orwell across Napoleon's first speech towards the start of *Animal Farm* and his second speech just over twenty pages later:

> **[C]omrades** [...] **We** are born, **we** are given just so much food as will keep the breath in our bodies [...] [T]he very instant that **our** usefulness has come to an end **we** are slaughtered. [...] **No animal** knows the meaning of happiness. [...] Why then do **we** continue in this

36 Sami Pihlström cautiously suggests that we can see the later Wittgenstein's 'we' as a 'socio-pragmatic reinterpretation of the transcendental self', while remaining neutral on what Wittgenstein's own view was (Pihlström 2015, 230).

37 For critical responses to idealist readings of Wittgenstein, see Dilham 1990, esp. Chapters 3 and 4, and Mulhall 2009. As Mulhall notes, Williams' reading is deeply inspired by the neo-Kantian reading of Wittgenstein in P. M. S. Hacker's first (1972) edition of *Insight and Illusion*, which Hacker comes to reject as 'misconstrued [...] exaggerated and distorted' in the 2nd edition (1986, ix); cf. A. W. Moore 2010, 209–12.

38 Ironically, the term 'shifter' was introduced by Jakobson as an account of the first-person *singular* (Jakobson 1957, 42–43), influenced by Russell's account of 'egocentric particulars' (viz. indexicals), which 'have a meaning relative to the speaker' (Russell 1940, 17).

39 See Brecht 1977, 28 (cf. Brecht 1998).

> miserable condition? [...] **Man** is the only real enemy **we** have [...] the only **creature** that consumes without producing. (Orwell 1945, 8–9)

> **Comrades**! [...] **You** do not imagine that **we pigs** are doing this in a spirit of selfishness and privilege? Many of **us** actually dislike milk and apples. I dislike them myself [...] Milk and apples (this has been proved by Science, comrades) contain substances absolutely necessary to the well-being of **a pig**. **We pigs** are brain-workers. It is for ***your*** sake that **we** drink that milk and eat those apples. (Ibid., 32)[40]

Even the 'you' of the second speech must remain a 'we' of sorts in a totalitarian system in which the 'I' is altogether eliminated. The best-known portrayal of this is to be found in Arthur Koestler's *Darkness at Noon*:

> The hours which remained to him belonged to that silent partner, whose realm started just where logical thought ended. He had christened it '**the** grammatical fiction' [*grammatikalische Fiktion*[41]] with that shamefacedness about the first person singular which the Party had inculcated in its disciples [...] he had never yet consciously tapped the word '**I**'. (Koestler 1940, 201)

The parallels between Wittgenstein and the author who would later write *The Ghost in the Machine*, named after Ryle's famous attack on the Cartesian self (itself indebted to Wittgenstein), are impossible to ignore:

40 In Napoleon's second speech, 'we pigs' have already begun to replace 'man', except for being portrayed as allies rather than enemy. It is worthwhile to compare this pig's use of 'man' with that of the human Mowgli in *The Jungle Book*: '"What is the good of a man," he said to himself at last, "if he does not understand a man's talk? Now I am as silly and dumb as a man would be with us in the jungle. I must speak **their** talk."' (Kipling 1894, 58).

41 While originally written in German, the book was first published in a last-minute English translation (and subsequently in Koestler's German re-translation of the English) as the original remained lost until Matthias Weßel discovered it in the Zurich Central Library in 2015. While there are hundreds of differences between the original MS and the version published in 1940 (Scammell 2016), Weßel has confirmed to me (private correspondence) that the original manuscript of Koestler's *Sonnenfinsternis* does indeed use 'grammatikalische Fiktion' (MS, 298–9; Koestler 2018).

> 'Aren't you nevertheless basically saying that everything except human behaviour is a fiction?' If I speak of a fiction, then it is of a grammatical fiction [*einer grammatischen Fiktion*]. (PI, § 307)

Like Nietzsche before him (see BGE, § 16, and WLN, I-87), Wittgenstein speaks of the 'I' as a kind of grammatical fiction. This is all the more true of 'us', even when individuated as precisely as 'Marlon Brando, Pocahontas, and me'.

Chapter 4

UNDERSTANDING THE LION FOR REAL

'Narnia, Narnia, Narnia, awake. Love. Think. Speak. Be walking trees. Be talking beasts. Be divine waters.' It was of course the Lion's voice. The children had long felt sure that he could speak: yet it was a lovely and terrible shock when it did.

C. S. Lewis, The Magician's Nephew, 1955

We gazed at each other his implacable yellow eye in the red halo of fur
Waxed rheumy on my own but he stopped roaring and bared a fang greeting.
I turned my back and cooked broccoli for supper on an iron gas stove

Allen Ginsberg, 'The Lion for Real', 1958

Prologue

Is it an accident that one of the most frequently quoted remarks by Wittgenstein is also one of the least understood? I do not propose to answer this question by conducting an investigation into our reasons for quoting,[1] although such a study would not be irrelevant to certain aspects of the one below. My focus will instead be on the contrast between the original philosophical context of § 327 of the typescript previously known as Part II of *Philosophical Investigations* (hereinafter PPF, § 327) and some of the conditions surrounding its incredibly muddled reception.

The published version of the remark in question is:

Wenn ein Löwe sprechen könnte, wir könnten ihn nicht verstehn. (PPF, § 327)

In her otherwise influential English translation of what became known as *Philosophical Investigations* (hereinafter PI), Parts I and II, Elizabeth Anscombe renders the claim as follows:

1 For sociohistorical explanations, see Finnegan 2011.

> If a lion could talk, we could not understand him. (PI, 223e)[2]

On the face of it, the remark seems absurd, and commentators have obligingly voiced numerous complaints against it. These frequently revolve around the thought that Wittgenstein did not know the first thing about animals:

> Wittgenstein once claimed, 'If a lion could talk, we would not understand him.' He seemed to assume that because the lion's consciousness is so different from ours, even if there were a spoken lion language, it would be too alien for us to understand. However, lions and many other animals do indeed communicate in their own ways, and if we make an effort to understand their communications, we can learn much about what they are saying. If Wittgenstein had gotten off his couch and actually watched animals, he might agree. (Bekoff 2007, 38)

> 'If a lion could talk, we could not understand him,' the philosopher Ludwig Wittgenstein once said. 'It's clear that Wittgenstein hadn't spent much time with lions', commented the gambler and conservationist John Aspinall. (Gray 2002, 52–3)

> Wittgenstein's oft-quoted aphorism [...] is implausible because lions, after all, are social mammals, predators, cousins of the familiar cat who has no difficulty speaking to us and being understood. Another remark of Wittgenstein's is more apposite: '[W]hat is the natural expression of an intention? – Look at a cat when it stalks a bird, or a beast when it wants to escape' [PI, § 647]. If Wittgenstein could not understand that cat, how could he interpret it as 'stalking'? (Clark 1991, 145–6; Clark 1997)[3]

But things are not so simple. One question is whether 'talk' is the correct rendering of '*sprechen*' or whether Wittgenstein might have had something

2 All other quotations from the *Investigations* are from the revised 4th edition, unless otherwise noted.

3 Cf. Clark 1991, 92. But see also Anscombe 1963, §2, 5, where she writes: 'Intention appears to be something that we can express, but which brutes (which, e.g. do not give orders) can *have*, though lacking any distinct expression of intention. For a cat's movements in stalking a bird are hardly to be called an expression of intention. One might as well call a car's stalling the *expression* of its being about to stop. Intention is unlike emotion in this respect, that the expression of it is purely conventional; we might say linguistic if we will allow certain bodily movements with a conventional meaning to be included in language. Wittgenstein seems to me to have gone wrong in speaking of the "natural expression of an intention".' (Emphasis in the original; for critical exegesis, see Moran and Stone 2009, esp. 135.)

like 'speak' in mind. It is difficult to ascertain whether his decision not to use the more colloquial 'reden' instead was more stylistic than semantic, the two German terms being closer in meaning than the English ones. At any rate, the issue cannot be settled in advance, without philosophical prodding. Another question is what exactly the referent of 'we' is here, assuming there is one at all. I shall be attending to these in due course. I wish to begin, however, with a comment on two alternative translations of '*könnten [...] nicht*'.

Would Not, Could Not, Should Not

A surprising number of writers (approximately 350 of them) attribute to Wittgenstein the considerably weaker assertion that if a lion could talk or speak we *would not* understand him or it.[4] These include Annette C. Baier, Marc Bekoff, Margaret Boden, Stephan Budiansky, Marcia Cavell, Stephen R. Clark, John Dupré, Douglas R. Hofstadter, Brian McGuinness, Iris Murdoch, D. Z. Philips and D. J. Richter (Baier 1985, 14; Bekoff 2007, 38; Boden 2006,1351; Budiansky 1998,vi; Cavell 1996, 129; Clark 1991, 92; Dupré 2002, 232; Hofstadter 1979; McGuinness 2002, 221; Murdoch 1992, 209; Philips 2004, 135; Richter 2004). In addition, H. O. Mounce, Roger Scruton, A. N. Wilson and more than 50 others opt for the more formal but otherwise identical 'should not' (Mounce 1989, 159; Scruton 1976, 94; Wilson 2004, 152). Both sets largely believe themselves to be quoting directly from Anscombe's translation,[5] a fact that points towards a potential case of collective misremembering.

There are two obvious factors that may (together or alone) help to explain this selective amnesia, although there are no doubt other contenders:

i. The claim has been taken out of context.
ii. Even in its weaker guise, the remark is frequently mocked and rejected as outright false.

I shall be arguing that these two factors go hand in hand because the remark is rendered implausible only if taken to be a statement about either (a) lions

4 Google searches reveal that more than 220 books, 130 different papers and countless blogs, etc. (totalling approximately five per cent of the total number of quotations), have 'would not' or 'wouldn't'. One out of four would-notters mistakenly (and tellingly) also translate 'ihn' as 'it' rather than 'him', in contrast to only one out of 55 could-notters (although part of the explanation for the latter statistic is that many of these are quoting Anscombe accurately).

5 The few who omit to reference it offer no explicit challenge to it either.

specifically or (b) wild animals in general, and such misreadings ignore the philosophical context in which the remark occurs. It is worth pointing out, at this point, that none of this is being offered as a defence of Anscombe. In fact, to anticipate, I later make a case for the revisions recently made to her translation by Joachim Schulte and Peter Hacker. First, however, we must determine what the remark is actually about.

Consider Thomas Nagel's justification for choosing bats as the stars of his famous paper 'What is it like to be a bat?':

> I have chosen bats instead of wasps or flounders because if one travels too far down the phylogenetic tree, people gradually shed their faith that there is experience there at all. Bats, although more closely related to us than those other species, nevertheless present a range of activity and a sensory apparatus so different from ours that the problem I want to pose is exceptionally vivid (though it certainly could be raised with other species). Even without the benefit of philosophical reflection, anyone who has spent some time in an enclosed space with an excited bat knows what it is to encounter a fundamentally *alien* form of life. (Nagel 1974, 435, emphasis in the original)

The criteria for being counted as alien here are primarily *behavioural* in a superficial sense unconnected with ethology or physiological studies. Similarly, the earliest occurrence of the lion remark in Wittgenstein's *Nachlass* is immediately followed by the words 'He [*Er*] becomes an enigma, enigmatic to us through a certain kind of behaviour'.[6]

It need not be pointed out that Nagel's paper is not about bats but about the nature of consciousness. Similarly, I wish to suggest that Wittgenstein's remark is not about lions (or wild animals in general) but rather about the nature of *understanding* and its relation to the behaviour of those we understand. Wittgenstein, on this account, takes himself to be presenting us with a case in which understanding would no longer be present, despite certain superficial behavioural similarities to cases in which understanding is not in doubt (the lion speaks, or at the very least talks). *Prima facie*, the lion seems like a good contender to take on the role of an 'alien form of life'. It is not as close to the average human as, say, a cat or a dog. *Pari passu*, it is not as easy to understand. But nor is the lion so far removed from us as to justify the suspicion that there might be nothing there at all for us to understand, as would be the case with a beetle or a fly. It is hardly surprising, then, that animal lovers confronted with the remark find it less persuasive than do those whose

6 MS 167, 12v–13r. There is no reason to think that '*Er*' does not refer to the lion here.

experience with animals is limited.[7] Hence also the sarcastic retort of the lion tamer who already presumes to understand the lion: 'You mean I would cease to understand him?'.[8]

The extent to which the knowledge and abilities of experts are relevant to Wittgenstein's remark partly depends on whether 'we' here refers to all members of the human race, or to the average person who is not an animal trainer or behavioural scientist. It equally depends on whether Wittgenstein is claiming that the 'we' in question could never understand the talking lion or merely that they *would* not understand it but *could*, should they undertake the relevant training. Either way – even if the very claim that Wittgenstein intended to make turns out to be factually false – this would not detract from what he is trying to do. Just as the force of Nagel's argument regarding the nature of consciousness does not rest on any empirical findings relating to bat experience, so Wittgenstein's point about the limits of understanding does not stand or fall with any ethological facts about lion behaviour.[9] In both examples, the form of life in question can easily be replaced with a 'higher' or 'lower' one until we are happy with the claim that the chosen animal's way of life is sufficiently alien to ours.

More tentatively, there are plausible literary catalysts for the lion remark. One is the spectacled, yawning Lion in Lewis Carroll's *Through the Looking Glass,* depicted by John Tenniel as standing on two feet. He asks Alice if she is animal, vegetable or mineral; insists on a fair portion of plum cake; and calls the Unicorn whom he fights for the King's crown a 'chicken'. Another is L. Frank Baum's turn-of-the-century fairy tale *The Wonderful Wizard of Oz,* featuring a cowardly lion who converses in English with various beings, including humans, a tin woodman and a scarecrow.[10] In William W. Denslow's accompanying illustrations, the lion looks ordinary, but it is anthropomorphized

7 [13] See also Beardsmore 1996, 41; Gaita 2002, 18–20; Osborne 2007, 70.

8 Of course, the lion's sudden use of language could shock the puzzled trainer into losing his or her previous understanding of it.

9 Similarly, the ethical lessons of ancient and monastic tales about intelligent beasts do not hang upon the scientific accuracy of the stories (see Osborne 2007, 138, 149).

10 A key theme of the book is that the lion is cowardly even though he regularly acts in the face of fear, the tin woodman is tender yet has no heart, and the scarecrow is wise but literally brainless. Baum's writing chimes nicely with the thought of the later Wittgenstein, who saw thought and feeling as abilities that were conceptually independent of the possession of any material states. In the sequel, *Ozma of Oz,* Dorothy also comes across a mechanical man called 'Tik-Tok' who 'Thinks, Speaks, Acts, and Does Everything but Live' (Baum 1907, 43; cf. PI, § 281, and Matthews 1977).

in the 1939 musical film.[11] The final possible influence, of course, is C. S. Lewis' *The Lion, the Witch and the Wardrobe.* Like the cowardly lion of Oz, Lewis' lion, Aslan, is presented to us as a normal English speaker (albeit one with a high-flown style) and depicted – in the accompanying illustrations by Pauline Baynes – as an animal. Though not published until 1950, it was written between 1939 and 1949, thus overlapping with the 1946–49 period in which Part II of the *Investigations* was written. Wittgenstein's 'lion' remark was first recorded in November 1948.[12]

It is likely that to Wittgenstein, the very supposition of English-speaking lions with whom one could converse was akin to the sort of nonsense we find in Edward Lear's poetry, various fairy tales and other parts of the work of Carroll, Baum and Lewis:

> 'But in a fairy tale a pot too can see and hear!' (Certainly; but it *can* also talk).
>
> 'But a fairy tale only invents what is not the case; it does not talk *nonsense*, does it?' – It's not as simple as that. Is it untrue or nonsensical to say that a pot talks? Does one have a clear idea of the circumstances in which we'd say of a pot that it talked? (Even a nonsense poem is not nonsense in the same way as the babble of a baby.) (PI, § 282, emphasis in the original)

Whether or not any particular utterance about a speaking lion is nonsensical depends on the context in which it is uttered. Wittgenstein's remark is perhaps best interpreted as the conceptual or 'grammatical' claim that there is no such thing as a speaking lion which 'we' could or could not understand.[13] On such an outlook, our failure to understand the speaking lion would not be on a par with that of a Greek person's failure to understand an Austrian. To give just one anticipatory example, we might fail to understand the lion because we do not even recognize that it has a language. As we shall see, this may be so even if the lion is speaking in words as opposed to roars and growls.

11 The lion retains this form in the recent West End musical, in contrast to the dog who (as in the book) tries to communicate with Dorothy only by barking.

12 Some months before, on 2 February, Anscombe had debated Lewis on the subject of miracles at the Oxford Socratic Club. For accounts of this encounter and its aftermath, see Reppert 2005 and Wolfe 2011.

13 If it is nonsense to say that we could understand a speaking lion, then it is arguably also nonsense to deny it (see Baker and Hacker 2009).

If a Lion Could Speak, Would It Sound Like Liam Neeson?

Baker and Hacker claim that a speaking creature with the appearance of a lion would not be a lion at all. The point is reminiscent of Erich Fried's poem 'Definition':

> A dog that dies
> and knows that it dies like a dog
> and who can say that it knows that it dies
> like a dog is a man. (Fried 1964)[14]

On this view, to imagine a lion *speaking* is to imagine a human being who is merely shaped like a wild animal:

> Of course, in a fairy tale a lion may speak. But then, as in *The Wizard of Oz*, the Lion is really a human being 'in the shape of a lion' (imagine the famous film, but with a real lion in the role of the Lion).[15]

In the case of *Narnia*, imagining a real lion in such a role is exactly what the filmmakers have done,[16] thus keeping closer to the vision of the original illustrations than did the musical film version of *The Wizard of Oz*. Are we to say that what is being imagined here is a human being (or whatever other English-speaking person we can allow ourselves to imagine) who not only looks like a lion but has also taken its actual form? Is it integral to the stories that we entertain the false supposition that it is a creature with lion vision, neurology, vocal cords, etc., that speaks English?

Daniel Dennett certainly thinks of Wittgenstein's lion in this way, although his precise objection alters across a series of books:

> Wittgenstein once said, 'If a lion could talk, we could not understand him' [...]. I think, on the contrary, that if a lion could talk, that lion would have a mind so different from the general run of lion minds, that

---

14 The translation is Georg Rapp's, as quoted by Hacker (1996, 413–4) in relation to PI, § 650.

15 Baker and Hacker 2009, 173, n. 1. The first edition (1985, 186, n. 1) adds the following thought: 'Or, as in the *Tales of Narnia*, God is a lion. But *that* is no stranger than God's being an old man with a long white beard!' Perhaps this was removed because it *is* stranger, for it is essential to the Christian religion that humans – but not lions – were made in the image of God and, consequently, that Jesus (whom Aslan is intended to represent allegorically) is the Word made *human* flesh. As such, he can be joyful, sad, depressed and so on; this is indeed no ordinary lion.

16 The animal speaks perfect English, using Ronald Pickup's voice in the BBC television series and Liam Neeson's in cinema films.

> although we could understand him just fine, we would learn little about ordinary lions from him. (Dennett 1991, 447)

> Ludwig Wittgenstein famously said, 'if a lion could talk, we could not understand him.' That's one possibility, no doubt, but it diverts our attention from another possibility: if a lion could talk, we could understand him just fine – with the usual sorts of effort required for translation between different languages – but our conversations with him would tell us next to nothing about the minds of ordinary lions, since his language-equipped mind would be so different. It *might* be that adding a language to a lion's 'mind' would be *giving* him a mind for the first time! Or it might not. In either case, we should investigate the prospect and not just assume, with tradition, that the minds of non-speaking animals are really like ours. (Dennett 1996, 18)

> Wittgenstein once said 'If a lion could speak, we could not understand him'. I disagree. If a monkey could speak – really speak a language – we could understand him just fine because, if a monkey could speak, his way of life would have to be very much more like ours than it is. (Dennett 1998, 306)[17]

A similar sort of worry has been raised by Budiansky:

> The philosopher Ludwig Wittgenstein made the famous observation, 'If a lion could talk, we would not understand him.' But that begs the question: if a lion could talk, we probably could understand him. He just would not be a lion any more; or rather, his mind would no longer be a lion's mind. (Budiansky 1998, xxi)

Insofar as a creature might be said to communicate in roars and growls, these claims are questionable. While it is arguably a stretch to extend the word 'talk' to describe the non-verbal forms that most non-human animals use to communicate orally, it is no accident that people are four times as likely to conceive of animals as talking as they are to conceive of them as speaking.[18] This lends support to those who translate '*sprechen*' as 'speak', for the hypothetical form of the remark reveals that Wittgenstein takes it as a given that

17 Note the switch from 'talk' to 'speak'.

18 This can be readily confirmed by a quick Google search (As of September 2024, there are approximately 735,000,000 results for 'animals talk' versus 299,000,000 for 'animals speak'). It is also worth noting that 'talk' may imply two-way communication (compare 'we had a talk' and 'it's good to talk' with 'he gave a speech' or 'he spoke to me').

lions are not able to do this. More importantly, we should in any case be wary of taking *per impossibile* claims at face value. One might as well claim that if walls had ears, they would not hear a thing because the ears would be made of brick or plaster, or to deny this on the grounds that if they had ears, they would be *human* walls, made of flesh and blood. Claims such as 'if a pot could talk it would have a mouth' are best seen as conceptual ones, not empirical statements to which one could respond with questions about the acoustics of porcelain.

With this in mind, let me focus more closely on the question of what Wittgenstein means by '*sprechen*'. Hans-Johann Glock offers two possible readings, suggesting that the second lends more plausibility to PPF § 327:

> On one reading, this means that we could not understand a lion who utters English sentences like 'I'm not interested in you, I've just eaten an antelope', which is obviously false (although one might, following Austin, question whether such a talkative creature could count as a lion). On a charitable reading, it means that if lions had a *feline* language of complex growls, roars, etc., we could never come to *learn* it. Why? Because their form of life, and their behavioural repertoire are so alien to us. We could not make head or tail of their facial expressions, gestures and demeanour. Moreover, our ability to interact even with a tame lion is strictly limited.[19]

Glock presents us with a false dilemma here. For the question is not whether the lion would talk in growls or words (including ones that sound just like German or English) but whether its lifeworld overlaps with the human one in a way that allows for a sufficient degree of shared concepts for us to be able to learn its language.[20] A language that is private to lions need not have feline syntax, nor need an accessible Lionese take the form of words or human-style gestures. How can we be sure that a speaking lion *would* say things like 'I've just eaten an antelope', even if it did utter propositions? Unlike the talking animals in Hollywood films and cartoons or the talking car in *Knight Rider*, real animals do not share most of our concepts, if they share any of them at all. It is consequently wrong to suppose, as Blaise Pascal did, that animals instinctively find the world to be as we conceptualize it:

---

19 See PI, § 282, quoted further below. This is not to deny that fantastical hypotheticals can reflect empirical facts. Hence the joke that if a dog could play poker, it would lose because its tail would wag whenever it had a good hand.

20 See Chapter 5.

> If an animal did with a mind what it does by instinct, and if it spoke with a mind what it speaks by instinct in hunting and in warning its mates that the prey is found or lost, it would certainly also speak about things that affect it more, as for example, 'Gnaw on this cord that is hurting me and [which] I cannot reach'. (Pascal (1670) 2005, L 105 [S 137], 30)

It begs the question to assume that if a lion could think and speak it would say things like 'gnaw on this cord for me' and 'fetch me an antelope', as opposed to 'milk my sugar' or some other form of ostensible nonsense. For to know what sorts of things the lion would say if it could speak is to already understand it. Another point worth observing is that if the feline language reading is combined with the 'would not' translation, the entire remark becomes trivially true, in contrast to Glock's (preferable) translation. What about the first reading? Notwithstanding the parenthesis on the concept of a lion (and we have already seen that Wittgenstein is uninterested in lions *per se*), is it as obviously true as Glock deems it to be that we *would* understand a speaking lionlike creature? Here we need, at the very least, to distinguish between understanding what the lion *says* and understanding the lion *itself*, for do we not often understand the words people say while failing to understand why on earth they should say such things, or at any rate have the thoughts they are expressing?[21]

The question is only partly rhetorical, because what we make of it depends on whether we are talking about expression meaning, utterance meaning or speaker meaning (to say nothing of communicative intention). In the case of expression meaning, we need to distinguish further between what the expression 'I'm not interested in you, I've just eaten an antelope' would mean in this context in (human) English and what it might mean in Lionese. Would we obviously understand the latter version of the expression? And how could we tell if the lion was joking, or being ironic, sarcastic, metaphorical, etc., unless we could also understand the practices that give meaning to its behaviour (including tone and gesture)?[22]

It is tempting to think that we could perhaps at least understand *what* the lion means to say without understanding *why* it is saying it, although this would admittedly not yet amount to understanding the lion itself. But Anscombe (1963) was right to argue that one cannot fully understand what

21 The next chapter considers Glock's positions on these matters in the detail they deserve.

22 Wittgenstein himself acknowledges this in connection with questions about understanding others that were troubling him as early as 1914.

someone did without understanding why she did it, for the latter can always feature in an informative redescription of the former. The same holds true of the things we say and why we say them.[23] This might have been what the young Wittgenstein had in mind, for example, when at the end of his 1929 PhD viva in Cambridge he allegedly told Bertrand Russell and G. E. Moore that they had failed to understand anything he had written in his *Tractatus*, a suspicion that became increasingly general as his work became more popular. This led him to announce in the Preface to the *Investigations* that he 'could not help noticing that the results of [his own] work [...] were [...] frequently misunderstood',[24] and he has also been quoted as having said that Ryle was one of just two philosophers who understood his work (Monk 1990, 436).[25]

In what way might the inability to understand a speaking lion differ from the inability to understand Wittgenstein when he speaks? Understanding comes in degrees, but we should not discount the possibility that Wittgenstein is working with a relatively demanding notion of understanding. This is evidenced both by his incredibly high personal standards for every aspect of life[26] and by remarks such as the following:

> It's important for our approach that someone may feel concerning certain people that he will never know what goes on inside them. He will never understand them. (Englishwomen for Europeans.) (CV, 74e)

Of course, feeling that we will never understand some people is compatible with in principle being able to do so (even if we never come to manage it).

---

23 I am thus in sympathy with traditional interpretations (e.g. Pitcher 1964, 243) insofar as they claim that we are not able to understand the lion's speaker meaning (let alone his communicative intention) because our forms of life are sufficiently different to render the lion's reasons opaque. This view has been criticized by von Savigny (1991, 111–12) for taking the lion remark out of context, but this misses the mark if Wittgenstein intended it to contrast with the remarks that precede it (see 'Cultures and Values' below).

24 If understanding the expression meaning of what people said were always sufficient for understanding them, there would be far less need for exegesis. Would our failure to understand the speaking lion also be a case of *mis*understanding? Insofar as there is something there to be understood, that would depend on whether we think that we understand it.

25 For whether or not Wittgenstein was merely being polite to Ryle's cousin, see Tanney 2009b, n. 1.

26 See Monk 1990, passim.

Cultures and Values

There are cultural complications relating to what we are disposed to understand when spoken to, as illustrated in the following passages from a humorous article in *The Economist* that demonstrates that 'a literal understanding of what someone says is often a world away from real understanding':

> [...] [W]hen a Briton says 'I hear what you say', the foreign listener may understand: 'He accepts my point of view.' In fact, the British speaker means: 'I disagree and I do not want to discuss it any further'. Similarly the phrase 'with the greatest respect' when used by an Englishman is recognisable to a compatriot as an icy put-down, correctly translated by the guide as meaning 'I think you are wrong, or a fool.' [...] [W]hen a Briton says 'by the way/incidentally', he is usually understood by foreigners as meaning 'this is not very important', whereas in fact he means, 'The primary purpose of our discussion is...' On the other hand, the phrase 'I'll bear it in mind' means 'I'll do nothing about it'; while 'Correct me if I'm wrong' means 'I'm right, please don't contradict me.' As the Brits see things, a Frenchman who says '*je serai clair*' (which literally means 'I will be clear') should be understood as meaning: 'I will be rude'.[27]

Clearly, our failure to understand the lion is more radical than the French person's failure to understand the Brit. There is a world of difference between a person from a different culture and a creature from a different species. But is it a difference in degree or in kind? The English-speaking French person does not understand the Brit, but surely he is *able* to. It can take years to overcome the cultural differences, but it takes only seconds to explain how each phrase is 'really' to be understood.[28] We, by contrast, are not able to understand the lion in this sense. But what kind of impossibility is this?

Anscombe's translation of 'könnten nicht' as 'could not' is both accurate and true to the aesthetic of Wittgenstein's remark. It also retains an important

27 Charlemagne 2004. For further discussion see http://www.thepoke.co.uk/2011/05/17/anglo-eu-translation-guide/; http://itre.cis.upenn.edu/~myl/languagelog/archives/001781.html.

28 A medieval monk would need to spend a considerable amount of time in our world in order to be able to understand someone who writes 'yr fbk account haz bin hacked dude' or 'wicked! text me if U head 2 bbq slapper, laterz', but he *could* come to understand the relevant concepts without the acquisition of any overarching new ability. The point about the lion, by contrast, is not just about the ever-changing, contextualist nature of language.

ambiguity in how we are to understand the modality in question, namely that of whether Wittgenstein is marking a *logical possibility* or simply noting a general *lack of ability*. Indeed, we may distinguish between the following three modalities:

1. Having an ability but not being able to exercise it
2. Lacking an ability that one can nonetheless acquire
3. Not even being able to acquire an ability.[29]

In their revised translation, Hacker and Schulte explicitly opt for the middle modality, rendering the remark as follows:

> If a lion could talk, we *wouldn't be able* to understand it. (PPF, § 327, my emphasis)

This is an interpretive translation (as opposed to one that seeks to preserve the ambiguities of the original), but a very convincing one. For, short of ascribing to lions a language private to themselves, there is no reason to think that a human could not in principle *acquire* the ability in question (e.g. by immersing herself in the form of life of another creature, perhaps from early childhood like Mowgli or Tarzan). Unlike the lion tamer, such a human might even come to resemble a lion in any number of ways, although this would undoubtedly involve *learning* to behave in ways that come naturally to other creatures. The extent to which such abilities may be acquired is an empirical question that Wittgenstein does not seem troubled by, presumably because he takes its answer to be irrelevant to the insight he is trying to convey.[30]

Most commentators also assume that 'we' refers to all humans, but it is clear from Wittgenstein's other writings (including some that we saw in Chapter 3) that he believes there to be groups of *people* that 'we' are not able to understand because we either lack the ability to do so or are prevented from exercising it:

29 For a rewarding discussion of the relation between abilities and their exercise, see Kenny 1993, 156; 2002, 59.

30 Haidt (2012), Prinz (2012) and Shweder (1991) all argue that it is in our human nature to be culturally malleable. This multiplicity may well extend to our understanding of conceptions held by non-human animals. Might any other animals share this malleability with us or is it unique to our (human) nature? This too is an empirical question.

> We tend to take the speech of a Chinese for inarticulate gurgling. Someone who understands Chinese will recognize *language* in what he hears. Similarly I often cannot discern the *humanity* in a man. (CV, 1)[31]

> We don't understand Chinese gestures any more than Chinese sentences. (Z, § 219)[32]

Wittgenstein singles out Chinese speech because it appears less human to 'us', or at least to him. As the narrator puts it in Lewis' *The Magician's Nephew*, 'what you see and hear depends a good deal on where you are standing; it also depends on what sort of person you are' (Lewis 1955, Chapter 10, 116). When Aslan and the other Talking Beasts begin to speak, they are understood not only by the Witch but also, to their own amazement, by several humans. The sole exception is Uncle Andrew, who 'tried to make himself believe that he could hear nothing but roaring' and soon 'couldn't have heard anything else even if he'd wanted to', hearing 'only barkings, growlings, bayings, and howlings' when the Beasts spoke in answer (ibid., 117).

Stephen H. Webb has argued that 'when uncle Andrew hears the animals speak, he can't understand them because he doesn't recognise them as belonging to the same community as his own [...] even when they are given the gift of human-like speech. Likewise, they can't understand him' (Webb 2005, 11). This may be true in Narnia,[33] but while one may undoubtedly fail to recognize sounds as speech, in the real world it is community membership – along with all that it entails – which makes the crucial difference, not one's recognition of it.

Wittgenstein seems comfortable talking of a 'we' that presumably excludes Western scholars of the Chinese language and that, *mutatis mutandis*, would also exclude lion ethologists, Mowgli, and so on.[34] Moreover, as Richard

---

31 We may, conversely, mistake decorative pseudo-inscriptions for the real thing.

32 Cf. LW II, 89: 'I wouldn't know, for instance, what genuine gladness looks like with the Chinese.' At the time when the CV remark was written (1914), Wittgenstein was far more sympathetic to solipsism than when he wrote the Z one (the earliest remark in *Zettel* dates from about 1929). The following passage from the earlier period betrays an acceptance of Russell's argument from analogy that he would later explicitly reject: 'Only remember that the spirit of the snake, of the lion, is *your* spirit. For it is only from yourself that you are acquainted with spirit at all' (NB, 85e, 20 October 1916).

33 For the view that his recognitional failure is the result of intellectual vice, see Kinghorn 2005. It is likely that Lewis borrowed this idea from ancient and monastic stories about beasts whose intelligence humans fail to perceive because of their false preconceptions (see Osborne 2007, 152–3).

34 Cf. Beardsmore 1996, 46.

Beardsmore has noted, Wittgenstein is also happy to clump human and non-human animals in the same cognitive and behavioural groups:

> Imagine a human being, or one of Köhler's monkeys, who wants to get a banana from the ceiling, but can't reach it, and thinking about ways and means finally puts two sticks together etc. (RPP II, § 224)

Beardsmore claims further that Wittgenstein aims to 'draw an analogy between communication between human beings of different groups and any hypothetical communication between humans and animals' (Beardsmore 1996, 42).[35] But it is evident from the passages that immediately precede the lion remark that Wittgenstein *does* see a radical break between the intra-human scenarios and those that cut across species:

> We also say of a person that he is transparent to us. It is, however, important as regards our considerations that one human being can be a complete enigma to another. One learns this when one comes into a strange country with entirely strange traditions; and what is more, even though one has mastered the country's language. One does not *understand* the people. (And not because of not knowing what they are saying to themselves.) We can't find our feet with them. [*Wir können uns nicht in sie finden.*[36]]
>
> 'I can't know [*Ich kann nicht wissen*] what is going on in him' is, all, a *picture*. It is the convincing expression of a conviction. It does not give reasons for the conviction. *They* are not obvious. (PPF, §§ 325–6, emphasis in the original)[37]

Simon Glendinning argues that here Wittgenstein is stressing a difference of *order* rather than one of mere degree (Glendinning 1998, 71). It would seem that while we *cannot* (are not able to) understand the lion, with the people it is only true that we *do not* understand them; we could in principle manage were we to live with them long enough. To understand human strangers, we need not acquire a new ability; we may currently lack their ways and concepts, but we already possess the ability to master them. By contrast, acquiring a new

35 His view is elaborated on by Sharpe 2005, 170 ff.

36 See von Savigny (1991, 110) for why the phrase does not just mean that we cannot 'get along' with them but, rather, that we are constantly surprised by their behaviour to the point of alienation.

37 'Both PPF § 325 and Z §§ 383–90 below are repeated here for the reader's convenience, without the additional emphasis used in Chapter Three. Note that the '*kann nicht*' of § 326 is but the expression of a conviction whose reasons are not at hand.

ability is exactly what would need to happen for us to understand the lion, at least according to Wittgenstein's demanding criteria for understanding. The contrast is missed by those who take Wittgenstein to be claiming that we 'would not' understand the lion.[38] We do not understand the humans in the sense that we *cannot now* find our feet with them, although presumably we *could* do so. The language suggests a failure to exercise an ability we already have by nature. By contrast, we must try to *acquire* the ability to find our feet with the speaking lion. This predicament is similar to the one we face when we encounter the opaque tribe in *Zettel*:

> Imagine that the people of a tribe were brought up from early youth to give no expression of feeling *of any kind.* [...] [A]n education quite different from ours might also be the foundation for quite different concepts. [...] What interests us would not interest *them.* [. . .] 'These men would have nothing human about them.' Why? We could not possibly make ourselves understood to them. Not even as we can to a dog. We could not [*könnten nicht*] find our feet with them. And yet there surely could be such beings, who in other respects were human. (Z, §§ 383–90)

The mention of the dog makes it clear that Wittgenstein does *not* have a human/animal divide in mind. So what is the distinguishing factor between this sort of case – in which 'we could not possibly' understand or be understood – and that of the strange people whom 'we do not *understand*' in PPF § 325? Catherine Rowett alludes to the lion remark in describing the temptation to think that 'there is a radical difference between the world experienced by a language user and that of any other'. On such an outlook, it is a mistake to assume that if a lion could talk it could give expression to the sorts of things we would understand because the world of the lion would be so different from ours. This linguistic reason is not to be confused with the 'form of life' argument offered above. At its most extreme, the linguistic view leads to the controversial claim that the lion has no world because it has no concepts, and all thought and perception are conceptual (Davidson 1984; Dennett 1979, 1995, 1996; McDowell 1996).[39]

38 Understanding the people in this context is not shorthand for understanding what they say when they speak. For the study in contrasts to work, we must take it that (as I have been arguing above) the same holds true of the lion remark.

39 For criticisms of this outlook, see Beardsmore 1996, 56; Blassime et al. 2012; Glock 2000 and 2006; Sandis 2006b, 13 and 2010, 30 ff. I have tried to show above that Dennett's concerns were, in any case, a red herring.

We have already seen that there is little in Wittgenstein to suggest that what he has in mind is an unbridgeable gulf between the experience of language users and that of other creatures. Accordingly, Rowett (then writing as Catherine Osborne) allows 'for more fruitful analyses of Wittgenstein's remark' (Osborne 2007, 65, 67), listing as an example John Dupré's claims that the lion remark 'develops the intuition that language is deeply integrated with non-linguistic practices and behaviour' and that '[s]ince lions, and other animals, lead wholly different lives, their hypothetical language could make no sense to us' (Dupré 2002, 232).[40] To this, Dupré adds:

> Suppose [...] that our lion found its voice and said something that we were (somehow) inclined to translate as 'I am in pain'. Why might we not be right in this translation, and thus understand the lion? One might imagine a Wittgensteinian answering that the role that such an utterance could, imaginably, play in the life of lions, and its relation to the natural leonine expressions of pain, would be different from the equivalent role of the English utterance in the life of humans. If this seems wholly implausible, it is perhaps because the behaviour associated with pain is so primitive that it really does extend to many non-human species without serious alteration. (Dupré 2002, 233)[41]

In MS 137, the lion remark is preceded by the note 'Zu S. 742 Tscr'. This refers to remarks now published as RPP II, §§ 566–9, which include the following thought experiment:

> But imagine people whose upbringing is directed toward suppressing the expression of emotion in their faces and gestures; and suppose these people make themselves inaccessible to me by thinking aloud in a language I don't understand. Now I say 'I have no idea what is going on inside them'. (RPP, II, § 568)[42]

The key to understanding creatures, on this outlook, is behaviour. This may, but need not, be linguistic. The important thing, it would appear, is that it is

---

40 Rowett also refers to Beardsmore (1996), discussed elsewhere in this essay.

41 This is not intended to show that Wittgenstein chose the wrong species for his example, for presumably the talking lion would not talk only of pain and may, in any case, have very different speech behaviour associated with pain (our behaviour is more likely to overlap at the more primitive level of groaning).

42 Joachim Schulte, who brought the note in question to my attention, pointed out to me that this version omits the phrase '*Welcher Fremde empfindet nicht so, wenn er nach England kommt?*' ['Which foreigner doesn't feel that way when he comes to England?'], connected to PPF § 325. See TS 232/MS 135–7, 1947–48.

an expression of 'the inner'. But is this not exactly what both Chinese gestures and lion roars are? It would seem that 'we' can find our feet only with certain forms of behaviour.

Epilogue

It is tempting to think that whereas the difference between Chinese and English people is cultural, that between humans and lions is biological. On this view, the difference of order that Wittgenstein seeks to mark is a biological difference, one that even the most knowledgeable ethologist could never overcome. But this view seems implausibly to commit him to the view that while no *individual* creature can have a language private to itself, it is not incoherent to suppose that a given *species* could have a language that is *in principle* inaccessible to members of certain other species.[43]

Wittgenstein famously does not think it conceivable that an individual can have a private language of his or her own.[44] Whether a species could, for biological reasons, have a language that is in principle private to itself is a somewhat different question,[45] as is that of whether lions might be such a species. This is not to say that Wittgenstein would have answered either positively, let alone that he would have been right to do so. On the contrary, he would maintain that this use of the concept of language would at best be a secondary one.[46] Moreover, there is no evidence whatsoever to suggest that PPF § 327 is motivated by empirical data about the *purely* biological obstacles of this sort. Indeed, Wittgenstein denies that we would conceive alien behaviour as being linguistic unless we could recognize some kind of pattern:

> Let's imagine that the people in that country carried on usual human activities and in the course of them employed, apparently, an articulate language. If we watch their activities, we find them intelligible, they seem 'logical'. But when we try to learn their language, we find it impossible to do so. For there is no regular connection between what they say,

43 Cf. G. Strawson 2010, 251 ff.

44 See Mulhall 2007 for related difficulties about whether we can even say what a private language is meant to be (cf. Pears 2006).

45 According to Bernard Williams, Wittgenstein is nonetheless committed to 'a transcendental idealism of the first person plural' (Williams 1974, 161). On this view, Wittgenstein's use of the term 'we' is primarily aimed not at privileging one human group over others or even humanity over other language-using creatures but at 'the plural descendent of the idealist I who also was not one item rather than another in the world' (ibid., 160). Cf. Dilman 2002, Hutto 1996, Malcolm 1982, Moore 1985.

46 See PI, § 282.

> the sounds they make, and their activities; but still these sounds are not superfluous, for if, for example, we gag one of these people, this has the same consequences as with us: without those sounds their actions fall into confusion – as I feel like putting it. Are we to say that these people have a language: orders, reports, and so on?
>
> There is not enough regularity for us to call it 'language'. (PI, § 207)

In MS 124 (208 ff.), in a remark preceding the one that appears at PI § 206, he writes:

> I come to an alien people and someone apparently gives an order in a language which I do not know; his gestures, voice and the situation suggest to me that it is an order. I hear these sounds or words from different people in different circumstances expressed in the same tone of voice, but I see no regularity in the reactions of the other to whom the words are directed. Would I call these orders?
>
> In the reactions to an order there must be uniformity. (Translation taken from Baker and Hacker 2009, 176)[47]

The activities the narrator perceives do not seem to be governed by any rules. Nor do they form evidence for the existence of a language that is private to the alien people, for we would only be inclined to assume that they have a language to the extent that their behaviour contains observable regularities. Regularities could, of course, occur in a fashion that renders them imperceptible to us (owing to speed or pitch, for instance), but the only evidence for this would be of a kind that was contingently inaccessible to us.

It is wrong, then, as we saw in Chapter 1, to accept that the relevant barriers are either *purely* biological or *merely* cultural or ethnological. What makes understanding possible is behaviour. Thus, MS 165 (quoted in Chapter 1) ties the identification of utterances as orders, answers, etc., to the surrounding actions and circumstances, and a similar passage in PI § 206 concludes that it is by means of '[s]hared human behaviour [*Die gemeinsame menschliche Handlungsweise*[48]]' that 'we interpret an unknown language'.

As we also saw in Chapter 1, the shared behaviour patterns that make others intelligible to us, even when culture-specific, are ultimately rooted in shared biology because they 'presuppose common perceptual capacities,

47 Cf. Baker and Hacker 1985, 190, which also includes the original German.

48 As noted in Chapter 1, see Hintikka and Hintikka 1986, 209; Ma and van Brakel 2016, Chapter 6; von Savigny 1991, 113–14 for an account of why Anscombe's rendition of this phrase as 'the common behaviour of mankind' is problematic.

needs and emotions'; this is why 'spherical Martians' would be incomprehensible to us (Glock 1996a, 128, quoted more fully in Chapter 1). Baker and Hacker agree, arguing that a lion's 'natural repertoire of behaviour and [...] behavioural dispositions' are 'too far removed' from those of humans (Baker and Hacker 2009, 173, also quoted at greater length in Chapter 1).[49] They go on to argue:

> In what manner does human behaviour aid us in interpreting an unknown language? It enables us to establish regular connections between the sounds they make and actions. For if such regularities are discernible, then it is plausible to see what is said as providing a reason for what is done. This provides us with the leverage for interpreting their words. But in the absence of any such discernible regularity (even though the noises they make do not seem superfluous) we shall not say these alien people speak a language. (Baker and Hacker 2009, 176)[50]

'Leverage' is the key term here, and what it requires is uniformity between the noises they make and their behaviour. *Pace* von Savigny,[51] the latter need not be behaviour that is in common with that of humans, let alone shared, so long as it is public in Wittgenstein's sense of the term.[52] That is to say, the behaviour must be observable and thus in principle shareable, viz. identifiable by others under the correct description. As Baker and Hacker put it, 'the publicity requirement on rules is that it be *intelligible* that another (the anthropologist) should learn the aliens' (or alien's) rule' (Baker and Hacker 2009, 177),[53] namely that they can in principle come to learn it. The problem, however, is not merely that feline noises do not count as speech but that even if lions did speak (in words or in any other way), we would not be able to understand them.

Shareable behaviour is a necessary but insufficient condition for understanding a creature. As we have already seen, it is all too easy to systematically misidentify behaviour, linguistic or otherwise. To recognize that someone has a language is not, *ipso facto*, to understand that language. But Wittgenstein is not presenting us with a theory of understanding that specifies necessary *and*

49 Cf. Baker and Hacker 1985, 186, n. 1. See also Baker and Hacker 1985, 328 ff, and 2009, 218 ff.

50 Cf. 1985, 189–90.

51 von Savigny 1991.

52 This remains compatible with something's being contingently hidden: 'If I were to talk to myself out loud in a language not understood by those present my thoughts would be hidden from them' (PPF, § 317).

53 Cf. Baker and Hacker 1985, 190.

sufficient conditions of success, nor is he offering an analysis of the concept of understanding, breaking it down to its most basic constituents. Rather, he is probing for *limiting cases* of resemblances associated with knowledge and understanding.[54] Are we able to understand Wittgenstein when he says that if a lion could talk, we would not be able to understand it? Are we meant to have a clear and specific vision of the scenario he speaks of, or is the supposed lion intended to be as nonsensical as a private language?

Lions are hardly spherical Martians, and Wittgenstein is not claiming that it is logically or metaphysically impossible to understand them. Nor does he have any interest in whether or not it is empirically impossible for even Mowgli to do so. Perhaps lions and humans can both learn (or be trained) to display behaviour that is not just shareable but actually shared. By and large, however, such behaviour does not come to them naturally[55] (with some aforementioned exceptions such as pain behaviour), and we should consequently wonder whether any learned shared behaviour makes the same kind of sense to each party.[56]

We may never fully understand Wittgenstein himself, but his lion has taught us much about understanding. Even if the latter could speak in words, it is conceptually problematic to assume that the average human being would be able to converse with it. Wittgenstein's behavioural approach may be contrasted with the following speculation by Deryck Cooke, whose 1959 book *The Language of Music* attempted to demonstrate that it is possible to decode the musical 'phrases' through which composers throughout history have expressed their emotions:

> Perhaps one day, after intensive research into the various aspects of the art – acoustical, physiological, psychological, and simply musical – it may be possible, by correlating many findings, to discover exactly what it is that music expresses, and exactly how it expresses it; but if the attempt is made, it will have to be guided by the most meticulous regard for absolute truth, especially in the psychological field, where the answer is likely to be found. [...] [I]t seems likely that the fundamental (i.e. psychological) 'content' of some musical masterpieces may be quite appalling and even horrifying; and when the language of music is finally deciphered, some terrible secrets may be revealed, not only

54 See PI, § 41.

55 The problem is magnified when it comes to making inferences about human motivation from experiments conducted on lab rats.

56 A similar point is expressed through the train game example in PI, § 282.

> about the particular composer, but about humanity at large. (Cooke 1959, 273)

Here, the prospect of understanding is a nightmarish one. Cooke's proposition is unsettling, but there is something amiss in the suggestion that we might be able to uncover what music expresses only by conducting an interdisciplinary investigation across psychology and neighbouring fields. As with philosophers, any given piece of music may or may not speak to us, but there is nothing (human, Lionese, musical, or otherwise) that cannot in principle be understood by one who is able to live with – as opposed to alongside – it. Regardless of whether the lion communicates via roars or words, then, we could in principle acquire the ability to understand it. But such things do not come naturally or effortlessly.

Chapter 5

ON SAFARI WITH GLOCK

BÊTES: Ah! si les bêtes pouvaient parler! Il y en a qui sont plus intelligentes que des hommes.

—Flaubert, Le dictionnaire des idées reçues

Prologue

Disclaimer: I have never been on safari with Professor Glock. His work on Wittgenstein, however, is the main reason I made the journey from the parklands of Oxford to the habitat of the Reading floodplains. I spent many – on some accounts, *too* many – happy years there as a graduate student in the University's philosophy department. Ever since those salad days, I have learned more from Hanjo than I could possibly express here; my gratitude to him is immense. Whatever criticism follows is intended to honour him, both as the author of some of my favourite philosophical texts and as the spirited conversationalist who can pull an argument apart while simultaneously scanning the restaurant table for any untouched desserts.

In 1996, my undergraduate self stepped into the basement of Blackwell's flagship bookshop on Broad St in Oxford and came out with a copy of Glock's *A Wittgenstein Dictionary* (1996a), priced at £10.99. It was within its pages that I first encountered the ideas I discuss in this essay. Towards the end of his entry for 'form of life (*Lebensform*)', Glock offers a brief exegesis of Wittgenstein's 'puzzling remark' that 'if a lion could talk, we could not understand him' (PI, 223).[1] At the time, I assumed that Glock's treatment of it was an undisputable orthodoxy. This was a *dictionary* after all, and I intended to use it to get through my final examinations. Some years later, I read his masterful paper 'On Safari with Wittgenstein, Quine and Davidson' (1996b), which was published around the same time as the *Dictionary*. The paper is a model of what

---

1 Glock quotes from the original 1953 Anscombe translation, which was the only one published at the time. The translation as revised by Schulte and Hacker in 2009 reads, 'If a lion could talk, we wouldn't be able to understand it' (PPF, § 327). I return below to questions of modality and to the perils of translating 'sprechen' as 'talk'.

philosophical writing can and should be: learned yet original, resolute but judicious, significant while light-hearted, its insights always perspicuous and its reprovals constructive. Upon reading it, I also realized that far from being standard, Glock's account of Wittgenstein was novel and important, both as an act of Wittgensteinian exegesis and as a piece of contemporary philosophical criticism.

Some years down the line, I nonetheless find myself at some distance from Glock's interpretation of the lion remark. This is a little awkward, for we both approach Wittgenstein's aphorism from a point of substantial agreement across an unlikely number of shared interests: Wittgenstein's later work, the nature of (human and non-human) animal thoughts and concepts, and philosophical anthropology at large (see, e.g., Glock 2000, 2006). My hope in this essay is to demonstrate that Glock's own understanding of Wittgenstein's method is best served by a different reading of the lion remark.

Glock's Lion

All but the final section of Glock's 'On Safari' is largely focused on explicating W. V. Quine's 'radical translation' and Donald Davidson's 'radical interpretation', with Wittgenstein appearing only as a third wheel for comparison. It is not until the paper's final section that Glock puts forth an interpretation of Wittgenstein's technical concept of a form of life as 'a culture or social formation' in which language games are embedded (Glock 1996b, 165). This final section is the focus of my essay. But whereas Glock appeals to the concept with the specific aim of building a powerful alternative to the philosophies of Quine and Davidson, I am concerned only with his interpretation of Wittgenstein. Quine and Davidson have been booted out of the safari and replaced by Glock and Sandis.[2]

I shall follow Glock (1996b, 170, n.1) in using 'radical translation' to refer simply to any attempt at understanding others that operates 'from scratch'. Both the scratchiness and the understanding in question are, however, a matter of degree. Indeed, both Glock and I read Wittgenstein as demonstrating that we always have something in common with any being we might begin to understand. Strictly speaking, then, there is no such thing as *fully* radical translation; it is just that some translations are more radical than others. My quibble with Glock concerns the radicality of translating the talking lion. This partly hangs on the question of what it might even *be* for a lion to talk, a

2 For the hope that one can 'transpose lessons from hermeneutic anthropology to hermeneutic ethology' see Glock 2023, 313.

question that is inextricably tied to what Wittgenstein meant his aphorism to convey. As one of his students puts it in Derek Jarman's 1993 film *Wittgenstein*, '[I]f we could understand him [Wittgenstein], I shouldn't think we'd have too much trouble with a lion'.

According to Glock, Wittgenstein's remark is best explained in light of the fact that 'we could never start the hermeneutical process unless "we" shared with the interpretees certain *forms or facts* of life' (Glock 1996b, 166, emphasis in the original). This is because 'understanding an alien language presupposes convergence not of beliefs, but of patterns of behaviour, which presuppose common perceptual capacities, needs and emotions' (Glock 1996a, 128). On both of these points, we are in full agreement. Indeed, my niggle presupposes a shared understanding of the nature of forms of life and their relation to radical translation.

Glock offers two possible readings of Wittgenstein's remark about the talking lion, each resting on a different understanding of what he means by '*sprechen*':

> On one reading, this means that we could not understand a lion who utters English sentences like 'I'm not interested in you, I've just eaten an antelope', which is obviously false (although one might, following Austin, question whether such a talkative creature could count as a lion). On a charitable reading, it means that if lions had a *feline* language of complex growls, roars, etc., we could never come to *learn* it. Why? Because their form of life, and their behavioural repertoire are so alien to us. We could not make head or tail of their facial expressions, gestures and demeanour. Moreover, our ability to interact even with a tame lion is strictly limited. For related reasons we 'could not find our feet' with human beings who give no expression of feeling of any kind, and would be completely at a loss with spherical Martians. (Glock 1996b, 166; see also 1996a, 128)

On the first interpretation Glock outlines, the lion remark effectively means that we could not understand a lion who *speaks* by uttering sentences in human languages such as English, German or Swahili. On the second interpretation, the term 'talk' would seem more apposite. People far more readily allow that animals *talk* to one another than that they *speak*, a fact that favours the 'speak' translation of '*sprechen*', given Wittgenstein's implication that lions are not able to perform the activity in question.[3]

3 In a published reply to an earlier version of this chapter, (Glock 2023, 312) maintains that there is no sharp contrast between talking and speaking in German and that 'it

Glock claims that the second reading is the more charitable because the first 'is obviously false'. By contrast, I wish to argue that Glock presents us with a false dilemma. The question, I believe, is not whether the lion would talk in growls or words (including ones that sound just like German or English) but whether its lifeworld overlaps with the human one in a way that would allow for a sufficient extent of shared concepts for humans to be able to learn its language. Even if Glock is right to think that all the concepts involved in stating 'I'm not interested in you, I've just eaten an antelope' can be attributed to an intelligent feline (Glock 2023, 313), we cannot be sure that a speaking lion would say such things because, unlike the talking animals in Hollywood films and cartoons, it may not share the relevant interests with us.[4]

What about the first reading? First, a creature that speaks in words need not be speaking a *human* language. Glock's contrast between human (word-based) and non-human (growl-based) communication ignores the possibility of a word-based language that is not an actual human one that the relevant native speakers would understand. This could be the case even if, by some cosmic accident, its words sounded *just like* those of an actual human language. We need to further distinguish between what the expression 'I'm not interested in you, I've just eaten an antelope' would in this context mean in English and what it might mean in Lionese.

Given that words and sentences in our own languages can completely change their meaning across time and place (see Sandis 2016), we should not expect the imaginary lion's spoken words to mean what a native speaker might instinctively take them to mean. If they did so by stipulation, we would not be dealing with a talking lion at all but with a human 'in the shape of a lion' (Baker and Hacker 1985, 186; cf. Dennett 1979, 1991, 1995, 1996), for no other creature would have a grasp of the required concepts.[5] It is through its behaviour and its behaviour alone that we could ever come to figure out what the lion might be saying, be it in words or growls.[6]

---

is definitely absent from German', but 'reden' more readily translates as 'talk' and 'sprechen' as 'speak'. For more on the distinction between speaking and talking, see Chapter 4.

4 As I argued in Chapter 3, the question of who 'we' are is tricky for Wittgenstein, and we should be suspicious of the thought that within the context of the lion remark, 'we' stands for *all* humans.

5 Cf. Schroeder (2019, 79–83). Glock (1996a, 166) makes the Austinian observation that it is debatable whether any creature with a natural language could count as a lion, whatever its appearance (see also Glock 2023, 313).

6 I am assuming (and assuming that Glock is assuming) that the growls and roars cannot be combined to express propositions. Whatever meaning they might carry is not conveyed in a word-like manner.

Talk Is Cheap

Wittgenstein is concerned not with linguistic comprehension but with interpersonal understanding. His point is not that we could not understand what the lion *says* but that we could not understand *the lion*. After all, we often understand the words someone utters while completely failing to understand the person.[7] Likewise, even if we did understand *what* the lion says (e.g. if it were speaking in English, German or Swahili), that does not mean that we would be able to understand *why* it would say such a thing, whether its speaker meaning coincided with the conventional meaning of the sentences it uttered and so forth. This is all assuming it is even possible to fully understand *what* someone is doing or saying without understanding *why* (cf. Anscombe 1957).

To complicate things further, we would (as with any human) need to be able to tell whether the lion was joking or being (for instance) ironic, sarcastic or metaphorical. We can do this only if we already share the relevant behavioural practices with it (e.g. in terms of gesture and tone) (see Glock 1996b, 166). But 'we' do not share a form of life with the lion; we simply don't have enough in common. And, indeed, as Wittgenstein's awkward remarks about 'the Chinese', 'Englishwomen' and 'Europeans' indicate,[8] 'we' does not stand for all humans but only for a contextually defined subset, one that would not obviously include lion tamers, let alone a Mowgli or a Tarzan (Sandis 2019a; cf. Schroeder 2019). While Glock is right to object that Wittgenstein 'is sometimes too impressed by the cultural diversity of gestures' (Glock 1996b, 167), he fails to note that there is no fixed 'we' who could or could not understand the speaking lion. Rather, 'we' functions as a kind of shifter in Roman Jakobson's sense, according to which the pronoun's referent 'shifts' depending on who is uttering it and in what context (Jakobson 1957; cf. Kursell 2010).

The same point may be approached from the opposite direction. The talking animals in, say, *The Jungle Book* or *The Lion King* are in many ways far closer to human animals than they are to the non-human ones they are presented as. They say things like 'good luck', 'he has no right' or 'it is unsportsmanlike'; they talk of 'taking orders', 'speaking the truth', 'buying for a price', 'miracles' and 'treasure'. However, none of these expressions involves concepts that an animal such as a lion or tiger could have.[9] Such fictions basically

---

7 See PPF § 325 (quoted fully in Chapter 4). There is a parallel here between understanding what someone *says* and what they *write* or, indeed, *sculpt*. Understanding a work of art and understanding the artist are two different things (see Sandis 2017a, 2017b).

8 See, for example, the opening remarks in CV.

9 Wittgenstein would have read tales of talking animals by the Brothers Grimm and would also, no doubt, have wondered what exactly was being imagined in Baum (1900),

portray humans in animal bodies. What prevents real-life lions from saying such things is not the inability to speak but a conceptual lack whose causes are largely biological. Non-human animals can be trained to share human practices only up to a point.

I am thus in sympathy with what Eike von Savigny (1991, 111) refers to as 'the received interpretation' (e.g. Pitcher 1964, 243), which is not so different from the one rejected by Glock in *A Wittgenstein Dictionary*:

> Let a lion be a competent speaker of some natural human language, competent in the sense preferred by linguists, namely, able to utter syntactically and semantically non-deviant sentences *ad libitum*. His utterances could not possibly be embedded in situations, reactions, and responses such that we could make sense of them. We should not be able to understand why he makes the utterances he makes or why he reacts to our utterances in this or that way. 'Good morning' would not come out when it would be appropriate for a greeting; 'thank you' might come as a reaction to a lash from a whip, and so on. These sentences, though perfectly good English, would not be used in the behavioural activities of greeting and thanking, and the lion in uttering them would not greet or thank someone. Hence these sentences would not have their standard English meanings, and the same would hold for any such utterances in so far as the lion does not share a form of life in which there are places for utterances with such meanings. In short: the lion does not share our form of life, and this is why we could not interpret anything he produces as an utterance that is translatable into a natural human language. (von Savigny 1991, 111–12)

At the very least, it seems to me correct to say that 'we' are not able to understand the communicative intention and speaker meaning of the lion precisely because our forms of life are sufficiently different to render the lion's reasons opaque. Von Savigny reproves such suggestions for taking the lion remark out of context (von Savigny 1991, 111).[10] But they are not doing so if Wittgenstein intended the remark to contrast with the remarks that immediately precede it.

Burroughs (1914), Carroll (1871), Kipling (1894) and Lewis (1950).

10 Simillarly, Severin Schroeder observes that 'people cannot resist the temptation of treating the sentence as an aphorism, that is, a saying that is to be interpreted on its own without any context' (Schroeder 2019, 80). In the previously published version of this paper, I made a complete botch of this footnote; I am relieved to have this opportunity to put things right.

I am here in agreement with Simon Glendinning, although we disagree on the precise nature of the contrast between Wittgenstein's human-to-human scenario, in which we *do not* understand the people of a strange country and *cannot* find our feet with them (PPF, § 325), and the human-to-lion scenario, in which we *could not* (or are not able to) understand the lion (PPF, § 327, emphasis added).[11] Glendinning suggests that Wittgenstein is here stressing a difference of *order* in the opacity that a human being 'can encounter in its respective relations with other human beings and other animals' (Glendinning 1998, 71). While we cannot find our feet with the strange humans, we presumably *could* do certain things that would render us capable of so doing. This suggests a failure to exercise an ability we already have. But even if we leave aside the contentious presumption that Wittgenstein's lion somehow stands for all non-human animals (see Chapter 3), the contrast does not seem as strong as Glendinning suggests. For it is not impossible for 'us' to *acquire* the ability to understand the speaking lion (see Chapter 4). Indeed, this predicament is similar to the one we face when we encounter the human tribe in *Zettel*, which 'we' are told is in some ways more alien to 'us' than a dog:

> Imagine that the people of a tribe were brought up from early youth to give no expression of feeling *of any kind*. [...] An education quite different from ours might also be the foundation for quite different concepts. [...] What interests us would not interest *them*. [...] We could not possibly make ourselves understood to them. Not even as we can to a dog. [...] (Z, §§ 383–90; emphasis in the original; quoted more fully in Chapter 4)

Von Savigny contends that the only thing that matters for Wittgenstein's argument is that we *could not* understand the lion. Accordingly, 'further explanations for why we could not understand him are unnecessary in this context; the lion example might as well be read as a supplement: "Why – if a lion could talk, we could not understand him either"' (von Savigny 1991, 113). In opposition to this sort of approach, I have been trying to suggest that the lion remark is the conclusion of an argument that precedes it. If that is right, then one cannot fully appreciate the remark's function without a proper understanding of the argument that leads up to it. While I therefore agree with von Savigny that the immediate context is key, we disagree about what the context reveals.

Von Savigny, Glock and I nevertheless all agree on a salient point, namely that neither the remark itself nor its wider context suggests that it is impossible to envisage mastering a language that is embedded in an alien form of life. On the contrary, Wittgenstein explicitly envisages such a scenario. According

---

11 I quoted both passages in full earlier in the chapter.

to von Savigny, it is sufficient that the behaviour of the objects of radical translation exhibit certain regularities, regardless of whether the interpreting subject shares any of them. But this cannot be right, either as an interpretation of Wittgenstein or as a hermeneutical truth. I thus concur with Glock's statement that

> like Quine and Davidson, Wittgenstein insists there are minimum requirements which a form of linguistic behaviour must meet in order to be intelligible to us. Our form of life need not be identical with that of the natives; after all, even if we leave aside Wittgenstein's fictional cases, we have managed to translate very remote languages such as Linear B, and to interpret very alien cultures, like that of the New Guinea head-hunters. But we could never start the hermeneutical process unless we shared with the interpretees certain forms or facts of life. (Glock 1996b, 166)[12]

As we shall see, however, while sharing these forms of life is crucial, it is not enough. What is shared is but the springboard for the acquisition of new abilities without which we would remain *incapable* of the relevant understanding.

Radical Translation and Forms of Life

Pace Quine and Davidson, radical translation is not a question of theory construction but of 'being introduced into a normative practice' (Glock 1996b, 164). To enter another's 'hermeneutical circle', we need some kind of access to the 'cultural and social formation' that constitutes their 'form of life' (Glock 1996b, 165; see also von Savigny 1991, 109). The term 'form of life' occurs just six times in Wittgenstein's published output. As Glock notes, he adopted it to refer to 'the intertwining of culture, world-view, and language', including 'patterns of behaviour' (Glock 1996a, 124–5).[13] Failure to understand another frequently results from the lack of a shared form of life. At the very least, one must have enough in common with others to be able to find one's feet with them (a task that is impossible in the case of Glock's beloved spherical Martians). As we saw in Chapter 4, Wittgenstein wonders whether we could

12 See also Glock 1996b, 171, n. 28.

13 The complete list, as detailed by Hacker (2015), is PI, §§ 19, 23, 241; *Nachlass*, MS 160, 51; PPF, §§ 1, 345.

recognize the giving of orders in an unknown language without seeing 'regularity' and 'uniformity' in people's reactions.[14]

If the activities that we perceive do not seem to be governed by any rules, they do not form evidence for the existence of a language which is private to the alien people, for we would be inclined to credit them with language only to the extent that their behaviour contains observable regularities. It is possible, of course, for these to occur in a fashion that renders them biologically (as opposed to metaphysically) inaccessible to us, although such obstacles can sometimes be overcome through the use of technology (e.g. infrared vision goggles). Either way, the *criteria* for the possibility of understanding are ultimately behavioural: to interpret an unknown language we rely on 'shared human behaviour' and 'very specific human actions' in the context of the surrounding 'circumstances'.[15] Moreover, the sense such behaviour makes to us, even when it is culturally specific, is ultimately rooted in biology, in our distinctively human needs and vulnerabilities.[16]

How does shared human behaviour aid us in interpreting an unknown language? By enabling us to establish regular connections between speech and action. This provides us with the leverage for interpreting others and, through this, to be in a position where we can be in receipt of reasons. In the absence of *any* such discernible regularity, 'we' cannot confidently say of the 'alien' people that they speak a language.[17] But even lions show sufficient regularity in the correspondence between their growls and their behaviour for one to take at least the crucial first step onto the ladder of understanding.

Von Savigny has pointed out that the pertinent behaviour need not be common to all (or even most) human beings (von Savigny 1991, esp. 113–17). What matters is that it be shared by both interpreter and interpretee. For this to be the case, its meaning must be public, in Wittgenstein's sense of the term; that is, the interpreter must in principle be able to learn it (see Baker and Hacker 2009, 177; cf. 1985, 190).[18] The worry, however, is not merely that feline noises do not count as speech but that even if lions did speak (in words or any other way), 'we' would not be able to understand them any more than

14 MS 124, 208 ff., translation from Baker and Hacker 2009, 176. Cf. Baker and Hacker 1985, 190, which also includes the original German.

15 PI, § 206, and MS 165, both quoted more fully in Chapter 1.

16 Baker and Hacker 2009, 173, inc. n. 1, quoted in Chapter 4 and at greater length in Chapter. Cf. Baker and Hacker 1985, 186, n. 1., 328 ff, and 2009, 218 ff.

17 Baker and Hacker 2009, 176; cf. 1985, 189–90.

18 This is compatible with some of the relevant evidence's being contingently hidden: 'If I were to talk to myself out loud in a language not understood by those present my thoughts would be hidden from them' (PPF, § 317).

we could if we were, *per impossibile*, to have direct access to their minds (see PPF, § 284; cf. Davidson 1984; Sandis 2019b; Schroeder 2019).

Shareable behaviour is a necessary condition for understanding others, but it is not sufficient. For reasons ranging from a disparity in the customary direction of nods (horizontal vs. vertical) to the structured misunderstandings in Jane Austen's *Pride and Prejudice*, behaviour lends itself to systematic misinterpretation. This leaves us far from understanding all cases of language use that we recognize as such. But, as noted in Chapter 4, Wittgenstein's exploration of understanding is neither an analysis of the concept nor a claim to offer necessary *and* sufficient conditions for its presence. Rather, it is a probing by way of limiting cases.

The lion remark is not really about lions at all, let alone animals in general; it is about the very notion of what it takes to understand another. The barrier to understanding the speaking lion is neither metaphysical nor epistemic. It is – like forms of life themselves – partly biological and partly cultural. Wittgenstein holds that it is virtually impossible to understand another being, not because of any *a priori* impossibility, but because it can be extremely hard to do so biologically, culturally and psychologically, depending on both the type and the individual.[19]

Epilogue

In advance of already understanding the lion, we cannot make assumptions about what it would say if it could speak. It is thus far from obvious that we would understand a talking – or even a speaking – lion. At the same time, Wittgenstein is not arguing for the logical, metaphysical or even empirical impossibility of doing so. It is conceivable that, with sufficient instruction or training, humans and lions could engage in shared behaviour. However, with certain exceptions, they do not do so naturally.

Human and many non-human animals alike do typically share certain basic biological features (birth, sex, hunger, death). These pave the way for what Glock refers to as 'behavioural universals' (Glock 1996b, 166) – that is, shared behaviour at a very general level (giving birth, eating, grieving, etc.). Such 'patterns of behaviour' in turn presuppose 'a framework of shared cognitive capacities, needs, emotions, and attitudes' (Glock 1996b, 169). This is so even when the related rule-governed practices differ wildly from species to

19 In keeping with this, Wittgenstein frequently complained that nobody understood him and/or his work. This was not vanity, for he just as often claimed that he was incapable of understanding other thinkers and/or their work (see Chapters 1 and 7).

species and, indeed, within subgroups of each (cf. Sharpe 2005; Vico (1725) 1999, §§ 332–3). Exclamations of hunger, gestures of disapproval, expressions of love and practices of mourning for the dead may differ radically across different periods and places, but the general practices are found in both human and many non-human forms of life, and it doesn't take much for outsiders to recognize them as such:

> It is for the most part straightforward to distinguish threatening and submissive gestures, since these are tied up with characteristic forms of human action, and the gesture of pointing is shared by all known [human] cultures (Glock 1996b, 167).

While most non-human animals are notoriously bad at understanding how *human* pointing works, studies in animal gestures show that many species (e.g. goats, elephants, apes and dogs) understand what it is to point.[20] More *to* the point, they can tell when we are being threatening and when we are being submissive, and we can do the same for them.

I have never been on safari with Professor Glock, but I'm sure that if we did go, we would both be able to distinguish a lion that was hungry from one that was full. The only trouble is that Hanjo can easily outrun me.

---

20 See, for example, Nawroth, Martin and McElligott 2020; Smet and Byrne 2013, 2020.

Chapter 6

UNDERSTANDING OTHER CULTURES (WITHOUT MIND-READING)

What kind of spider understands arachnophobia?

Robert Wyatt, 'Free Will and Testament'

Prologue

If the past is a foreign country, then it is plausible to expect the conditions for understanding contemporary cultures that seem alien to us to parallel those of historical understanding. R. G. Collingwood famously suggests that such understanding involves 'the re-enactment of past thought in the historian's own mind' (Collingwood 1946, 216–17, 301).[1] This view finds recent expression in Bettina Stangneth's proclamation that 'to understand someone like Eichmann, you have to sit down and think with him. And that's a philosopher's job' (Schuessler 2014, x). Such *thinking with* does not imply any agreement of opinion. Its task is to see things from within a system of concepts and values that is alien to one's own.

This essay attempts to illustrate the thesis that intercultural understanding requires a parallel sharing of thought processes. It does so through an exploration of recent attempts to make sense of the ghost narratives that emerged in the aftermath of the 2011 Tōhoku earthquake and tsunami. With a little help from Wittgenstein and Geertz, I suggest that understanding the thoughts of another culture is not a question of mind-reading but rather one of conceptual immersion.

The Universe of Human Discourse

Does one enter the mind of another culture, past or present? How *could* one? It has become popular to use the expression 'mind-reading' as a shorthand for understanding another person's thoughts. This is not a harmless figure of speech but a misleading portrait of communication that has its contemporary

1 For exegesis, see Chapter 7 and Sandis 2011a.

roots in John Locke's theory of human understanding, which considers all thoughts to be private in that they 'cannot be laid open to the immediate view of another' (Locke 1689, Book IV, Chapter XXI, § 4).[2] Accordingly, 'to communicate our Thoughts to one another, as well as record them for our own use, Signs of our *Ideas* are also necessary' (ibid.).

Locke believed that human understanding requires the translation of inner thoughts into a shared language. This enables communication with recipients, whose minds, in turn, translate our words into their own hidden thoughts.[3] Locke coined the term 'Σημειωτική' (*Semeiotike*) for his accompanying doctrine of signs, 'the business whereof is to consider the nature of signs the mind makes use of for the understanding of things, or conveying its knowledge to others' (Locke 1689, Book IV, Chapter XXI, § 4). The term gave rise to what Margaret Mead would term 'semiotics' (Mead 1964, 279; Sebeok 1964, 5, 275), which also influenced the works of Barthes (1964), Jakobson (1960), Kristeva (1984) and Sebeok (1976).[4] It would also influence Claude Lévi-Strauss' structuralism (1963), the symbolic anthropology of Geertz (1973) and the semiotics of translation of Eco (1975) and Steiner (1975).

Geertz, however, rejects Locke's thought that the purpose of signs is to translate our private thoughts. In so doing, he embraces the later Wittgenstein's dictum that 'shared human behaviour is the system of reference by means of which we interpret an unknown language' (PI, § 206). The primary task of the anthropologist is not to explain this behaviour but rather to observe and describe it. The results of this task involve the registration and analysis of public signs that lie at the core of the 'symbolic systems' constituting culture:

> Culture is public because meaning is. You can't wink (or burlesque one) without knowing what counts as winking or how, physically, to contract your eyelids, and you can't conduct a sheep raid (or mimic one) without knowing what it is to steal a sheep or how practically to go about it [...] [T]he aim of anthropology is the enlargement of the universe of human discourse. (Geertz 1973, 13–14)

Some form of understanding could, indeed, emerge from such a process, but it should not be projected onto it. According to Geertz, we can 'gain empirical

2 I elaborate on this theory in Sandis 2019a, 243 ff.

3 This notion of privacy – which is shared by the early Wittgenstein – is a relatively weak one in which thoughts remain *in principle* communicable. Despite its many problems, the account is not vulnerable to the private language argument of PI §§ 203–315 (see Tejedor 2014, 16–22).

4 This is not to minimize the earlier influence of Saussure and Peirce.

access' to cultural practices 'by inspecting events' (Geertz 1973, 17). This distinctively one-way characterization of the anthropologist's job is deemed by some to be more objective than the two-way interactive model. Arguably, however, one cannot fully grasp another culture without actively participating in it.[5] This places certain limits on historical understanding (where one is logically limited to re-enactment), as well as on the understanding of behaviour that we do not want to immerse ourselves in (for e.g. moral reasons).[6]

Whereas Geertz's approach is an uneasy blend of Locke and Wittgenstein, Steiner is clearly wedded to a theory that is Lockean through and through:

> Any model of communication is at the same time a model of translation, of a vertical or horizontal transfer of significance. No two historical epochs, no two social classes, no two localities used words and syntax to signify exactly the same things, to send identical signals of valuation and inference. Neither do two human beings. Each living person draws, deliberately or in immediate habit, on two sources of linguistic supply: the current vulgate corresponding to his level of literacy, and a private thesaurus [...] Thus, a human being performs an act of translation, in the full sense of the word, when receiving a speech-message from any other human being. Time, disparities in outlook or assumed reference, make this more or less difficult [...] 'Translation', properly understood, is a special case of the arc of communication which every successful speech-act closes within a given language. (Steiner 1975, 45–7)[7]

Steiner makes explicit what was implicit in Locke, namely the view that every act of communication involves translation from a private language to a shared one and that differences across cultures and their languages merely exacerbate a difficulty that is present even in the ideal scenario of communication

5 See Tejedor 2023. The traditional observational model was contested by Margaret Mead's controversial approach in *Coming of Age in Samoa* (1928), in which she undertakes 'to identify herself so completely with Samoan youth that she gives a lucid and clear picture of the joys and difficulties encountered by the young individual in a culture so entirely difficult from our own' (Boas 1928, xv). Mead's form of identification anthropology lies somewhere between the one-way and two-way models. The latter finds its clearest statement in Joy Hendry's *An Affair with a Village*, in which her anthropological engagement is introduced as a long-term personal *relationship* (Hendry 2021, iii). Intentional or otherwise, the accord, here, with the work of Jiddu Krishnamurti (1992; 2010, 111) is striking.

6 For the notion of 'behavioural immersion' as it appears in pedagogy, see Giambatista and Hoover 2009.

7 Cf. Eco 1976, 1986.

between identical twins who grew up together. For Steiner, each culture has a unique body of shared secrecy buried within its language.

Contemporary debates on mind-reading assume all this as a given. The only contested question is how people's thoughts are being accessed in the first place. Philosophers disagree about whether access to other people's 'mental contents' is primarily gained with the help of data inferences (attribution theory and theory-theory)[8] or through the use of emotional tools such as empathy (simulation theory).[9] Against the grain, I argue that the dispute rests on two misguided assumptions: (1) that understanding others is a matter of accessing the so-called 'contents' of their minds and (2) that the success of such a procedure is a matter of employing the right rational and/or emotional tool, which becomes a key to another's inner theatre.

Wittgenstein famously quips that 'if God had looked into our minds, he would not have been able to see there whom we were speaking of' (PPF, § 284). But how else are we meant to access the thoughts of another person if not through some form of mind-reading? If even God cannot do it, what hope have we mortals? Following Geertz, I maintain that the relevant understanding does not require 'long-distance mindreading' (Geertz 1973, 14) but rather a deep immersion in an altogether different way of life. This involves learning more about the background, education, traditions, practices, interests and concepts of others, which, unsurprisingly, becomes harder to achieve with age.[10]

Following Geertz and other symbolists, I hold that understanding is not a matter of cracking some symbolic code but of being *with* others – actually thinking and acting *with* them, not merely observing and reporting on their behaviour.[11] To a certain extent, such understanding may be acquired indirectly, by means of books, films and the testimony of those who do the 'fieldwork'. When it comes to the distant past, one can but imagine what it must have been like to partake in their practices. And in the case of violent or fascist cultures, one may inch closer by going undercover. But this all falls short of the complete cultural immersion and conceptual enlightenment in which the anthropologist is not so distinct from a layperson who immerses

8 E.g. Carruthers 2011, 1; Malle 2004, 106; Morton 2003.

9 E.g. Baron-Cohen 2011, 12; Coplan and Goldie 2011, ix; Stueber 2006.

10 Cf. Z, §384–90, quoted further below. Hence Wittgenstein's 1949 confession to Piero Sraffa: 'The older I get the more I realize how terribly difficult it is for people to understand each other' (WC, 410, 450; discussed in Sandis 2015a).

11 For why Wittgenstein's morphology is ultimately incompatible with symbolic anthropology, see Palmié 2018, 8 ff.

themselves with abandon in a new school, workplace or neighbourhood or in their partner's extended family.

Real Presences in Japan

At 2:46 p.m. Japan Standard Time on 11 March 2011, the Tōhoku undersea earthquake triggered a 120-foot-high tsunami that hit the east of the Oshika Peninsula, in turn causing a nuclear meltdown at the Fukushima Daiichi Power Plant. The entire event – commonly referred to as 3.11 – killed more than 18,000 people within six minutes.[12] Most of them were crushed, burned or swept out to sea. Many of the bodies were never retrieved, and soon thereafter, people began to see ghosts.

Taxi drivers reported despondent passengers requesting rides to abandoned buildings and then disappearing; there were sightings of mud-plastered figures walking around; fire engines were regularly called out to deserted locations; groups of soaking-wet people were seen standing in doorways on sunny days or walking on the beach dressed in coats at the peak of summer; some survivors claimed to be possessed by multiple spirits, including those of animals from the power plant district; others heard voices for days on end, received calls from deceased loved ones on their mobile phones or witnessed the toys of deceased children moving autonomously. The variety of these supernatural experiences is considerable. For the most part, however, the dead were not there to haunt the living but rather to bring them comfort (Harding 2018a, 494; 2018b; Parry 2014, 2016; Shuji 2017).

At first sight, this may all seem surprising for a country that self-identifies as staunchly secular and rationalistic, but the phenomenon led to a revival of Japanese ghost stories ('Kaidan') through storytelling evenings, writing competitions and new anthologies (see Parry 2014). Whatever experiences people were having should be partly understood against this cultural backdrop. Cultural historian Chris Harding spoke with people from the area, including chief priest Jikisai Minami:

> *JM:* The dead are a *very real presence* [...] there's only one difference between the real and the virtual. With something virtual you can

12 According to National Centers for Environmental Information, 'Japan National Police Agency reported 15,899 deaths, 2,527 missing and presumed deaths, and 6,157 injuries for the Great East Japan event' not long before its 10th anniversary (https://www.ncei.noaa.gov/news/day-2011-japan-earthquake-and-tsunami). Bodies were still being identified as late as March 2021 (https://www.aljazeera.com/news/2021/3/5/body-of-woman-missing-in-japan-2011-tsunami-finally-identified).

> switch it off whenever you want, you can switch it on whenever you want. Something real is different. You can't control it […] Something that's real appears regardless of human actions, of our intentions or feelings. But some people can change your actions even after they are dead.
> *CH:* Sometimes we talk in our country of a dead person being real in the sense of remembering them very vividly. Are you talking about remembering someone vividly or are you talking about something else?
> *JM:* If you're remembering someone you can conjure them up in your mind, on demand. This is different. It's not on demand. Even if you want to forget someone who's died, they appear. You can't control it. *They really exist.* Just as powerfully as that table, sometimes even more so. It's completely different from them existing in memories. It's not a spiritual question of the soul. It's a question of the existence of a deceased person, with whom you have a relationship. They are a *very real presence.* If you turn that into a conventional, almost trite story about the souls of the deceased, you lose that vivid sense of reality. It wouldn't make sense anymore.
> *CH:* I would probably make quite a fine clear distinction between a living person and a dead person […]
> *JM:* The living aren't that real a presence […] you can't say that the living are real and the dead are virtual. They're the same. People insist on making futile distinctions about death […] – either ghosts exist, or it's all about grief; either we appear again somewhere else, or we don't – because on the whole they have yet to understand life: its reality and also its unreality. (Harding 2019, my emphasis; see also Harding 2018a, 406)

Independently of Harding, British foreign correspondent Richard Lloyd Parry interviewed Reverend Kaneta, a Zen priest performing 'exorcisms' on those claiming to be possessed:

> *RK:* Personally I do believe in them, but from an academic point of view we cannot explain whether ghosts exist or not. […] I don't think it really matters whether you believe in the literal existence of ghosts […] [W]hat's more important is that these experiences feel genuine to those who've had them, and they express very sincere emotions and genuine needs, but I also think it expresses, in the end, a reconciliation with death and with the dead and maybe even a way forward out of the disaster for this place […] I think it's natural to see ghosts […] [S]eeing or hearing the dead is nothing strange. It isn't a case of believing or not believing […] You would struggle to understand what is going on.

> *RP:* I'm trying to work out whether it's psychological on the one hand or whether something is really happening in the world on the other. Do you have a different way of looking at it?
> *RK:* All of us, even if our eyes are good, there are limits to what we see. If there are people whose eyes or ears are better attuned than normal, then that's fine. From a Buddhist point of view, it's the coming together of lots of causes and elements in the world that gives us all the appearance of existence. Lots of people don't see ghosts [...] Rather than believing or not believing it's about consciously engaging [...] Not about true or false but sharing an emotional experience.
> *RP [narrating]:* One of the things that [...] came up more and more as I travelled north was people's bafflement at the black-and-white way that I (and probably a lot of people who come from a background like mine) tend to see the world. (Parry 2016)

Instead of seeking to *explain* such phenomena in terms of a mass psychogenic illness, collective delusions and so on, Parry rightly considers a sociohistorical exposition of the resurgence of religion, superstition and/or spirituality after a great personal or national trauma. But it would be erroneous to allow such expositions to altogether displace the straightforward description of how supernatural terminology is being used here, namely the observation of what the specific Japanese people in question are actually *doing* with their words. If 'we do not understand' people, it might not be 'because of not knowing what they are saying to themselves' but instead because 'we cannot find our feet with them' (PPF, § 325–7).

While the English language embraces a variety of words such as 'spectres', 'apparitions', 'spirits' and 'ghosts', their meanings are not as distinct as those of the various Japanese terms for supernatural beings:

Ayakashi: yōkai that appear above the surface of a body of water
Bakemono: supernatural creatures
Bakeneko: changed cats (single-tailed feline *yōkai*)
Bōrei: departed spirits
Funayūrei: boat spirits (*onryō* who have died at sea)
Fuyūrei: floating spirits
Gaki: hungry ghosts (Buddhist tradition)
Goryō: vengeful (often martyred) aristocratic ghosts
Ikiryō: living spirits (disembodied, wandering souls of the living)
Jibakurei: earth-bound spirits
Jikininki: human-eating ghosts (Buddhist tradition)

Jiko bukken: condemned properties associated with an accident or incident
Kaibyō: supernatural cats
Nekomata: two-tailed mountains or domestic feline *yōkai*
Obake: shapeshifting *yōkai*
Onryō: vengeful spirits
Reikon: souls or spirits
Shiryō: dead spirits (souls of the dead)
Shinritekikashi bukken: black property or psychologically harmful property (haunted)
Tamashī: souls
Ubume: mothers who have died in childbirth
Yōkai: strange apparitions
Yūrei: faint spirits (ghosts) of people who died in an unexpected, violent way
Zashiki-warashi: parlour children (ghosts of children)

Translations of these terms are by no means inadequate, but they can easily be misleading. 'Is it even possible to translate the language games constitutive of other forms of life into those we find ourselves immersed in?' Stephan Palmié asks, and 'at what cost do we attempt to override their incommensurabilities?' (Palmié 2018, 2).

In Western culture, the concept of a haunted house largely exists in fiction, with the few examples of real-life apparitions often being the effect rather than the cause thereof. By contrast, the existence of 'incident buildings', 'accident buildings', 'psychologically harmful property', 'death rooms' and so on in contemporary Japan has a huge effect on the property market. These stigmatized properties are extremely difficult to rent or sell and are consequently 30–40 per cent cheaper, even though they are not considered 'haunted' in the Western sense (for instance, they might have been built recently on unproblematic land). It is sufficient that the former occupant died of unnatural causes or simply reported the property as psychologically harmful.[13] According to Japanese real estate legislation, an estate agent has a legal obligation to inform the tenant or buyer that the property is '*Jiko Bukken*'. Many estate agents list such properties in a special section, and banks assign them a low mortgage value.[14]

13 There are several subsets of Jiko Bukken properties: https://blog.gaijinpot.com/jiko-bukken-reasonable-rent-apartment-incidents/

14 https://japanpropertycentral.com/real-estate-faq/what-is-a-jiko-bukken-property/

We must also not assume that the people who were interviewed speak for their entire region or faith, let alone for all of Japan. It is natural to want to capture 'what the Japanese thought [think?]', but the supposition that they share a unified *conception* (as opposed to concept)[15] of a ghost is just as problematic as thinking that the ancient Greeks had a unified conception of the gods.[16] It is normal for such notions to be contested within any particular society.

This raises the question of what it means to share a concept. One may attempt to contrast the Japanese concept of a ghost with 'the Western' or perhaps even 'the British' or 'distinctively English' concept of a ghost; to be sure, when we examine the cultures' respective histories, we encounter various differences and similarities in the ghost stories narrated and recorded within each culture, reflecting histories that for over a century – from Lafcadio Hearn's *Kwaidan* (1904) to Hideo Nakata's *Ring* (1998) and its American remake *The Ring* (Verbinski 2002), as well as Hayao Miyazaki's *Spirited Away* (2001) – have been marked by cultural fusion and assimilation.[17]

According to Hearn (who became a Japanese citizen and took the name Koizumi Yakumo), Japanese Buddhists do not share the 'Western' concept of an individual ghost that continues living after bodily death (Hearn 1896, 137). This is because the Japanese belief in reincarnation does not allow for individualist notions of 'the self', which is considered instead to be an amalgam of ancestral spirits.[18] However, it does not follow from this that the Japanese generally have no concept of an individual ghost. Instead, both the living and the dead are believed to consist of multiple entities (Hearn 1896, 141), in a similar sense to that expressed in Section 51 of Walt Whitman's Emersonian 'Song of Myself' (Whitman 1856). The real difference, as Hearn himself points out, is that in the West, ghosts 'are thought of – as our collections of folk-lore bear witness – rather with fear than love', whereas the Japanese feeling towards the returned dead is 'a feeling of grateful and reverential love' (Hearn 1896, 169):

> Were there suddenly to arise within us the absolute certainty that our dead are still with us, – seeing every act, knowing our every thought, hearing each word we utter, able to feel sympathy with us or anger against us, able to help us and delighted to receive our help, able to love us and greatly needing our love, – it is quite certain that our conceptions of life and duty would be vastly changed. We should have to recognize

15 See Sandis 2019b, 147 ff.

16 See Sandis 2009b.

17 See Davisson 2020, 159 ff.

18 See Hearn 1896, 141, 151–2.

> our obligations to the past in a very solemn way. Now, with the man of the Far East, the constant presence of the dead has been a matter of conviction for thousands of years: he speaks to them daily; he tries to give them happiness; and, unless a professional criminal he never quite forgets his duty towards them. (Hearn 1896, 170)

The above description entails that there is such a thing as *the* shared 'Western', 'English' or 'Japanese' concept of a ghost. It is tempting, at this juncture, to declare that the concept of a ghost is one of family resemblance. However, although it may be true that no necessary and sufficient conditions could cover all uses of the word 'ghost', I am not convinced that the notion of a 'family resemblance concept' is useful here – or anywhere else for that matter. The notion is frequently attributed to Wittgenstein, but he never used the phrase himself, for good reason. Moreover, he applies the simile of 'family resemblance' to *words*, not concepts.[19] The phrase 'family resemblance concept' suggests that there exists a special subclass of concepts that stubbornly resist analysis. The implication is that there is something special about such concepts that distinguishes them from ordinary ones. But we should not expect the uses of *any* word in ordinary language to be bound by necessary and sufficient conditions.[20] Only precise technical concepts are immune to the fluidity of everyday language.

'Us' and 'Them'

If we are to have any hope of understanding post-tsunami ghost narratives, we must leave all our cultural, linguistic and psychological presumptions at the door. This is one of the main insights in Wittgenstein's *Remarks on Frazer's Golden Bough*. As Joy Hendry puts it, '[O]ne of the problems is that we generally

19 PI, §67. See also PI, § 65. The metaphor of family resemblance is a peculiar one for Wittgenstein to have chosen. As Beardsmore (1992) argues, members of human families resemble one another *because* they are related; games, by contrast, form families because they resemble one another. The order of explanation has been completely reversed. If there is anything to the family analogy, it is the fact that families themselves, similar to concepts, have no clear borders. We can talk of *the* family of Wittgenstein if we like, just as we can talk of *the* concept of a game, but we should not let this mislead us into thinking that we cannot sensibly make a more refined distinction between overlapping families, whether they are human or conceptual.

20 We cannot, of course, rule out in advance the possibility that some words may be used in accordance with such criteria. The point is that, even in such a case, there is no reason to expect that the usage will always remain so stringent, unless it is highly technical.

apply our own standards of judgement when we look at Japan. It is of course difficult to do anything else' (Hendry 1995, 1). But who are 'we', anyway?

Parry (2016) speaks of 'people who come from a background like mine' (see previous section for full quotation); Hendry writes of 'our own standards', and Wittgenstein frequently refers to 'us' and 'them' (Z, §§ 219, 383; CV, 74).[21] In all of these cases, the plural pronoun refers to something along the lines of 'we Westerners' or 'we Europeans, excepting some peasant communities'.[22] Leaving aside our previous concerns about there being all that much in common in the practices of people across entire nations, let alone continents, I wish to focus here on Western perceptions of 'the East'. 'We' have undoubtedly come a long way since *The Golden Bough*, which infuriated Wittgenstein owing to passages such as the following:

> According to a native account, the origin of the power of Melanesian chiefs lies entirely in the belief that they have communication with mighty ghosts, and wield that supernatural power whereby they can bring the influence of the ghosts to bear. If a chief imposed a fine, it was paid because the people universally dreaded his ghostly power, and firmly believed that he could inflict calamity and sickness upon such as resisted him. As soon as any considerable number of his people began to disbelieve in his influence with the ghosts, his power to levy fines was shaken. (Frazer 1890, 84)

> They employ thorn bushes for bed and pillow, in order to keep away the ghost of the deceased; and thorn bushes are also laid all around their beds. This last precaution shows clearly what the spiritual danger is which leads to the exclusion of such persons from ordinary society; it is simply a fear of the ghost who is supposed to be hovering near them. (Frazer 1890, 207)[23]

Wittgenstein's response has several distinct facets:

> Frazer: '[...] That these operations are dictated by fear of the ghost of the slain seems certain [...]' [212]. But why does Frazer use the word 'ghost'? He thus evidently understands this superstition only too well,

21 These and other remarks are discussed at length in Chapter 3.

22 See Chapter 3. Cf. Das 2020, 44, 198 ff.

23 See also Frazer 1890, 84. Maurice O'Connor Drury read out parts of the first volume of the third edition (1906–15) to Wittgenstein in 1929. In 1936, Wittgenstein acquired a personal copy of the 1922 abridged version (see Klagge and Nordmann 1993, 115 and Palmié 2018, 1–2). There are over 50 separate occasions in the abridged version alone where Frazer refers to ghosts.

> since he explains it with a superstitious term familiar to him. Or rather, he could have seen from this that there is something in us, too, that speaks in support of such observances on the part of the savages.[24] – When I, who do not believe that there exist, anywhere, human-superhuman beings whom one can call gods – when I say: 'I fear the wrath of the gods,' then this shows that I can mean something with this [utterance], or can express a sentiment that is not necessarily connected with such belief. (RFGB, 44, § 18)

> I would like to say: nothing shows our kinship to those savages better than the fact that Frazer has at hand a word as familiar to us as 'ghost' or 'shade' to describe the views of these people [...] [T]he strangeness of this relates not only to the expressions 'ghost' and 'shade', and far too little is made of the fact that we count the words 'soul' [*Seele*] and 'spirit' [*Geist*] into our own civilized vocabulary. Compared to this, it is a minor detail that we do not believe that our soul eats and drinks. (RFGB, 48, § 23)

Heonik Kwon recently objected that

> [i]n Wittgenstein's view, the descriptive strategy of *Golden Bough* is problematic: On the one hand, it contents itself with a mere listing of forms of magical beliefs rather than trying to situate a particular belief within a specific cultural context that gives meaning to the belief. By assigning the idea of ghosts to a belief in magical power, on the other hand, *Golden Bough* projects a distance of presumed civilizational maturity between such magical beliefs and the ideas of higher religions [...] The issue is not so simple, however. The attribution of the concept of soul to the description of magical beliefs is not separate from *Golden Bough* but very much part of its making [...] Therefore, the substitution of 'spirit' for 'ghost', as Wittgenstein suggests, is much more than a question of translation. It involves a great shift of perspective in the rebirth of anthropology as a modern social science between the late Victorian era and the early twentieth century. Seen from this angle, it is not sufficient to argue, as Wittgenstein does, that the concept of spirit is more appropriate than that of ghost. (Kwon 2018, 90) [...] [H]e seems oblivious, unlike Frazer, to the fact that 'spirit' is a problematic concept, and that

24 It is upsetting that Wittgenstein retains Frazer's use of this word, although he does at least complain that 'Frazer is far more savage than most of his savages' (RFGB, 44, § 19).

> hidden in the modern concept of 'spirit' is a history of the purge of the concept of 'ghost' from civilized society. (Ibid., 95)[25]

I do not wish to dispute Kwon's analysis.[26] Instead, I wish to focus on a different aspect of Wittgenstein's criticism of Frazer, regarding the background, education, traditions, practices, interests and concepts of others.[27] Frazer's error was to take local references to 'ghosts' and interpret them from an English background, as opposed to interpreting them within the context of the various local practices and traditions of the people he was writing about. As Frazer's own biographer puts it:

> He wrote vast, assured tomes about primitive religion and mythology without ever leaving the library. He based his comprehensive theories on the often crude and ethnocentric reports of explorers, missionaries, and traders. He lacked the idea of culture as the matrix, both conscious and unconscious, that gives meaning to social behavior and belief, and thus had no qualms about comparing terms of culture from the most disparate times and places. He was a hard-line rationalist who used ethnographic facts to try and knock the last nail in the coffin of religion in the name of objective science. If from time to time he achieved a kind of prophetic power, it is because he was the spokesman for an imperialist confidence that has now been swept away. It is no wonder that no one wants him for a professional ancestor. (Ackerman 1987, 1)

Palmié notes that 'Wittgenstein opposed a now bygone tendency' in Frazer 'to rationalize – according to metropolitan European standards of reason – what used to be called "ostensibly irrational beliefs" and practices in the non-Western world, or Europe's own peasant periphery' (Palmié 2018, 3). Such 'scientific rationality' ultimately backfires on the very forms of belief one blindly thought immune to it. Hearn puts it best:

25 Cf. Harding 2018b, in which JM says that '[t]alk of "spirits" or "souls" is often too trite, too easy'.

26 For the Japanese notion of 'spirit', see Hearn 1896, 140 ff.: 'To many persons it must seem that the idea of Soul as an infinite multiple would render impossible any idea of religion in the Western sense [...] [I]t is the use of the English word "soul", not understood at all as we understand it, which creates the false impression' (cf. Hearn 1896, 169).

27 Cf. Z, § 384–90, quoted further below. Hence Wittgenstein's 1949 confession to Piero Sraffa: 'The older I get the more I realize how terribly difficult it is for people to understand each other' (WC, 410, 450, discussed in Chapter 1). In the same letter, Wittgenstein writes: 'For certain people to understand each other, one has to think *not* of the few occasions on which they meet, but of the differences of their *whole lives*'.

> Those who hope to substitute their own Western creed in the room of one which they wreck by the aid of knowledge borrowed from modern science, do not imagine that the arguments used against the ancient faith can be used with equal force against the new. (Hearn 1896, 118)

Would an alien anthropologist observe any real difference in kind between Japanese attitudes towards the reality of ghosts and the engagement of millions of Westerners with daily horoscopes, or, for that matter, Christian sacraments? Parry romanticizes the notion that unlike 'us', the Japanese do not see the supernatural in black-and-white terms. But whom is he really speaking for?

Epilogue

This essay opened with a quotation from Geertz's *The Interpretation of Cultures*, a book that explicitly brought Wittgenstein's philosophy to the attention of anthropologists and urged that 'it is through the flow of behaviour – or, more precisely, social action – that cultural forms find articulation' (Geertz 1973, 17). The meaning of what we say and do thus 'varies according to the pattern of life by which it is informed' (Geertz 1973, 14). Such patterns are not hidden away in our minds but lie open to view for all to see, even if, prima facie, we cannot make sense of them.[28]

Wittgenstein begins not with 'I' but with 'we', and from there, he moves to understand 'them'. These 'others' may seem stranger, if not completely alien, and in extreme cases, we cannot even find our feet with them. However, there is never any question of what we would need to do in order to attempt to. The answer is not accessing their 'mental content' but acquiring a better grasp of the relationships and activities at which their reasoning is directed. Instead of beginning with a Lockean account of one-on-one communication and attempting to extend it to cultural understanding, Wittgenstein dives straight into the social. His is a 'we-first' philosophy.[29]

I am not an anthropologist. And I write this not from Japan but from a basement apartment in London. The aim of this essay has not been to make any kind of contribution to the understanding of Japanese society but rather

28 For an explanation of why the 'cannot' here does not imply logical or metaphysical impossibility, see Sandis 2012a, 151–2.

29 Katja Behrens (2018) makes a similar point in the philosophy of action. Philosophers operate with an 'atomistic' understanding of action that they use as a model for collective action. But paradigmatic action is already social, and it is the near-solipsistic individual action considered in abstraction that requires a special account.

to critique certain accounts of understanding others – accounts forged in the grip of a philosophical portrait of communication that goes against what should be obvious to anyone who has ever made a sincere attempt to master a previously foreign concept.

The statement that to understand another culture we need to spend time with them is so banal that it is somewhat embarrassing to write. Even Frazer believed that this much is true. But what has become obvious to anthropologists remains opaque to philosophers. Perhaps when they go on vacation or attend conferences abroad, philosophers understand all too well how intercultural understanding is achieved. But when they return to their desks and armchairs and start pondering how communication is possible in the first place, strange theories emerge. Theories of belief are far stranger than any belief in supernatural presences.

Chapter 7

PERIOD AND PLACE: WITTGENSTEIN AND COLLINGWOOD ON UNDERSTANDING OTHERS

Prologue

What it takes to understand radically different others lies at the heart of the philosophies developed by Collingwood and Wittgenstein at roughly the same time.[1] Their approaches differ in three ways that are *prima facie* significant but ultimately prove to be little more than a divergence in emphasis. This is particularly remarkable in light of the fact that the two thinkers are frequently thought to stand at opposite ends of the methodological spectrum with respect to the value of metaphysics.

First, there is the difference between period and place. Whereas Wittgenstein typically considers examples of (chiefly fictional) people from geographically distant strange lands, Collingwood concentrates specifically on the thought and action of past figures from the history of Western civilization. This relates to the second difference between them, which is that Collingwood is primarily interested in *individuals*, whereas Wittgenstein focuses on *collectives* of people. The third, arguably greatest, difference is in their conceptions of what understanding involves. For Collingwood, this is a matter of *re*-enacting the practical reasoning of those concerned; Wittgenstein, by contrast, seems to think that it requires a serious *immersion in the other's form of life*, a feat more – on some views *only* – feasible with one's contemporaries.

We must nonetheless view their approaches to understanding others as complementary rather than opposed. For one thing, it is plausible to expect parallel conditions for understanding the foreign present and the local past (as in historical understanding). As the famous opening line of L. P. Hartley's

1 Wittgenstein's Preface to *Philosophical Investigations* (PI) is dated January 1945; Collingwood's *The Idea of History* (IoH) was originally published in 1946. Both had been working on these uncompleted (posthumously published) masterpieces for years and would continue to develop their ideas until their early deaths. For literature on various resemblances between the two philosophers, see Boucher 1995, n. 42.

The Go-Between contends, 'the past is another country, they do things differently there' (Hartley 1953, 1). We must also take care not to exaggerate the differences between their interests. Wittgenstein does not focus solely on understanding one's contemporaries, and Collingwood was certainly interested in cultural beliefs and practices, as exemplified in his historical works as well as in his doctrine of absolute presuppositions (arguably inspired by Evans-Pritchard[2] but connected to the 'hinge propositions' of Wittgenstein's *On Certainty*[3]) and in his critique of anthropology.[4] *Pari passu*, not all of Collingwood's pronouncements are about individuals, and, as we shall see, Wittgenstein's more personal worries about understanding others focus explicitly on the thought of individuals.

While Wittgenstein does not adhere to anything resembling Collingwood's method of re-enactment, there are deep commonalities in how they conceive of the relation between thought, action and explanation. Both philosophers resist the temptation to assume that the thoughts of others are inner mental events that are in principle hidden from us. Rather, actions are the observable expressions of our thoughts and desires, and it is in principle possible for one person to have *the very same thoughts* as another. However large the psychological or cultural obstacles to this might be, they are ultimately *contingent* in nature.

The task of both the historian and the anthropologist, so conceived, is not to establish facts and offer causal explanations for them but to explore what a

2 James Connelly (2013, 413–14) notes that the doctrine may have been influenced by *Witchcraft, Oracles, and Magic Among the Azande*, which Collingwood read in manuscript form for the university press. For comparisons between Evans-Pritchard and Wittgenstein, see Winch 1964, 22 ff.; cf. MacIntyre 1962, 1964.

3 Bernard Williams (Williams 2006, 355 ff.) contends that 'absolute presuppositions structure practices' and that 'Collingwood should have acknowledged more than he did in this connection what in relation to Wittgenstein is called the primacy of practice'. In his *Remarks on Frazer's Golden Bough*, 'our' presuppositions are claimed to be no better (or worse) than those of allegedly primitive people who 'only possess a peculiar interpretation of the phenomena' (RFGB, 141). This approach culminates in the remarks in *On Certainty* (e.g. §§ 341, 343, 655) that 'hinge propositions' are arguably not propositions at all but akin to heuristic maxims for interpreting phenomena. As Danièle Moyal-Sharrock argues, these 'hinge certainties' are *not* inferred from experience and do *not* function as grounds but rather as the 'scaffolding of our language games' (Moyal-Sharrock 2005, 80–2; cf. Hamilton 2014, 104 ff.

4 Collingwood 2005 and Collingwood (1939) 2013, Part II; see also Connelly 2009. As the editors of *The Philosophy of Enchantment* point out, 'some of the points made by Collingwood in his critique of early anthropology are mirrored in Wittgenstein's almost contemporary notes made on the *Golden Bough*, also little known and most fully published only in 1993' (Collingwood 2005, lxvi).

situation means or meant to those whom one is trying to understand. As Peter Winch would later put it, 'the way to understand events in human history [...] is more closely analogous to the way in which we understand expressions of ideas than it is to the way we understand physical processes' (Winch 1958, 123–4).[5] In this methodological approach, Collingwood and Wittgenstein are as close as two coats of paint.

Understanding Through Re-enactment

According to Collingwood, the explanation of past action requires a reconstruction of the thought and reasoning that led up to it. Without this, our knowledge is limited to the occurrence of bodily events and, as such, lacks understanding. Given that the re-enactment involved inevitably occurs from a different perspective, it takes on a critical form:

> The history of thought, and therefore all history, is the re-enactment of past thought in the historian's own mind. This re-enactment is only accomplished, in the case of Plato and Caesar respectively, so far as the historian brings to bear on the problem all the powers of his own mind and all his knowledge of philosophy and politics. It is not a passive surrender to the spell of another's mind; it is a labour of active and therefore critical thinking. The historian not only re-enacts past thought, he re-enacts it in the context of his own knowledge and therefore, in re-enacting it, criticizes it, forms his own judgment of its value, corrects whatever errors he can discern in it. This criticism [...] is an indispensable condition of the historical knowledge itself [...] [T]he thought which re-enacts past thoughts [...] criticizes them in re-enacting them. (IoH, 216–17)

The clue to what re-enactment itself consists in is provided some pages later:

> Suppose, for example, [the historian] is reading the Theodosian Code, and has before him a certain edict of an emperor. Merely reading the words and being able to translate them does not amount to knowing their historical significance. In order to do that he must envisage it as that emperor envisaged it. Then he must see for himself, just as if the emperor's situation were his own, how such a situation might be dealt with; he must choose to see the possible alternative, and the reasons for choosing one rather than another; and thus he must go through the

5 I consider Winch's somewhat uncharitable interpretation of Collingwood in Chapter 8.

> process which the emperor went through in deciding on this particular course. Thus, he is re-enacting in his own mind the experience of the emperor; and only in so far as he does this has he any historical knowledge, as distinct from a merely philological knowledge, of the meaning of the edict. (Ibid., 283)

Without such re-enactment, we can at best only *chronicle* events. But the missing element is not a discrete thought or intention that hides behind an otherwise clear meaning. In the case of a philosophical text, for instance, its meaning can only be understood once one has seen 'what the philosophical problem was, of which his author is here stating his solution [...] re-thinking for himself the thought of the author' (ibid.).[6] To achieve this, we must 'come prepared with an experience sufficiently like his own to make those thoughts organic to it' (IoH, 300).[7]

In what sense are we supposed to go through the *same* process of thought as the person we are trying to understand? Collingwood's readers today must themselves adopt strategies of re-enactment in order to find out what Collingwood actually meant by that. As we cannot make sense of what it would be to go through the same *particular* process, it is tempting to assume that Collingwood has in mind a thought process of the same *type*. Nothing could be further from the truth:

> When I read Plato's argument in the *Theaetetus* against the view that knowledge is merely sensation, I do not know what philosophical doctrines he was attacking; I could not expound these doctrines and say in detail who maintained them and by what arguments. In its immediacy, as an actual experience of its own, Plato's argument must undoubtedly have grown up out of a discussion of some sort, though I do not know what it was, and been closely connected with such a discussion. Yet if I not only read his argument but understand it, follow it in my own mind by re-arguing it with and for myself, the process of argument which I go through is not a process resembling Plato's, it actually is Plato's so far as I understand him correctly. (IoH, 301)

The rethinking of a thought, then, is identical to its critical consideration. So understood, the practice shares elements with the Pyrrhonic method of holding a belief without assenting to it. Collingwood is here explicitly rejecting

6 See also Collingwood 1939, 53–76.

7 In Sandis 2011, I try to show that Collingwood here strikes a balance between empathy and detachment.

the (still) dominant view that identity, as opposed to mere resemblance, is either a matter of strict numerical (token-token) identity or an instantiation of a universal type in a token copy.[8] Instead, he maintains that one may go through the *very same* thought process as Plato just by reasoning in *exactly the same* way as he did. A thought process, after all, is but a reasoning process, and we cannot rule out that two people at different times and places might, in principle, reason in exactly the same way. How might such sameness be ruled *in*? We find a ready-made example in Jorge Luis Borges' story about Pierre Menard, who sets out to write the *Don Quixote* from scratch, initially by *being* Miguel de Cervantes (learning Spanish, returning to Catholicism, forgetting the history of Europe from 1602 to 1918, etc.) but finally coming to write the ninth and 38th chapters of Part I and a fragment of Chapter 22 through his own experiences.[9]

This *through*-ness is what Collingwood calls *immediacy*, which he contrasts with *mediation*:

> [Thought] is both immediacy and mediation. Every act of thought, as it actually happens, happens in a context out of which it arises and in which it lives, like any other experience, as an organic part of the thinker's life [...] [I]n addition to actually happening it is capable of sustaining itself and being revived or repeated without loss of its identity [...] [W]hat we think is not altered by alterations of the context in which we think it [...] [I]n their immediacy, as actual experiences organically united with the body of experience out of which they arise, Plato's thought and mine are different. But in their mediation they are the same. (IoH, 300–1)

Collingwood's thought that two people can have the very same thought is itself shared by Wittgenstein. But Wittgenstein's remarks on this are unconcerned with overcoming any pragmatic difficulties which might be presented by period or place, seeking instead to establish a logical possibility in the philosophy of mind. This is not because Wittgenstein has no interest in the first set of worries. It is just that we must look elsewhere in his work to find them, in what we might call his philosophy of understanding. As we shall eventually see, however, the two areas of enquiry are not unconnected. Wittgenstein's philosophy of mind both completes and is completed by his philosophy of understanding. To appreciate how this completion itself completes the

8 For the type/token distinction in Collingwood, see D'Oro 2000, Saari 1989, Van der Dussen 1995.

9 Borges 1939.

thought of Collingwood, we must first take a brief excursion into the relation of thought to action.

From Thought to Action

Wittgenstein notoriously takes issue with the commonsense assumption that two people cannot have the same pain:

> 'Another person cannot have my pains.' – Which are *my* pains? What counts as a criterion of identity here? Consider what makes it possible in the case of physical objects to speak of 'two exactly the same', for example, to say 'This chair is not the one you saw here yesterday, but is exactly the same as it'. In so far as it makes *sense* to say that my pain is the same as his, it is also possible for both of us to have the same pain [...] 'But surely another person can't have THIS pain' – the answer to this is that one does not define a criterion of identity by emphatic stressing of the word 'this'. Rather, what the emphasis does is to suggest the case in which we are conversant with such a criterion of identity, but have to be reminded of it. The substitution of 'identical' for 'the same' (for instance) is another typical expedient in philosophy. (PI, §§ 253–4)

The view here is that we are being presented with two different language games, neither of which is *in itself* justified or unjustified, correct or incorrect, though their comparative proximities to everyday parlance are instructive. It is all too easy to become so fixated by a philosophical or scientific picture that we fail to recognize that there are other, equally legitimate, ways of seeing the same thing. A related danger is that of switching between two different conceptual schemes in mid-thought, as illustrated in the following example by P. M. S. Hacker:

> The reasoning is confused, for two different language-games are being crossed [...] 'pain in my leg' does not determine a location in the same way as 'penny in my pocket' does. Hence we should be suspicious of the claim that since A's pain is in his foot and B's pain is in *his* foot, therefore their pains are in different places. (Hacker 1990, 21)

As David Boucher, Wendy James and Philip Smallwood demonstrate, Collingwood's undated paper 'Observations of Language' isolates 'the identity of language in near-Wittgensteinian terms' (Collingwood, 2005, xvii, 18, n.1). Collingwood here writes:

> It is a mistake to think of it as having certain properties or powers in itself and apart from the 'using' of it: for since it is an activity, not an instrument, it does not exist save in being 'used'. (Collingwood 2005, 18)

Boucher et al. note that while there is no evidence that Collingwood knew of Wittgenstein's ideas (meaning that he may have formulated his views of language independently), we find additional parallels in *The Principles of Art* and *The New Leviathan*:

> One does not first acquire a language and then use it. To possess it and to use it are the same. We only come to possess it by repeatedly and progressively attempting to use it. (Collingwood 1938, 250)

> A word is not a sound or group of sounds [...]; it is a sound or group of sounds having its own meaning, namely what a person using that word means by making that sound. (Collingwood (1942) 1992, 41)

Unlike Wittgenstein, however, he would not have had any problem with the claim that 'you cannot have my pain' *per se*. This is because pain, for Collingwood, is a sensation and therefore strikingly different from thinking in not being a 'directional activity' (Collingwood 1938, Chapter 8).[10] Accordingly, the spatiotemporal criteria that apply to the having of the sensation do not apply to what Collingwood means by 'thought', viz. *what* is thought rather than the thinking of it.[11]

We are now in a better position to explore how rethinking past thoughts is meant to help with the understanding of historical figures and, *mutatis mutandis*, with the explanation of their actions. As already noted, Collingwood maintains that without a reconstruction of the reasoning that led up to action, the historian's knowledge is limited to that of the occurrence of bodily events. Without re-enactment, we can capture only a record of statements that *chronicle* events:

> The processes of nature can [...] be properly described as sequences of mere events, but those of history cannot. They are not processes of mere events but processes of actions, which have an inner side, consisting of processes of thought; and what the historian is looking for is these processes of thought. All history is the history of thought. (IoH, 215)

10 See Asad 2012, 49 for complications relating to emotion.

11 For the *locus classicus* of this distinction, see White 1972.

Thoughts, for Collingwood, are but aspects of the actions which can be used to characterize them. Accordingly, there are no hidden 'inner' thoughts which lie behind – and causally precede – actions:

> The historian, investigating any event in the past, makes a distinction between what may be called the outside and the inside of an event … By the inside of an event I mean that in it which can only be described in terms of thought: Caesar's defiance of Republican law, or the clash of constitutional policy between himself and his assassins [...] [A]n action is the unity of the outside and inside of an event [...] [The historian's] main task is to think himself into this action, to discern the thought of its agent [...] For history, the object to be discovered is not the mere event, but the thought expressed in it. To discover that thought is already to understand it. After the historian has ascertained the facts, there is no further process of inquiring into their causes. When he knows what happened, he already knows why it happened. (Ibid., 213–14)

While Collingwood couches his position in Hegelian terminology,[12] there is an obvious parallel here with Wittgenstein's contention that nothing is hidden (PI, §§ 243–316). William Dray captures this aspect of Collingwood's philosophy of mind and action very well by comparing his philosophy of mind to that of Ryle:

> [F]ar from considering explanatory thoughts as unobservable events, he regarded them as having no existence at all apart from the events which expressed them. In this connection, his views are much closer to those of his successor in the Chair of Metaphysical Philosophy of Oxford, Gilbert Ryle, than has always been supposed. Suggestive in this connection is his vigorous attack on what he called 'the metaphysical theory of mind' – the conception of it as a non-physical substance, rather than a complex of activities. (Dray 1980, 12)[13]

If action is ontologically inseparable from thought, then one cannot even begin to understand or explain action without understanding the thoughts

12 See Sandis 2011a, 12–15. For parallels between Hegelian and Wittgensteinian approaches to the philosophy of action, see Laitinen and Sandis 2010b: 6–7; Taylor 1979, 2010.

13 In a similar spirit, Giuseppina D'Oro (2003) argues that Collingwood's philosophy of mind offers a viable account of the irreducibility of the mental that has been mistakenly regarded as one of Ryle's targets; see Collingwood (1933) 2008, 253–326, for his correspondence with Ryle.

that form part of its constitution. Given this tight connection, the question of whether beliefs and 'pro-attitudes' are *causes* of intentional behaviour does not even arise. This is because it makes no sense to look for nomological relations between the inner and outer aspects of one and the same event. One may, of course, observe correlations between various inner and outer characterizations, but the latter are not what the historian is trying to explain, for the job of the historian is to explain *action* – and thereby also *thought* – not mere movements of material bodies. A unified account of neuroscientific explanations of every single bodily movement of some person does not constitute a biography.

Actions, for Collingwood, are not identified through – let alone *with* – bodily movements, but by the *thought(s)* they express. When he speaks of actions having an interior aspect that events lack, this is arguably a metaphorical way of expressing the Aristotelian point that in attempting to understand any given action we may ascribe a practical syllogism to its agent. Such syllogisms are reconstructed reasonings that help to explain the agent's action by disclosing *what* she was doing. They need not either accompany or precede the act, which they are not entirely separate from. Hence Collingwood's claim that when historians know *what* happened they already know *why* it happened ('for the historian there is no difference between discovering what happened and discovering why it happened').

A related thought would later be echoed by Wittgenstein's pupil G. E. M. Anscombe in her account of explanation by re-description:

> The description of something as a human action could not occur prior to the existence of the question 'Why?', simply as a kind of utterance by which we were *then obscurely prompted to address the question.* (Anscombe 1957, 83, § 46, emphasis in the original)

Whether or not Collingwood had recognized that explanation is sensitive to description, what is clear is that, despite his reference to the 'inner', he joins Wittgenstein and anticipates Anscombe in taking his point about action's being the outer *expression* of thought to debunk a causalist approach to explanation that was already gaining prominence:[14]

> This does not mean that words like 'cause' are necessarily out of place in reference to history; it only means that they are used there in a special sense. When a scientist asks 'Why did that piece of litmus paper turn pink?' he means 'On what kinds of occasions do pieces of litmus paper

14 For Collingwood's place in the history of the reasons/causes debate, see Chapter 8 and D'Oro and Sandis 2013.

> turn pink?' When an historian asks 'Why did Brutus stab Caesar?' he means 'What did Brutus think, which made him decide to stab Caesar?' The cause of the event, for him, means the thought in the mind of the person by whose agency the event came about: and this is not something other than the event, it is the inside of the event itself. (IoH, 214–15)[15]

Collingwood's methodological approach here is once again eerily close to that of Wittgenstein, as described above.[16] With this in mind, let me now outline Wittgenstein's approach to understanding others before relating it back to that of Collingwood.

Sharing Lives

Whereas Wittgenstein's published writings on forms of life refer to entire communities of people, his personal obsession with the difficulty of understanding others focuses on individuals[17] and as such lies closer to the interests that Collingwood is best known for.[31] Conversely, passages such as the following, from a letter Collingwood sent to Ethel Collingwood shortly after his arrival in Indonesia on 31 November 1938, could have easily been written by Wittgenstein:

> It is a very odd thing, this idea that one entire civilization should be so related to another that any member of the first is given a title of nobility by any member of the second. It doesn't mean that either *understands* the other, for they don't; nor that the dominant people beat the natives at their own game and win their respect that way, for that again doesn't happen; it does mean, however, that the natives recognize the strangers as people whom they can see to be obeying a stern and exacting law, living for an idea & not for a good time, living hard & not taking things easy. And I don't think that this is true any longer. I don't think

15 For his alternative way of capturing the nature of action explanation, which does not resort to the inside/outside metaphor, see Collingwood (1940) 1998, 285–9.

16 It is even closer and, along with Wittgenstein's, served as a forerunner to the kind of descriptive metaphysics that (Strawson 1959a) would pioneer in the aftermath of Wittgenstein's heyday. The largest difference between them is that the latter replaces *historical* metaphysics with 'a massive central core of human thinking' which, unlike Collingwood's absolute presuppositions, 'has no history' because 'there are categories and concepts which, in their most fundamental character, change not at all' (ibid., 10; see also Hacker 1996a, 176).

17 I explored this contrast in Chapter 1.

> that people hereabouts look up much to Europeans. (James 2013, 522; emphasis in the original)

In response to a letter from C. L. Stevenson, Wittgenstein writes, 'I'm sorry you must do a lot of the history of philosophy for it will hardly help you to clear up your own muddles'. It would be precipitous to dismiss this as preposterous without making a little effort to understand the thought behind it. The pleasing irony is that *part* of the reason for Wittgenstein's doubts that the history of philosophy will help with one's personal philosophical muddles is a deep pessimism about our power to readily understand the thought of others. This difficulty becomes particularly salient when we are trying to understand people who lived in the distant past and spoke a different language, both literally and metaphorically. Hence Wittgenstein's pessimistic comment to C. L. Stevenson, in a letter written upon hearing that Stevenson was 'supposed to have a fairly intimate knowledge of the history of philosophy' (WC, § 162) for an examination he was preparing for:

> Really to understand other peoples [sic] thoughts or to learn from their confusions is *enormously* difficult, especially if they lived long ago [...] The only thing to do is to tell *yourself that you don't understand what exactly they were at* [...] (WC, § 165, 218 December 1933; emphasis in the original)[18]

In the arena of the history of ideas, we are all latecomers seated up in the gods, with restricted viewing; but at least we got in. Wittgenstein undoubtedly found the ideas on show – at least as incarnated in our *reception* of them – too thoroughly muddled to be of use to anybody. The letter to Stevenson reveals why he also took it to be an extremely hard and perhaps thankless (but not altogether hopeless) task to re-evaluate standard interpretations of past texts. Indeed, he seems to have acquired many of these second-hand, with the exegetical disinterest of a first-year undergraduate, a stance fortified by his curious apathy with regard to whether other philosophers had previously entertained the same thoughts as he (Wittgenstein TLP, 26; 1953, viii).[19]

Wittgenstein would have approved of Collingwood's pronouncement that '[e]very piece of writing is primarily addressed by the writer to himself' (Collingwood (1933) 2008, 209) and that, as Bernard Williams has put it, 'you could not understand what was being said by an author unless you understood [...] the question that he was trying to answer' (Williams 2006, 344).

18 This stance arguably explains Wittgenstein's lifelong claim to 'not wish to judge' how far his efforts 'coincide with those of other philosophers' (TLP, Preface).

19 For a deeper exploration of Wittgenstein's ambivalent relation to the history of philosophy, see Glock 2005.

While he liked to spot congenial features, Wittgenstein cared little whether what *he* saw in (say) Plato, Spinoza, Hume, Schopenhauer or Freud coincided with what *they* had in mind; what mattered was that it was there to be found.[20] This is a celebration, not of the death of the author, but of the life of the reader. As such, it is immune to Collingwood's chastising of the scissors-and-paste teacher whose 'claim to know what question the author is asking is a fraud which anyone could expose by asking for his evidence' (Collingwood (1939) 2013, 71).[21]

Another instructive anomaly is Wittgenstein's precise juxtaposition of the *historical* with the *personal*. This is complicated by the *prima facie* tension between his anti-scepticism about *knowledge* of other minds and his pessimism in private correspondence about *understanding* (or being understood by) other people.[22] The contrast reveals that, for Wittgenstein, while it is *metaphysically possible* not only to understand another person's thought but also to have *that very same thought*, it is *in practice almost impossible* to do so. Hence Wittgenstein's remark, in a later letter to Sraffa (23 August 1949), that 'it's impossible, or almost impossible, for certain people to understand each other' because of the 'differences of their whole lives' (WC, 410, 450).

The problem of understanding, we are reminded, is not limited to period and place but permeates our daily lives. Collingwood's thoughts on generation gaps. reveal a stance consonant with Wittgenstein's appropriation of Nestor's line that 'the thing about progress is that it always seems greater than it really is'[23]:

> If a community of fish-eaters had changed their method of catching fish from a less to a more efficient one [...] this would be called an example of progress. But from whose point of view is it an improvement? [...] [T] he older generation will see no need for the change knowing as it does that life can be lived on the old method. And it will also think that the old method is better than the new; not because of irrational prejudice, but because the way of life which it knows and values is built round

20 Von Wright (1955, 543–4) writes that '[f]rom Spinoza, Hume, and Kant he said that he could get only occasional glimpses of understanding', whereas 'he did read and enjoy Plato'.

21 The passage also includes an incidental mention of Wittgenstein, in the same breath as Plato and Kant.

22 See Chapters 1 and 4 for how Wittgenstein's cryptic remark about the speaking lion may serve as a point of contact between the two domains.

23 For exegesis, see Cahill 2006.

> the old method [...] To him, therefore, the change is no progress but a decadence. (IoH, 325)

The thought that bridging such life-gaps is *almost* – but not quite – impossible is testimony to Wittgenstein's view that the difficulty here is not metaphysical but psychological. Indeed, as early as the *Tractatus*, Wittgenstein sees no difficulty in the idea of having or thinking the same thought as another:

> *Dieses Buch wird vielleicht nur der verstehen, der die Gedanken, die darin ausgedrücht sind – oder doch ähnliche Gedanken – schon selbst einmal gedacht hat.* (TLP, 26)[24]

If the qualification 'or similar thoughts' marks any kind of hesitation at all, it is of a psychological (not philosophical) nature. Indeed, Wittgenstein has such a high standard for thought that he finds it is hard for writing to express thoughts at all (TLP, 28), let alone ones that have not already been anticipated in some way. It is highly improbable, on this view, for one person to fully understand the thought of another. Nonetheless, it remains possible, precisely because two people can share the same thought. Wittgenstein presents us with no theory here, but it is clear that two such people must share much else in their lives in common for this to be the case. Whereas Collingwood emphasizes the *reasoning* that led to the thought in question, Wittgenstein highlights the importance of shared *forms of life*.

In his book *Historical Explanation: Re-enactment and Practical Inference*, Rex Martin compares what he presents as Wittgenstein's idea that the 'content' of practice founded on game-forms can be neither true nor false to Collingwood's doctrine of absolute presuppositions (Martin 1977, 209–10; Collingwood (1940) 1998, Part I). His aim is to show how 'action explanations constitute a practice, a language-game' (Martin 1977, 203), thereby integrating his modified version of Collingwood's account of re-enactment as the reconstruction of practical reasoning with G. H. von Wright's theory of practical inference.[25]

This takes us to the heart of the distinction between explanation and understanding. Martin laments:

24 Ogden translates this as 'This book will perhaps only be understood by those who have themselves already thought the thoughts which are expressed in it – or similar thoughts' (1922, 27); Pears and McGuinness as 'Perhaps this book will be understood only by someone who has himself already had the thoughts that are expressed in it – or at least similar thoughts' (TLP-R, 3).

25 For a sympathetic, yet pertinent, critique of von Wright's account, see Anscombe 1974.

> Von Wright has provided no real role for understanding in his account of the logic of action explanations [...] [He] has failed to integrate understanding into his account of the teleological explanations of actions. (Martin 1977, 94)

He subsequently argues that while von Wright provides a corrective to Collingwood's allegedly distorted role of understanding by showing that 'an action-explanation derives its force not just from facts in perspicuous connection but from these facts *when placed within their proper framework*, the framework provided by the basic schema' (ibid., 95, emphasis in the original) and that we can view re-enactment as 'the *way* of establishing facts that will satisfy the conditions of the schema for action-explanation' by showing 'that these particular facts do "fit together"' (ibid., 96), it is here that Wittgenstein comes to the rescue, by providing the schema which lies at the foundation of the language game or practice.[26]

Martin defines understanding as 'the ability, given a particular set of facts, to construct an unforced narrative' (Martin 1977, 94). This to be contrasted with the psychological construal of understanding as an *experience* of some kind (e.g. of having 'got it'). To understand another, on this view, is to be able to render their words and deeds intelligible via a narrative that lends itself naturally to the given facts, as opposed to one which is forced upon them like some ill-fitting puzzle piece that ostensibly completes the sky. The ability need not be exercised, of course. We might *immediately* see the meaningfulness in another's conduct; but the criteria for judging whether we in fact do so are tied to being able to explain it to another.

In the case of distant periods and cultures, nothing is immediate, at least not conclusively so. Here is how Isaiah Berlin characterizes a typical challenge:

> We must therefore ask ourselves what the world must have been like for those to whom such use of language, which is almost meaningless to us, made sense [...] Transpose ourselves [...] [It is] only with the most agonising effort that we can even attempt to enter the mentality into another world [...] [T]o our remote ancestors ploughs actually appeared to have teeth; rivers, which for them were semi-animate, had mouths: land was endowed with necks and tongues, metals and minerals with veins, the earth had bowels, oaks had hearts, skies smiled and

26 Martin equates the two, but this infelicity need not concern us here. In next chapter of the same book, he explicitly compares historical explanations to cultural ones without mentioning any of Wittgenstein's numerous remarks on understanding others.

frowned, winds raged, the whole of nature was alive and active. (Berlin 1974, 344–5)[27]

Martin argues persuasively that the problem of other periods (viz. how to understand the past from the radically dissimilar perspective of the present) is structurally identical to the problem of other cultures (viz. how to understand another culture given ethnocentric distortion) (ibid., 217).[28] The possibility of history thereby hinges on the same kinds of transcendental abilities as the possibility of anthropology. Martin contends that Collingwood's idea of a 'changing human nature' that 'conceived of a set of thoughts and actions common to men at one time turning into a wholly different set for other men at a later time' (1977, 216) rules out transhistorical generalizations from the outset. This is a mistake, in his view, because we can come to understand others only by appeal to schemata of practical inference that have transhistorical application.[29]

It is precisely here that Wittgenstein can come to Collingwood's rescue. What the social understanding requires is not the Winchian application of any kinds of rules of inference which 'favour a static picture of a fully functioning and coherent system' (Williams 2006, 357) but an immersion in their form of life. In the case of other periods, this can be simulated only through re-enactment. It is a false dilemma to think that understanding a radically different person or culture must be either completely impossible or a mere matter of locating some norms and making the relevant inferences. Understanding is a matter of degree and can be difficult to attain properly

27 A book-length treatment of a cultural example akin to Berlin's historical one may be found in Lear 2006. One difference between Berlin and Collingwood is that the former places a greater emphasis on the notion of empathy; for Collingwood's influence on Berlin, see Bevir and Choi 2015, 334–56.

28 See also Danto 1965, 201–56; 1966; Hanson and Martin 1973. Danto distinguishes between the explanatory need for general laws and that for narratives. In his book, he mentions Collingwood only once, alongside Croce and Dilthey, all identified as 'Historical Idealists [...] unanimous in insisting upon a radical distinction between the behaviour of human beings and non-human entities, and a corresponding radical distinction between the groups of disciplines which respectively study these two allegedly distinct kinds of behaviour' (Danto 1965, 205). Notwithstanding the complicated exception of animal thought (see Chapter 4), this puts Wittgenstein in the very same 'radical' boat.

29 In his later work, Martin (2013, 259) writes that '[t]he place to look in order to find models or sympathetic examples of Collingwood's idea that basic presuppositions couldn't be verified would be [...] not logical positivism [...] but rather strong critics of that doctrine, like Wittgenstein or Quine'; for Collingwood's response to logical positivism, see Williams 2006, 353–4.

even with those closest to one, not to mention one's own self. But it is, in principle, always possible to share a way of living with another and thereby also come to share their thoughts.

Wittgenstein uses 'forms of life' to refer to regular, shared forms of living (Hacker 2015, § 3), but the concept readily extends to cover a particular individual's unique way of living. So understood, a form of life need not be an entire community's way of living but can be simply that of an individual. If 'to imagine a language is to imagine a form of life' (PI, § 19), might this not also apply to the language of a particular person? This would not be a private language in Wittgenstein's principled sense but the distinct language of a particular person nonetheless.

The alternative understanding of Wittgenstein's forms of life as 'part of our inflexible biological human nature'[30] is implausible, both as an interpretation of Wittgenstein and as a philosophical view in its own right. This is not to say that biological differences cannot underlie or enable cultural ones, just that the everyday difficulty of understanding others is not based on biology. The dilemma between a difference in forms of life that is purely biological and one that is merely cultural is a false one. It is ultimately both natural and nurtured behaviour that provide the leverage for understanding others (Baker and Hacker 2009, 173, inc. n. 1; see also 218 ff.). Wittgenstein uses examples such as giving and responding to orders in MS 165 (quoted n Baker and Hacker 2009, 177; 1985, 191) and PI, § 206. Glock (1996a, 128) points out that even such culturally specific conduct is ultimately rooted in biology: '[U] nderstanding an alien language presupposes [...] common perceptual capacities, needs and emotions [...] we would presumably be at a loss with spherical Martians' (Glock 1996a, 128). (All of these passages are quoted at length in Chapter 1.)

We need not worry then, as Martin does, whether or not human nature is constant. What matters is that Wittgenstein shares Collingwood's thought that the actions of individuals should be understood against a background of shared assumptions that may be culturally specific. In this respect, it is a moot point whether or not Wittgenstein would ultimately reject Collingwood's historical metaphysics, for even Strawson's substitute account of core (transhistorical) concepts is in keeping with contextualist anthropology.[31] Indeed,

30 The phrase – but not the view – belongs to Glock (1996a, 124–5).

31 Both the Humean and the Kantian strands of Strawson's approach to concepts may be at odds with Collingwood's wholesale rejection of the uniformity of human nature, but neither of them undermines the explanatory importance of shared particulars. In his review of William Dray's *Laws and Explanation in History*, Strawson accordingly argues that while some 'general knowledge of human nature' is relevant to

we could even acquire the elusive ability to understand a speaking lion if we successfully immersed ourselves in its non-human form of life.[32]

Epilogue

It is common and not entirely mistaken to think of Collingwood as a metaphysician and Wittgenstein as the anti-metaphysician *par excellence*. The followers of the latter would form a crucial part of the ordinary-language backlash to the British idealist movement, with whose tail end they associated Collingwood. Given all this, it is pretty remarkable that Collingwood and Wittgenstein developed strikingly similar views on what it takes to understand another person independently of one another during the same period of years.

While they go about this in strikingly different ways, this is not a case of reaching the same conclusion through different, let alone incompatible, routes. Far from it, the two philosophers reasoned in similar ways when considering the relation of thought to action and that of both to explanation and understanding.

I began this chapter by highlighting a number of contrasts in *focus* between Collingwood and Wittgenstein. These were (i) period vs. place, (ii) individual vs. collective and (iii) re-enactment vs. forms of life. It turned out that not only were these superficial differences of emphasis, but Wittgenstein's philosophical anthropology provides the glue that makes Collingwood's anti-transhistoricism stick.

---

historical explanation, there are no covering laws of human behaviour for it to appeal to (Strawson 1959b, 266). He also chastises Dray for (apparently) failing to distinguish between 'reconstructing a calculation and endorsing it as a correct calculation' (ibid., 267; see Dray 1963, 72, 83 for his response).

32 See Chapter 4.

Chapter 8

ONE FELL SWOOP: SMALL RED BOOK HISTORICISM BEFORE AND AFTER DAVIDSON

Prologue

Donald Davidson begins his landmark paper 'Action, Reasons and Causes' by contrasting his so-called causalist account of reason-giving explanations of action with the views of a large number of then-prominent philosophers, all of whom were writing from within a loosely Wittgensteinian tradition. These are dismissed in one fell swoop:

> In this paper I want to defend the ancient – and commonsense – position that rationalization is a species of causal explanation. The defence no doubt requires some redeployment, but it does not seem necessary to abandon the position, as has been urged by many recent writers [fn: Some examples: Gilbert Ryle, *The Concept of Mind*, G. E. M. Anscombe, *Intention*, Stuart Hampshire, *Thought and Action*, H. L. A. Hart and A. M. Honoré, *Causation in the Law*, William Dray, *Laws and Explanation in History*, and most of the books in the series edited by R. F. Holland, *Studies in Philosophical Psychology*, including Anthony Kenny, *Action, Emotion and Will*, and A. I. Melden, *Free Action*]. (Davidson 1963, 3)[1]

In a later essay, Davidson acknowledges Carl Hempel's deep influence on his views while re-affirming the contrast to the volumes in Holland's series:

1 The full Holland series ran as follows: 1. Hamlyn 1957; 2. Geach 1957; 3. Peters 1958; 4. MacIntyre 1958; 5. Winch 1958; 6. Malcolm 1959; 7. Melden 1961; 8. Armstrong 1962; 9. Kenny 1963; 10. Alexander 1963; 11. Bennett 1964; 12. Kovessi 1967; 13. Fingarette 1969; 14. Penelhum 1970; 15. Dilman and Phillips 1971; 16. Drury 1973; 17. Teichman 1974; 18.Wilkes 1978; 19. Bambrough 1979; 20. Newell 1986; 21. Donagan 1987. From here onwards, any general reference to small red books is intended to apply to nine of the first ten (published by 1963), the exception being Armstrong, whose sympathies were far removed from those of the others.

> In December of 1961 Hempel gave the presidential address at the annual meeting of the Eastern Division of the American Philosophical Association. The title was 'Rational Action'. In that address, Hempel argued that explanation of intentional action by appeal to the agent's reasons does not differ in its general logical character from explanation generally; in taking this position, he was swimming against a very strong neo-Wittgensteinian current of small red books. (Davidson 1976, 26)[2]

The contrast is not imaginary, although we shall come to see in due course that it is subtler than Davidson lets on. As we shall see, numerous books in Holland's series defend the view that the relation between an agent's reason(s) and her action(s) should be understood not causally but logically, normatively, conceptually and/or hermeneutically. In this they are united by various forms of what might reasonably be termed anti-scientism. The books do not have a clearly articulated and specific target here – certainly no definition of scientism is ever provided – but there is a general suspicion of any philosophy that attempts to answer questions relating to human minds and actions by appeal to models stemming from natural science, such as physical mechanisms.[3] Here is how one reviewer at the time characterized this movement:

> The entire series adds up to nothing less than a major philosophical revolution set off by Ryle's *Concept of Mind* and Wittgenstein's *Investigations.* No doubt devotees of natural science will regard this development as more of a counter-revolution, since modern philosophy began with the liquidation of purposive concepts from natural science while the goal of this new movement is to expunge pseudo-mechanistic concepts from the language of human affairs. The illuminating discoveries made by the writers of these monographs should have a profound effect on psychology and the social sciences, in revealing the absurdity of all attempts to model them on the natural sciences. (Abelson 1963, 616)

In what follows, I first outline the sense in which this anti-scientistic outlook may be plausibly described as *historicist.* I next argue that despite this unity and a related allegiance to what has come to be known as the 'logical connection argument', there remain some sharp disagreements to be found across the books that Davidson so readily grouped together. These differences are

2 The allusion is, of course, to Mao Zedong's 'little red book'. For a proto-Davidsonian approach to Wittgenstein's influence on the small red books, see Cerf 1962, 558.

3 Some of the authors controversially assume that any appeal to causation counts as evidence for this. I return to this issue further below.

frequently underscored by numerous insightful distinctions that have been largely ignored by post-Davidsonian philosophers of action, to the detriment of the subject. In defending a selection of these, I shall eventually suggest an approach to the explanation of action that steers clear of the Scylla of scientism without crashing into the Charybdis of the historicism in question.

Explanation and Understanding

In the 1950s and 1960s, much of the debate concerning action explanation was conducted within the philosophies of history and social science.[4] The term 'historicism' has confusingly been used to describe both the view that the explanation of historical action appeals to laws of history (which may or may not be distinct from natural laws)[5] and the diametrically opposed view that – unlike explanation in the natural sciences – historical explanation is not lawlike at all.[6] It is only in this latter sense that I shall be using the term here. So understood, historicism has been further defined as the view that 'historiography is characterized as a matter of understanding or interpreting events [...] treated as distinct from the aim of explanation or prediction within the natural sciences' (d'Amico 2011, 243).[7]

Defenders of this mode of historicism have included Oakeshott (1933), Croce (1938), Collingwood (1946), and Dilthey (1961).[8] In the words of G. H. von Wright, their common protest 'is directed against the application to history of a category which is at home in the natural sciences' (von Wright 1971, 201).[9] This outlook – in unexpected alliance with both Wittgenstein and eighteenth-century Christianity – figures as a strong influence on many of the red book authors, although not all would accept the points about either

4 For details and wider context, see D'Oro and Sandis 2013b, 17–21.

5 Karl Popper dismissively uses it in this sense (Popper 1945, 1957).

6 As if this weren't confusing enough, the term has also been used to characterize 'any position which promotes historical thinking in philosophy and warns against ignoring or distorting the past' (Glock 2005, 238). I shall not be concerned with this altogether different debate here, although its complicated relation to Wittgenstein and those whom he inspired is not without interest (and is hinted at in the first quotation by Cerf further below).

7 Cf. Bevir 2009, 211–24.

8 The leading contemporary defender of this variety of historicism is Giuseppina D'Oro (2007, 2011, 2012).

9 Von Wright's own view of the debate about causation in history is that a significant part of it is due to conceptual and terminological muddles. Ironically, his student Fred Stoutland would later give the very same diagnosis of the debate between von Wright and Davidson (Stoutland 1999, 191–208).

prediction or understanding as outlined above.[10] In a characteristically cynical review of the first six volumes of the series, the Princeton phenomenologist Walter Cerf captured this strange inheritance as follows:

> [T]he *Studies in Philosophical Psychology* are not, to be sure, studies in rational psychology. They contain no explicit commitment to metaphysics, in whatever sense of the term, no commitment, explicit or implicit, to a priori knowledge and certainly no proofs of the substantiality and immortality of the soul [...] [but] [t]he Christian tenor of eighteenth-century rational psychology is still audible in the antiscientistic (but not antiscientific) message of the *Studies*: Beware the encroachments of the natural sciences upon the specifically human. Winch presents us with a veritable declaration of independence of the social sciences from the natural [...] All this sounds rather like Dilthey (even though, quite typically, none of the six seems to be acquainted with him), who tried to separate a non-scientistic psychology, 'understanding' or 'hermeneutic' psychology, from explanatory psychology. However, Dilthey did not, I believe, wish to restrict explanatory psychology in any way, while some of our authors, out-diltheying Dilthey, go so far as to contend that no explanatory theory of the natural science variety has any logical business in the domain of the specifically human [...] [M]an is set apart from nature. Behind their anti-scientistic attitude towards psychology is an antinaturalistic conception of the nature of man [...] the belief that the methods of the natural sciences are in principle inadequate to an understanding of what is specifically and essentially human. (Cerf 1962, 537–8, 556)

Dilthey's own statement of his rather technical distinction between explanation ('Erklären') and understanding ('Verstehen') is axiomatic in its brevity:

> We explain nature, but understand the life of the soul. (Dilthey 1961, vol. 5, 144)

On Cerf's reading of this outlook, human history and psychology may be treated as both natural sciences (NS) that are the province of event explanations (E) *and* human sciences (HS) concerned with our understanding (U) of people:

10 The relation of both tenets to the history of philosophy of action is detailed in D'Oro and Sandis 2013b.

Psych/Hist

‖ ‖

E U

‖ ‖

NS HS

To understand a person, in the sense in question, is to render her intelligible, for example via some narrative that helps us make better sense of her. This is not to offer a causal explanation of anything. Conversely, one may provide a causal explanation of an action understood as a natural event without contributing to our understanding of the mind or soul of the agent behind it.[11]

Cerf maintains that the red book authors go much further than this in distinguishing between two kinds of explanation: the natural (NE) and the human (HE). In so doing, they reserve the term understanding (U) for the latter. Crucially, this domain comprises the entire domain of history and psychology. These are deemed not amenable to scientific explanations, whose nature is by definition causal (C):

Explanation

‖ ‖

NE HE

‖ ‖

Science (C) Psych/Hist (U)

11 It should be noted that neither Dilthey's outlook nor that of the small red books is limited to the explanation of human action. For example, Hamlyn (1957) applies it to his approach to perception, and Malcolm (1959) to dreaming. I restrict the discussion merely so as to stay on topic.

This account of the relation of small red book historicism to Dilthey is by and large a plausible one. Nevertheless, authors differ in the details of their accounts, and it is difficult to ascertain how much of the disparity is ultimately terminological. Which of the resulting views may be dubbed anti-naturalistic, for example, seems to be a moot point. This should not surprise us, given the variety of things that we might contrast 'natural' with. As Jennifer Hornsby writes:

> [W]e need to consider carefully this thought that persons and their actions are part of nature. It seems right when we point out that nothing supernatural needed to have happened for human beings to evolve, and that it is a natural fact about people that, for instance, they have the abilities they do, and thus a natural fact that there are actions. Such considerations ensure that a naturalistic view of ourselves is in order [...] but they do not help to place our actions in a world 'of nature' if a world 'of nature' is to be thought of as constituted independently of the human beings that occupy it. (Hornsby 1997, 73–7)

The small red book use of Dilthey is sometimes (e.g. in the case of Winch) filtered through a related debt to Collingwood (and by extension Hegel). On Collingwood's view (which may be traced back to Hegel[12]), all actions have an inner (psychological) and an outer (behavioural) side, only the second of which is amenable to study by the natural sciences. The two sides are not related causally in any standard empirical sense. Rather, as independently also hinted at by Wittgenstein (1953, §§ 335 ff.; 1967, §§ 53–60), the latter is an *expression* of the former:

> [A]n action is the unity of the outside and inside of an event [...] To the scientist, nature is always and merely a 'phenomenon,' not in the sense of being defective in reality, but in the sense of being a spectacle presented to his intelligent observation; whereas the events of history are never mere phenomena, never mere spectacles for contemplation, but things which the historian looks, not at, but through, to discern the thought within them. In thus penetrating to the inside of events and detecting the thought which they express, the historian is doing something which the scientist need not and cannot do (Collingwood 1946, 213–14)[13]

12 See Laitinen and Sandis 2010.

13 Cf. von Wright 1971, 87–8.

Though receptive to much of this, Winch is worried by the role in providing understanding that he takes Collingwood to ascribe to re-enactment. I quote at some length in order to do justice to the nuances of his position:

> Collingwood's conception of all human history as the history of thought [...] is no doubt an exaggeration and the notion that the task of the historian is to re-think the thoughts of the historical participants is to some extent an intellectual distortion [...] But Collingwood is right if he is taken to mean that the way to understand events in human history [...] is more closely analogous to the way in which we understand expressions of ideas than it is to the way we understand physical processes [...] Collingwood [...] says that the aim of the historian is to think the very same thoughts as were once thought [...] But though extinct ways of thinking may, in a sense, be recaptured by the historian, the way in which the historian thinks them will be coloured by the fact that she has had to employ historiographical methods to recapture them. The medieval knight did not have to use those methods in order to view his lady in terms of courtly love: he just thought of her in those terms [...] And naturally, it is even more impossible for me to think of *his* lady as he did. Nevertheless, Collingwood's view is nearer the truth than is that most favoured in empiricist methodologies of the social sciences, which runs somewhat as follows [...] [T]he historian unearths [...] data and presents them to his more theoretically minded colleagues who then produce scientific generalizations and theories establishing connections between one kind of social situation and another [...] [S]ocial relations must be an unsuitable subject for generalizations and theories of the scientific sort to be formulated about them: Historical explanation is not the application of generalizations and theories to particular instances: it is the tracing of internal relations. (Winch 1958, 123–4)[14]

I shall return in the next section to Winch's more positive argument, but it is worth pausing here to observe that his interpretation of Collingwood is uncharitable. This is because –as we already saw in the previous chapter – the view in question is not as metaphysically mysterious as Winch supposes. In Collingwood's own words:

> [F]or the historian there is no difference between discovering what happened and discovering why it happened [...] [H]ow does the historian

14 Winch has more positive things to say about Collingwood in later work (e.g. Winch 1964, 14).

> discern the thoughts which he is trying to discover? [...] [B]y re-thinking them in his own mind [...] This re-enactment [...] is not a passive surrender to the spell of another's mind; it is a labour of active and therefore critical thinking. The historian not only re-enacts past thought, he re-enacts it in the context of his own knowledge and therefore, in re-enacting it, criticizes it, forms his own judgment of its value, corrects whatever errors he can discern in it. (Collingwood 1946, 177, 215)[15]

This view comes remarkably close to that later found in Anscombe, quoted in the previous chapter:

> The description of something as a human action could not occur prior to the existence of the question 'Why?', simply as a kind of utterance by which we were *then obscurely prompted to address the question.* (Anscombe 1957, 83, § 46, emphasis in the original)[16]

With Croce, Dilthey and Collingwood also came the idea that historical understanding requires empathy of some kind. Thus, for example, Isaiah Berlin would later write of Vico and others that they were guided by

> [t]he very notion that the task of the historian was not merely to establish facts and give causal explanations for them, but to examine what a situation meant to those involved in it, what their outlook was, by what rules they were guided... not merely knowledge of facts and events, but understanding – Einfühlung, empathy – is required. (Berlin 1974, 355–6)

Whether or not understanding requires empathy has since been a matter of considerable debate.[17] Whatever the right answer may be, the small red book emphasis on understanding has been vindicated to the extent that empathy has in recent years become a major topic of philosophical research. The victory, however, is arguably a Pyrrhic one, for the standard approach to empathy remains stubbornly reductive: empathy is a tool we use to gain access to the informational content of other people's mental states (which double as their motivating reasons).[18]

---

15 The view is taken further by Dray (1957, 108 ff).

16 For the view that Collingwood's views here are also in unexpected alliance with those of Hegel, Dray, C. Taylor, Wittgenstein and Ryle, see Sandis 2011a.

17 See Bevir 1999, Sandis 2011a and Stueber 2006.

18 This view is, for example, endorsed in many of the essays in Coplan and Goldie 2011. In their introduction, Coplan and Goldie explicitly relate the empathy research agenda to various movements in the history of ideas, including historicism (under the

My aim in this section has been to give a taste of the sense in which many of the small red books may be said to be historicist. It is now time to focus on some of the particular claims about reasons for action to which Davidson objected. While these are situated within the framework outlined above, I hope to demonstrate that they ultimately hang on additional considerations. For reasons of space, I shan't be able to properly rehearse the arguments of each of the authors here, so I shall hint at some of the diversity while focusing on those I find most insightful. I begin with a cluster of moves collectively known as the 'logical connection' argument. This centrepiece of anti-causalism was understandably a chief target of Davidson's. I shall be maintaining that while Davidson was right to criticize the negative argument at the centre of this cluster, he ignored a positive argument that, albeit more peripheral, contains the seeds of a fruitful approach to the relation between actions and the reasons for which we perform them. In so doing, he threw the anti-causalist baby out with the historicist bathwater.

The Logical Connection

The historicist framework of the small red books lends itself to the view that actions are not mere pieces of bodily movement to be explained according to mechanistic laws of nature. Whatever one makes of this outlook, it is important to remember that the anti-causalism that Davidson was combatting was not about action explanation in general but about explanation in terms of the agent's reasons for acting as she did (from here onwards 'agential reasons'):

> [S]ome philosophers have concluded that the concept of cause that applies elsewhere cannot apply to the relation between reasons and actions, and that the pattern of justification provides, in the case of reasons, the required explanation. (Davidson 1963, 9)

Indeed, some of the philosophers Davidson has in mind here (e.g. R. S. Peters) deny that agential reasons are causes, while allowing for causal explanations of human behaviour that appeal to motives and other factors which they distinguish from agential reasons. Moreover, even Davidson was later careful to state that the mantra 'reasons are causes' should not be understood as a strict metaphysical statement about causal relations but, rather, as a point about the necessarily causal aspect of the explanatory role of reasons. Unlike causal

label 'hermeneutic tradition').The fact that none of the small red books is mention anywhere in the volume (and many others like it) is a sign of the how widespread the collateral damage of Davidson's attack has been.

relations, causal explanations are sensitive to description (Davidson 1967, 149–62).[19] Davidson's account is arguably anti-scientistic in maintaining, *pace* Hempel, that there are no strict psycho–physical laws and that the explanation of human action requires no knowledge of purely physical ones. This understanding of the relation between psychological and physical aspects of the world (viz. anomalous monism) in some respects resembles the views of Hegel, Collingwood and Dilthey.[20] Be that as it may, Davidson's insistence that the explanations in question only work if backed by strict physical laws (which we may be ignorant of) is enough to distance him from the mode of historicism defined at the outset of 'Explanation and Understanding' above.

An important bone of contention here between Davidson and the red book authors is the latter's appeal to the so-called 'logical connection argument', according to which the relation between reasons and causes is not causal but internal, logical, conceptual, intrinsic, hermeneutic and/or normative.[21] The most famous proponent of this anti-causalist stance was Melden. His influential version of the argument connects the logical connection point with the aforementioned division of action into inner and outer parts related by expression, not causation:

> [T]he very notion of a causal sequence logically implies that cause and effect are intelligible without any logical internal relation of the one to the other [...] The interior event which we call 'the act of volition' [...] must be logically distinct from the alleged effect – this is surely one of the lessons we can derive from a reading of Hume's discussion of causation. Yet nothing can be an act of volition that is not logically connected with what is willed – the act of willing is intelligible only as the act of willing whatever it is that is willed (Melden 1961, 52–3).[22]

19 (McLaughlin 2013) argues that while explanations in terms of primary reasons are causal, Davidson is wrong to infer from this that rationalization is a species of causal explanation. For a small red book take on the relation between explanation and description in science, see Chapter 6 of Alexander 1963.

20 For two distinct ways in which Davidson's account of action and its explanation is arguably not far removed from that of Hegel, see Knowles 2010 and Quante 2004.

21 Unhelpfully, many of these different attributes are frequently run together across the red books.

22 The argument is inspired by PI and Ryle 1949, 106–11, but variations of it may be found in Anscombe 1957, §§ 19, 29; Hampshire 1959, 166 ff.; Kenny 1963, 76 ff.; Peters 1958, 27 ff.; Winch 1958, 124. A later version appears in White 1967.

In a larger red book published in a different Routledge series,[23] von Wright points out that while this point is frequently made by reference to willing or intention, it ought to apply equally well to decisions, desires, motives, reasons and so on (von Wright 1971, 95). Indeed, Davidson rehearses Melden's argument as follows:

> Since a reason makes an action intelligible by redescribing it, we do not have two events, but only one under different descriptions. Causal relations, by contrast, demand distinct events. (Davidson 1963, 13–14)

It is worth remembering here that at the time of writing 'Actions, Reasons, Causes', Davidson agreed with Anscombe's claim that the intention with which an action is performed 'does not refer to an entity or state of any kind' (Davidson 1980, xvii). He came to abandon this view in his 1978 paper 'Intending'. His objection to the logical connection argument is not that no such connection exists but that it doesn't preclude a causal one. His line of argument hangs on his aforementioned distinction between causal relations and causal explanations (the latter, but not the former, being sensitive to description):

> To describe an event in terms of its cause is not to confuse the event with its cause, nor does explanation by redescription exclude causal explanation. (Ibid., 14)

To this he adds that '[i]n any case there is something very odd in the idea that causal relations are empirical rather than logical [...] The truth of a causal statement depends on *what* events are described' (ibid., emphasis in the original). As Frederick Stoutland later put it, 'the mere fact of a logical connection doesn't rule out a contingent relation between intentions and the occurrence of what fulfills them' (Stoutland 1970, 125). Stoutland influenced his teacher, who concluded that while 'those who advocate what has become known as the Logical Connection Argument are substantially right', it is not obvious 'whether anybody has yet succeeded in presenting the argument quite convincingly', and '[s]ome versions of it are not only unconvincing but manifestly defective' (von Wright 1971, 93).[24]

So, is there anything to be said for the logical connection argument? Its negative claim that a logical connection cannot also be causal is, at best, difficult to establish. But the positive claim that in citing reasons we explain

23 See D'Oro and Sandis 2013b, 35, n. 46.

24 This argument should be distinguished from his view that actions are logically/conceptually/intrinsically connected to their *results* (ibid., 87–8).

action by pointing to non-causal facts or relations is more promising. An earlier incarnation of this positive suggestion may be found in Winch's talk of 'internal relations' at the end of the long passage quoted above. Winch further holds that reasons are akin to norms in that to act on a reason is to follow a rule of some kind. Understanding why someone acted as they did, on this view, is a matter of understanding the cultural norms which help to render the action in question intelligible. This explains both his sympathy for Collingwood's general approach and his scepticism towards the latter's appeal to a method of re-enactment. According to Winch, what we need to do is not share the beliefs of those we are trying to understand but, rather, get to grips with the sociocultural norms which provide the normative framework within which the action took place.

On the above view, understanding others does not require the use of empathy as some kind of emotional instrument that provides us with an access pass to their 'mental contents' but, rather, a normative immersion which enables us to find our feet with one another (Wittgenstein 1967, §§ 383–90). This insight – which goes against the popular grain of understanding as a form of 'mind-reading'[25] – has been all but lost among the debris of the logical connection argument. In the previous section, I suggested that this Wittgensteinian approach to the relation between reasons-explanation, rule-following and cultural practices fits well with Collingwood's insight into historical *understanding*. It remains vulnerable, however, to a serious objection against the thought that reasons can explain action merely by virtue of rendering them intelligible in such ways. It is to this challenge that I now turn.

The Causal Constraint

In arguing that the 'primary' reason for an action is its cause, Davidson was looking for a criterion to distinguish between the reasons one actually acts upon and other reasons we might have and which we might have acted upon. Such reasons are capable of rendering our actions intelligible in the sense that they offer what he calls an *interpretation* of why we might have acted upon them. The interpretation 'fits [an action] into a familiar picture', e.g. by demonstrating that it would have been rational or appropriate.[26] However, this

25 See, for example, Nichols and Stich 2003.

26 While rejecting her view that one can explain an action simply by putting it 'in a certain light', Davidson nonetheless follows Anscombe 1957, 21 in holding that showing its 'desirability characteristic', e.g. why it would be *tempting* (even if vicious or otherwise inappropriate) to perform it, is sufficient for rendering an action intelligible. Hempel, by contrast, uses the phrase 'render intelligible' in a stricter sense which

form of removal from puzzlement is insufficient to explain why we *actually* acted as we did, for we may have not acted for those reasons at all:

> [A] person can have a reason for an action, and perform the action, and yet this reason not be the reason why he did it. Central to the relation between a reason and an action it explains is the idea that the agent performed the action because he had the reason. Of course, we can include this idea too in justification; but then the notion of justification becomes as dark as the notion of reason until we can account for the force of that 'because'. (Davidson 1963, 9)

It is this point that Davidson adapts from Hempel, who has the following to say about it:

> To show that an action was the appropriate or rational thing to have done under the circumstances is not to explain why in fact it was done [...] [T]he presentation of an action as being appropriate to a given situation, as making sense, cannot, for purely logical reasons, serve to explain why in fact the action was taken. (Hempel 1974, 102, 105)[27]

Unlike Hempel, Davidson maintains that rationalization is 'a species of causal explanations'. By this he means that we have failed even to rationalize an action if the reason we offer for it turns out not to have been its cause. But this difference is really semantic. Davidson is using the term 'rationalize' as a success verb which conventionally implies successful explanation of why an event[28] actually occurred. Hempel, by contrast, uses it to mean 'render intelligible', where this can clearly fall short of the aforementioned kind of explanation. Both philosophers agree that a reason may render an action intelligible without being its cause.

This point, it seems to me, is indisputable. Consequently, there is a burden on the anti-causalist (or 'intentionalist', to use von Wright's (1971, 95) term for

---

requires rationality. Nothing I say in this essay hangs on which one of them is right, although it seems obvious to me that Davidson is on the side of ordinary parlance here (not that he cared much about that).

27 See also Hempel 1942, 1962.

28 For now, I leave aside the vexed question of whether or not actions are events. Collingwood and Winch seem happy to use the term, but they arguably do so in a sense that is significantly different from Davidson's. I argue below that giving the reason for which one acted is an altogether different exercise from explaining why the event of one's acting occurred. While this point differs in detail from those of the red book authors, I shall in due course employ such distinctions to gesture at a way forward out of the impasse between Davidson and the small red books.

those who take the connection between intention and action to be logical or conceptual) to demonstrate what marks the difference between a reason that explains an action and a reason that (merely) renders it intelligible, if not the fact that one of these additionally functions as a cause.

One answer to this question, to which Kenny and Melden are in different ways both reasonably sympathetic, is to defend a version of agency according to which reasons relate to actions via the agency of those who choose to act upon them. So while Melden subscribes to the 'logical connection' argument, it is ultimately his account of agency that enables him to state that 'it is a fundamental mistake to suppose that the causal model employed in the natural sciences will fit the everyday explanation of actions in terms of intentions, interest, desires, etc.' (Melden 1961, 199). A young Annette Baier (then Stoop) took exception to Melden's dismissal of what he termed the 'Humean model' of causation, rightly objecting that 'until Melden has told us precisely what he means by a Humean cause we do not know whether he is right or wrong in maintaining that a logical connexion precludes such a causal connexion' (Stoop 1962, 248).[29] Be that as it may, Melden's alternative positive account – a constitutivist account of agency as a non-causal form of truth-making (to which I shall briefly return) – has been unjustly neglected.

A complementary line of resistance is to be found in the pluralistic account of action explanation provided by R. S. Peters, who distinguishes between four different kinds of explanation:

(a) *'His' Reason Explanations*: 'what *end* he had in mind (ibid., 4) [...] *[H]is* reason – whether real or not – entails that a man is conscious of his objective' (ibid., 9).

(b) *'The' Reasons Explanations*: 'a way of calling attention to the law or assumed law that a given case falls under. His reason may coincide with the reason. *The* reason why Jones crossed the road might in fact be his desire for tobacco. This would then be his *real* reason' (ibid., 8).[30]

29 In her later work, Baier argues that Hume's own view of action explanation fits uneasily with the Davidsonian causal model (Baier 2009). I have argued for a similar view, although I don't share Baier's understanding of what Hume meant by 'cause' (see Sandis 2019a).

30 An anonymous referee has suggested that it is scientistic to explicate '*the* reason explanations' in terms of causal laws. Whether or not this is the case partly hangs on how strict the laws in question are supposed to be. But even if Melden were to embrace a form of scientism here, this embrace would not be all-encompassing, for he asserts that there are other legitimate forms of explanation that cannot be reduced to this model.

(c) *Causal Explanations*: 'When there is some kind of deviation from the rule-following model [...] the appropriate answer [...] may be in terms of a causal theory' (ibid., 10).[31]

(d) *End-state Explanations*: 'Such explanations [...] do not give a man's reason for eating but the reason why he eats' (ibid., 21).

While we may not wish to endorse this precise way of carving things up, a pluralism along these general lines is a viable contender for the best approach to the sorts of questions we have been pursuing. The first lesson to note is that these are not four different explanations of one and the same thing, namely action or behaviour. As Peters maintains, '[t]here are many *different* sorts of questions which can be asked about human behaviour and the differences [...] are such that an all-embracing theory is inappropriate' (Peters 1958, 3).[32]

Consider, for example, (a) and (b) above. Philosophers have tended to conflate these, typically subsuming both under the notion of a 'motivating reason', which is often taken to be interchangeable with that of an 'explanatory reason'. In the case of Davidson, a 'primary reason' is meant to both motivate my action and explain it as well as justify it 'in some anaemic sense'. Moreover, it is meant to be my reason, namely a reason upon which I act and which can serve as a premise in a practical syllogism (whose conclusion Davidson takes to be an action). This is quite a lot to ask of one single entity (if that is even what reasons are), and Davidson doesn't seem to have considered the possibility of distinguishing between 'his reason' explanations and 'the reason why' explanations of action.[33] This leads to some irresolvable tensions in his account, as evidenced in the following claim:

> Your stepping on my toes neither explains nor justifies my stepping on your toes unless I believe you stepped on my toes, but the belief alone, true or false, explains my action. (Davidson 1963, 8)

The sentence suggests that what explains my action is not *what* I believe (viz. that you stepped on my toes) but my believing that you did so. But if we ask what would rationalize my action, the former would be a better candidate

31 Cf. Melden 1961, 184.

32 For a very positive review of Peters' book, see Thomson 1959.

33 Davidson famously leaves room for the possibility that an agent can be mistaken about what 'his' reasons are, but this would not be a case of 'the' reason's differing from 'his' reason. On the contrary, to be mistaken about what *your* or anybody else's reasons are, on Davidson's view, is to identify them with beliefs and pro-attitudes that are not 'the' reason for the act in question.

than the latter, especially if we are to follow Davidson in calling this 'the agent's reason'. Davidson himself fudges the issue:

> [T]here is a certain irreducible though somewhat anaemic sense in which every rationalization justifies: from the agent's point of view there was, when he acted, something to be said for the action. (Ibid., 9)

The trouble is that what is to be said for the action, the sort of thing that can figure in my deliberations, is a consideration that I act upon, something that I believe to be the case, not *my believing* it to be so.[34] Davidson switches between the following five characterizations of a 'primary reason' with no qualms:

1. The agent's reason for doing what he did (ibid., 3)
2. The reason that rationalizes the action (ibid., 3)
3. The reason that explains the action (ibid., 3)
4. The reason why an agent did something (ibid., 4)
5. The agent's reasons in acting (ibid., 11).

It is far from obvious that these are interchangeable, let alone that they are all in the business of explaining one thing – e.g. why A acted or why the event of her acting occurred. More importantly, for our purposes, Davidson has failed to provide philosophers such as Peters with an argument explaining why the agent's reasons in acting should also act as a cause of her action. Indeed, it isn't even clear why the agent's reasons should explain her action.

Davidson is looking for an all-in-one reason where there are multiple notions to distinguish between and things we might wish to explain. Each sense of 'reason' is tied to a different sort of question we might ask about action or behaviour. *Pari passu*, to say that one is explaining an action, even under a certain description, is to not yet specify what it is about the action that one is wishing to explain.[35] For example, it is arguably one thing to ask my reason for putting on rubber gloves and quite another to ask why the event of my putting on rubber gloves occurred. On a constitutivist account of action such as (say) Melden's, one can maintain that the latter event occurred just *because* I put the rubber gloves on, in the sense that my putting on the gloves *is* my making it the case that the event of my putting on the gloves occurred.

34 See Dancy 2000, 126 ff. For the anaemic sense in which the latter might be said to rationalize, see Smith and Pettit 1997. But if this really is all Davidson has in mind, he is not entitled to identify it with a reason for which the agent acts (Sandis 2012a, 73–4).

35 This general point about explanation has been made by Achinstein (1975). I relate it to action explanation in Sandis 2012a, 2012b.

This explanation of my action event doesn't cite *my* reason for putting them on. Conversely, my reason (e.g. that I was preparing to wash up the dishes) may not in itself explain why the event of my acting occurred, let alone why it did so as and when it did.

Taking on board both Hempel's and Melden's distinctions, then, we should differentiate between at least the following four explanatory aims:

1a) Rendering what happened intelligible: explaining why an action *might have occurred*
1b) Explaining why an action *actually occurred*
2a) Rendering it intelligible why someone acted as she did
2b) Explaining why someone *actually* acted as she did.

So what exactly is the difference between the (1)s and the (2)s (i.e. between explaining or rendering intelligible why an event of someone's acting occurred and explaining or rendering intelligible why someone actually acted as she did)? One apparent difference is that only the second set of sentences explicitly mentions an agent. But it would be begging the question against those causal theorists of action who identify agents with collections of psychological states (e.g. Buckareff 2011) to assume that agency is absent in the first set of examples. The difference is rather one of ontological structure: if I can make it true that my action of raising my arm occurs *by* raising my arm, then once I realize this, my reason for raising my arm could just be in order to make it true that the action of raising my arm occurs.[36] Yet what explains its occurrence will not be this reason but, rather, the fact that I raise my arm. The reason why the event occurs will just be that I performed the relevant action, whereas my reason for performing the act in question will be in order to ensure that the event of my performing it occurs.

Epilogue

The variety of nuanced distinctions relating to reasons and action to be found in the small red books points towards a pluralistic approach that rejects the dichotomies between causalism and anti-causalism, historicism and ahistoricism, scientism and anti-scientism. I have tried to show that the arguments offered by Melden and Peters are not restricted to the main negative thesis of the 'logical connection argument' account, which Davidson rightly dismissed.

36 For a defence of view that the things we do or actions we perform are not events, see Hornsby 1980.

The argument is at its strongest when presented more positively – as it is by Dilthey et al. – from within the wider framework of human understanding. Hempel and Davidson's objection to this move was that the resulting account of explanation was not so much false as incomplete. I have argued for an alternative means of completing it, to be found within the variety of subtle conceptual distinctions discoverable within the small red books themselves. These have largely been forgotten,[37]and the philosophy of action will be all the worse for it until the anti-causalist baby has been rescued from the historicist bathwater.

I have defined historicism as the view that 'historical explanation is not lawlike at all'. But if we are to espouse pluralism about action explanation, this view must be rejected in favour of one that allows that historical explanation *can* but *need not* be historical in character, depending on one's precise explanatory aims.[38] To appreciate this is to steer clear of the Scylla of historicism without crashing into the Charybdis of scientism.

37 Two exceptions are Glock 2014 and Tanney 2009b.

38 Under the influence of Anscombe, Paul Ricœur has similarly argued that there are various equally legitimate types of historical explanation, each corresponding to a different use of 'because' (Ricœur 2004, 182–8).

Chapter 9

IF AN ARTWORK COULD SPEAK: AESTHETIC UNDERSTANDING AFTER WITTGENSTEIN

Prologue

'I could only stare in wonder at Shakespeare; never do anything with him', writes Wittgenstein in *Culture and Value* (CV, 84e). This is not because he understands Shakespeare but has no instrumental use for him. Rather, Shakespeare does not *speak* to him any more than a talking lion would (see Chapters 1 and 4.) Whatever is happening in Shakespeare, Wittgenstein claims to not really get it. The confession is not a criticism of either Shakespeare or himself but a statement of aesthetic alienation:

> I am *deeply* suspicious of most of Shakespeare's admirers. The misfortune is, I believe, that he stands by himself, at least on the culture of the west, so that one can only place him by placing him wrongly (CV, 84e).

The study of Shakespeare and his cultural milieu has progressed significantly since Wittgenstein's time, but to the modern Austrian philosopher the Elizabethan playwright was nothing less than an enigma. The failure to understand Shakespeare *qua* artist is akin (but by no means identical) to the failure to understand him *qua* person. *Mutatis mutandis*, the failure to understand an artist's works is akin to the failure to understand a person's actions. This is not because artworks are actions but because both are things that we produce intentionally, with varying degrees of success.

What – if anything at all – is it to understand a play, a symphony, a sculpture or (*pace* Barr 2016) an event? What does getting it or not getting it amount to? The failure to grasp something is not a matter of being left out of knowing some kind of secret fact (phenomenological or otherwise), as in Wrede's *The Messianic Secret* (Wrede 1901). Rather, it is like the tortoise's failure to understand what it is for one thing to logically follow another. 'Whatever Logic is good enough to tell me is worth writing down', says the Tortoise to Achilles

(Carroll 1895). Yet, his understanding of whatever Achilles writes down falls perilously short of understanding what is going on when he does so.

Just as understanding a person is not a matter of understanding what she is saying, so understanding a work of art is not a matter of understanding what it is saying, assuming it is saying anything at all. Wittgenstein might understand the words of Shakespeare's texts, yet fail to understand the works themselves. Must this amount to a failure to understand what Shakespeare is saying or doing? The question is too ambiguous to merit an answer without due clarification. But this much is true: you might understand *what* I am saying, but fail to understand me because you cannot fathom *why* I would say it. If so, my writing will not speak to you. Two people may be speaking to each other without either's speaking to the other in this metaphorical sense.

What I tell you may either help you to understand me or stand as an obstacle to this, intentionally or otherwise. By the same token, understanding me may both help you to understand what I am saying and impair your ability to do so (e.g. if I am speaking out of character). An artwork may similarly both reveal and obscure the artist, as well as be revealed or obscured by her. The analogy is trickier to maintain with non-linguistic art, but the temptation to think that art always contains some idea to be understood, that is, that all art is ultimately conceptual, runs deep. I wish to steer us away from this temptation without entirely abandoning the idea that the appreciation of art can involve a kind of 'getting it'.

Understanding Art

In his paper 'Art and Philosophy', Wittgenstein's student and friend Rush Rhees draws analogies between grasping a work of art and philosophical understanding. In both cases, he claims, the person seeking understanding is not at all interested in how a certain notation – for example, a string of words or musical notes – is being used. While allowing that what is said in one form of art is impossible to say in another, Rhees nonetheless holds that 'to understand a painting or a poem or a song is to understand its ideas (to grasp it)' (Rhees 1969, 138). I hope to demonstrate how this view is indicative of a troubling failure to grasp what art even is.

There have been numerous analogies between art and language. Without altogether rejecting the possibility of seeing art as language, Garry Hagberg warns that these analogies are only ever as good as the model of language one is working with in the first place. If one's theory of linguistic meaning is misguided, the analogy will give rise to highly distorted views of art.[1] Hagberg is equally sceptical about the very question of what it is for a work of art to have meaning, at least under a popular understanding of meaning:

> The question what is the meaning of a work of art, where 'meaning' carries an implicit analogy with language and where in turn language implies a fundamental separability of meaning from materials, is a question that ought to be treated with extreme caution. (Hagberg 1995, 74)

He explicates:

> If an entity of a suspiciously ill-defined metaphysical nature is presumed to exist as the meaning of a work, aesthetic discussion will not proceed along fundamental lines: instead of asking what we mean by artistic 'meaning', we merely ask what critical approach best captures that meaning. (Hagberg 1995, 74)

Hagberg's critique of the assertion that 'art is the *language* of emotions' as concealing 'delicate falsehoods within unassailable truths' is good as far as it goes, but he nonetheless holds onto the thought that '[i]t is, and ought to be, an undeniable truth that art possesses meaning' (ibid.; emphasis in the original). I wish to assail this assumption. Art no more has meaning than lacks it. If having meaning is a matter of containing ideas, being about something, or there being something it is to understand a work of art *qua* art (as opposed to *qua* historical artefact, for example), then of course one can understand that a painting is a painting in a particular genre, that a novel is set in a particular place and time and so on, but none of this amounts to understanding the work of art itself. This is because there is no such thing as *the* correct understanding of even the most trivial work of art.[2]

This is not to rule out radical misunderstandings or interpretational abuse.[3] Art is not meaningless, for it is a category mistake to say of a particular

1 Hagberg appeals to the later Wittgenstein to attack a number of overlapping analogies that I will here simply dismiss as '-ismized' by labelling them, without any additional argument of my own, as forms of ineffabilism (Hagberg 1995, Chapter 1), cognitivism/idealism (Chapter 2), experientialism (Chapter 3), intentionalism/mentalism (Chapter 4), correlativism (Chapter 5), solipsism (Chapter 6) and/or atomism (Chapter 7). While many of these -isms form part of my own target here, my main objection is to their wider common assumption that art is a language at all, at least in any sense that is not utterly loose and empty. (There is not a single philosophical proposition that is not true in *some* weird sense; the question is whether the sense in question is of any value.)

2 My critique here takes further the arguments in Chapters 2 and 3 of Hagberg 1995.

3 See Pole 1972, 157.

painting, jazz tune or sculpted frieze that it either has or lacks a meaning. Does it follow that artworks cannot be understood or misunderstood? Appreciation certainly does not require understanding the meaning of anything. Failure to appreciate a wine, for instance, is not a failure to understand the wine itself. J. L. Austin writes:

> The goldfinch cannot be assumed, nor the bread suppressed: we may be deceived by the appearance of an oasis, or misinterpret the signs of the weather, but the oasis cannot lie to us and we cannot misunderstand the storm in the way we misunderstand the man. (Austin 1979, 112)[4]

What of artworks? Are they more like people or storms? One can radically misunderstand a satire by taking it at face value or mistaking its intended target. However, 'getting' its satirical nature and intended target does not amount to understanding the artwork *tout court*. An artwork is not reducible to any ideas associated with it. Moreover, I may understand such ideas perfectly but just not *get* the artwork in question because it does nothing for me; it does not speak to me even after I have made it talk.

As with any object, vegetable, project or even life itself (Taylor 1970, 264 ff.),[5] one can of course assign an artwork genuine meaning – not just a personal meaning it might have for oneself,[6] but a public one that can be shared. Such meaning is deeply intertwined with meaningfulness.[7] However, understanding is not a matter of correctly describing how things are, as if the existence of what is to be understood is entirely independent of our understanding of it. This is not to say that anything goes but only that, as G. E. R. Lloyd puts it, 'We should not assume at the outset that there is just one simple truth of the matter to be had, let alone one to which we happen to have exclusive access ourselves' (Lloyd 2012, 118; see also 101 ff.). This should be distinguished from the greatly mistaken outlook that understanding art is a matter of finding one's own meanings and interpretations, commonly found in journalistic writing such as this:

> [T]hinking about possible meanings [...] is a process of interpretation. It's not a science. It's not about finding the 'right answers', but about

4 Cf. Grimm 2016. For a revisionary reading of Austin's original argument about knowledge of other minds that may be extended to cover aesthetic understanding, see McMyler 2011, § 6.

5 A promising alternative to Taylor's voluntaristic conception may be found in Wisdom 1965, discussed in the Epilogue below.

6 See Ground 1989, 66.

7 See Goldie 2012, 17–25, and Sandis 2017b, § I.

> thinking creatively about the most plausible understandings of a work. The key here is context. The broader context of an artwork will help make sense of what you've already observed. Much of the information about context is usually given in those dull little labels that tell you the artist's name, the title of the work and the year. And there are often other valuable morsels of information included too, such as the place and year an artist was born. (Meshaum-Muir 2014)

Understanding art is not a matter of 'correct interpretation', for there is no fixed set of ideas to be found and understood in any artwork. If we are to talk of meaning here at all, we must allow that new meanings may be acquired in time, leading to re-evaluations.[8] This is not anti-realism but a multilayered pluralism that is compatible with 'the common pursuit' of true judgement (Eliot 1923; Leavis 1952). A Marxist reading of a book may be valuable, but almost never *qua* providing *the* correct understanding of it. There are overlaps here with Joseph Margolis and Michael Krausz's multiplism (critical pluralism), which combines interpretive relativism with cultural realism. Margolis, however, treats the self as actually being a sort of text, rather than as merely analogous to one:

> We ourselves are texts, if we view ourselves – our thoughts and deeds – as the individuated expression of the internalized enabling structures of the larger culture in which we first emerge, are first formed, as the apt selves we are, apt for discovering how the language and practices of our society course through our every deed. In this sense, selves are the paradigmatic agents of linguistic and lingual uttering; also, metaphorically (historically), they 'are' the legible utterances of their age: Goethe, Napoleon, Rousseau, Goya, for instance. (Margolis 2001, 156)

However, human beings are not texts of any sort, and to understand another person is not to understand a text. To understand another person – a matter of degree, not kind – is to know what makes them tick, to get how they think and feel about certain things and why. To be sure, some people are an open book, while we do not know how to read or at times even interpret the behaviour of others. By and large, however, we do not read others in even a metaphorical sense.

8 For (Leavis 1936), this is largely a matter of readjusting a work's place within the canon. Such a refusal to set any evaluation in stone need not lapse into the postmodernist's perpetual deferral of meaning. Leavis' own proposal for an aesthetic judgement's *entitlement* to universal assent takes a more Kantian route, as noted by (Moyal-Sharrock 2016b, § 6).

In earlier work, Margolis argues for a strong analogy between understanding people and understanding artworks (Margolis 1980, 44).[9] There is indeed a nice parallel between understanding what someone *says* and what they *write* or, indeed, *sculpt*. Understanding what a person says, though, is not the same thing as understanding *them*. When Wittgenstein remarks that if a lion could speak we could not understand it (PPF, § 327), he does not mean that we couldn't understand *what* the lion says (e.g. if it was speaking in English[10]), but that we would not be able to understand *why* it would say such a thing, whether its speaker meaning coincided with the expression meaning of the sentences it uttered and so forth.[11]

Wittgenstein held that it was virtually impossible to understand another person, not because of any metaphysical or epistemic barrier, but because it is *psychologically* difficult to do so.[12] Understanding others requires some degree of immersion in their form(s) of life, so that we may find our feet with them. Does understanding an artwork require the same? What would count as the artwork's form of life? Rhees suggests that to understand any particular poem, '[y]ou have to know the life to which these remarks and phrases and expressions belong' (Rhees 1969, 137).[13] He is here referring to the practices and conventions of the genre:

> What is said in a sonnet [...] could not be said at all, unless there were other sonnets and other poems [...] It was possible for Drayton to write a great sonnet or a weak one because people were writing and have written poetry [...] because poetry already had the relation to the rest of language which it did [...] And if I had never seen or heard a poem in my life, then I'd not understand a great poem if you showed it to me [...] I doubt if anyone has understood German poetry unless he knew German music; or French poetry without French painting. (Rhees 1969, 137–9)

9 Cf. Hagberg 1995, 180 ff.; Strawson 1966, 202. If individual people are like art objects, does that mean that identifiable groups (the Dutch) are like art types (the Dutch School)?

10 There is, of course, the difficulty of knowing whether the English-sounding phrases are really English as we know it. Wittgenstein rightly thinks of the supposition that something can be a lion yet speak English as nonsense (see Chapter 4).

11 See Chapter 4 for how to understand the modality at hand.

12 See Chapter 1.

13 By contrast, 'religious ideas are what the treatment in painting or in sculpture *does* to those themes. The ideas the work of art has are not ideas it received *from* religion. They are ideas it contributes *to* religion' (Rhees 1969, 140).

However, we need not accept Rhees' surprisingly cognitivist framework to deny, as F. R. Leavis does,[14] that works of art are self-contained. To the limited extent that we may talk of understanding a piece of music, I can hear it for the first time and truly *get it* in a way that no amount of scholarship can help with. There is a disanalogy here between understanding music and understanding that 2 + 2 = 4, which, as Richard Wollheim puts it, 'may be self evident [...] but not to someone ignorant of what addition is' (Wollheim 1968, 89). There is a sharp contrast here between understanding artworks and understanding people. The analogy has got us so far but can go no further.[15] We are at a dead end.

On Not Getting It

In Rhees' view, there is a language of music, poetry, sculpture, etc. (each with a variety of dialects), and to be able to understand a particular song or poem, one must speak the language and be well-versed in the dialect. The view implies further that there is something that artworks, like sentences, are *about*:

> Art is serious in its 'ideas'. A piece of music is written in musical phrases or in music, as a poem is written in language and poetry [...] What is said in poetry cannot be said in ordinary speech, unless it is a bad poem [...] What is said in a sonnet (say Drayton's 'Since there's no help, come let us kiss and part') could not be said in any other form. (Rhees 1969, 136–7)[16]

Rhees' account may be subdivided into the following five theses:

1. Works of art can always be understood.
2. To understand art is to understand its idea(s).
3. To understand its idea(s) is to understand what is said in the work of art.
4. This cannot be said in ordinary speech.
5. What is said in one artwork may not be said in any other form either – for example, using different (artistic) language.

14 See, for example, Leavis 1936, 1969, 1974. For further criticism of cognitivist approaches, see Chapter 2 of Hagberg 1995.

15 If it could go further, we could allow that while language can help with this, words often fail us. Indeed, it frequently hinders understanding, a point Weil (1959) and Murdoch (1992, 281 ff.) hint at.

16 Cf. Cooke 1959.

For all his talk of inextricability, the view remains that there is something a novel or lyric says (or that an artist says with it) that is not identical to the words used to say it; something the artwork is about, which in turn gives it its purported meaning.

Such ideas take us down the short but troubling road from Claude Lévi-Strauss's structural anthropology (which seeks to crack the code of any narrative by uncovering the underlying structures of its elements (e.g. Lévi-Strauss 1958, 1978)) to A. J. Weberman's Dylanological Method (which claims to 'have cracked the enigma code of Dylan's lyrics' (Weberman 2005, ii)). However, the institutions of meaning are too holistically 'bound up with the common practices that shape the way we act and talk' to be codifiable (Descombes 2014).[17] There is no skeleton key to the kingdoms of meaning; there are no secret codes to crack.

The view that the language of art may be deciphered and translated is defended by Deryck Cooke:

> When we try to assess the achievement of a great literary artist, one of the chief ways in which we approach his [sic] work is to examine it as a report in human achievement. We feel that, in his art, he has *said* something significant in relation to life as it is lived; and that *what he has said* [...] is as important as the purely formal aspect of his writing. Or rather, these two main aspects of his art – 'content' and 'form' – are realized to be ultimately inseparable: *what he has said* is inextricably bound up with how he has said it. (Cooke 1959, ix; emphasis added)

Such is also the approach of Nelson Goodman, who argues that '[a]esthetic experience is cognitive experience distinguished by the dominance of certain symbolic characteristics' (Goodman 1968, 262). Indeed, Goodman explicitly holds that we can quite literally *map* and decipher the languages of art, and Cooke aims to do just this with music:

> [I]f we continually argue about the 'emotional content' of this or that composition – we should not therefore despair of ever finding an

17 Elsewhere, Descombes argues against the notational view of the novel as an 'art of language' in which we find Proust's '"ideas" about life, about love, or about the world' (Descombes 1992, 90 ff.). Descombes embraces the pluralism of different readings/interpretations of a novel and argues against 'essentialist poetics' that 'seek the essence of literature' (ibid., 93). If we differ on anything, it is that I wish to distance myself from the thought that the institutions of art are institutions of meaning, as well as the accompanying view (indebted to Dumont 1983) that human beings can themselves be institutions of this kind.

> objective basis to work on. It may be that we have just not found a way of understanding this language, and that much of our interpretation of it is simply misinterpretation [...] This book is an attempt to bring music back from the intellectual-aesthetic limbo in which it is now lost [...] by beginning the task of actually deciphering its language. It attempts to show that the conception of music as a language capable of expressing certain very definite things is not a romantic aberration, but has been the unconscious assumption of composers for the past five-and-a-half centuries at least. (Ibid., xi)

Leaving aside problems regarding universal unconscious assumptions and the idea of *any* language's remaining static enough to be decipherable, we should reject the claim that something definite is being said by a particular composition, such that understanding the composition is a matter of unearthing what it is saying. Naturally, there are things about an artwork that one can understand (e.g. its theme, structure and devices), but this would not be to understand it in the sense in which we can understand another human being.

To think that you cannot truly understand a work of art unless you get what it is about is not to get art at all. Bob Dylan jests in this direction, channelling Magritte (see Gablik 1976, 11):

> Bob Dylan: It's not that it's so difficult to be unspecific and less obvious; it's just that there's nothing, absolutely nothing, to be specific and obvious *about*. My older songs, to say the least, were about nothing. The newer ones are about the same nothing – only as seen inside a bigger thing, perhaps called nowhere. But this is all very constipated. I do know what my songs are about.
>
> Nat Hentoff: And what's that?
>
> Bob Dylan: Oh, some are about four minutes; some are about five, and some, believe it or not, are about eleven. (Cott 2006, 101)

Dylan's infamous San Francisco television press conference, the year before (3 December 1965), is a master class in deflecting questions of artistic meaning from the outset:

> – *What's your new album about?*
>
> – Oh it's about, uh – just about all kinds of different things – rats, balloons. They're about the only thing that comes to my mind right now. (Ibid., 65)
>
> – *Your songs are supposed to have a subtle message.*

> – Subtle message? [...] Where'd you hear that?
>
> – *In a movie magazine.*
>
> – Oh my God! Well, we won't – we won't discuss those things here. (Ibid., 66)

The idea that all the songs to date or the last album might all be about one thing (constituting a concept album par excellence) is at once both preposterous and inviting:

> [E]very song tails off with 'Good luck – I hope you make it'. (Ibid., 68)

The trappings of a more focused artistic intentionality are recognized by Jon Landau, writing about Dylan's then newly released *John Wesley Harding* LP:

> Dylan manifests a profound awareness of the war and how it is affecting all of us [...] This doesn't mean that I think any of the particular songs are about the war or that any of the songs are protests over it. All I mean to say is that Dylan has felt the war, that there is an awareness of it contained within the mood of the album as a whole. (Landau 1968)

Even Dylan would not deny that you might write a commissioned sonnet about your grandmother and that it might turn out to also be about mortality.[18] But does this aboutness exhaust its meaning? Does it exhaust our understanding of the sonnet? And if someone doesn't know that it is about your grandmother, do they fail to understand it? When Dylan sings 'you've got a lot of nerve to say you are my friend' or 'a hard rain's a-gonna fall', there may have been an original person or event that moved him to write the lines. But by the time the song is finished, this initial cause need not mean that the song is about something so specific. In time he may forget what motivated it. Does he thereby cease to understand his own song?[19]

What would count as a full or even adequate understanding of something? The question forms part of a more general puzzle of circularity that many gallery and museum curators face: the viewer's understanding of any given object is typically dependent on the specialized knowledge of the curator, archaeologist, anthropologist, ethnographer or other expert about the

---

18 For why the intention constraint on representation makes little difference to aesthetics, see Wollheim 1968, 35 ff.

19 Does the song change every time that Dylan updates a line or tune? Theorists will wish to wheel in their favoured accounts of aesthetic metaphysics at this point. But life is too short for endless debates about questions of aesthetics whose answer is surely 'in one sense yes, and in another no' (see also Gallie 1955).

objects themselves. Yet, the artefacts themselves will inevitably be part of the evidence for understanding other cultures. The only way forward involves a reflective equilibrium between our knowledge of the objects we discover and that of the social context in and for which they were originally created and used. These two areas of knowledge and understanding are epistemically interdependent: a reassessment of either will alter our perspective of the other (see Sandis 2014). This much is true of artworks and artefacts *qua* historical objects. However, their appreciation *qua* artworks cuts loose from such concerns.[20]

Does understanding what an artist produces require that we understand the artist 'behind the work'? Attempts to understand the artwork through the artist are mirrored by attempts to understand the artist through the artwork. This trouble disappears once we abandon the notion that understanding an artwork is a matter of understanding the ideas that the artist seeks to communicate, a view that would literally transform all art into conceptual art. Nothing in art is hidden. And yet, understanding what an intelligible critic says about a work of art is still a far cry from sharing in their understanding of it.

Transport Studies

Contemporary philosophy leaves little space for a theory of understanding that is distinct from theories of knowledge and explanation.[21] This is partly due to the assumption, found in Locke among others, that understanding another is a matter of obtaining information about their mind (see Chapter 2). But is this true? It helps to here compare the understanding of others to self-understanding. The traditional view that understanding oneself is a matter of acquiring information or knowledge via some kind of privileged introspective access to the 'contents' of our own minds is deeply implausible. Self-understanding is inseparable from our relationships to the people, objects and institutions that make up our world.[22] Hence the common phenomenon of better understanding oneself after one has lost something integral to one's life, such as one's job, child, reputation, abilities, property, dreams or ambitions.

20 In this I am diametrically opposed to those who claim that '[t]o appreciate particular works [of art] we need some understanding of their background' (Pole 1972, 152). For a populist application of this approach, see Schama 2006; cf. Sandis 2017b.

21 See Hertzberg 2005 for the relation of (a different sense of) understanding to both knowledge and explanation.

22 Cf. Cockburn 1990.

As with self-understanding, the understanding of others comes from a shared communion that cannot be reduced to propositional knowledge. Eleonore Stump (2010) argues that the experiential knowledge of persons is transmitted through stories. I remain more sceptical about the truth value of the narratives we deliver. Autobiography reveals how our attempts to understand are inextricably tied to the desire to conceive of our lives as having purpose and direction. While these may produce the *feeling* of understanding, we have overwhelming reason to mistrust the tales we spin to ourselves (which is not to deny that we may comprehend ourselves better by reading old letters, diaries and the like).

While still dominant, the Lockean notion of understanding as the obtaining of information of some kind has also been attacked by Stanley Cavell:

> Talking together is acting together, not making motions and noises at one another, not transferring unspeakable messages or essences from the inside of one closed chamber to the inside of another. (Cavell 1969, 33–4)

G. H. R. Parkinson (1977) dismisses the view of understanding that follows from Locke's theory of communication as 'the translation theory of understanding'. In a paper in the same volume, Timothy G. Potts characterizes the model of meaning communication that falls out of it as 'a branch of transport studies' in which ideas are transported from one person's mind to another via sentences or art, encoded into a common language by the speaker or artist and then decoded back into that of the hearer or observer (Potts 1977, 92).[23] Potts nevertheless accepts that sounds carry messages, and perhaps he would say the same of artworks too. However, if an artwork carried a message in this sense, it would have to be the sort of fanciful secret message hypothesized about in paperback novels such as Dan Brown's *The Da Vinci Code.* Granted, such things are possible, but such codes would not give us *the* meaning of the artwork in question any more than a Bible referred to by spies speaking in code may be said to carry the meaning of their exchanges.[24]

This view has recently resurged in standard contemporary accounts of empathy as a kind of emotional tool that provides one with an access pass to people's 'mental contents', which in turn double as their motivating reasons,[25]

23 See also Hagberg 1995, 66–7; Stewart 1977; Vesey 1977, ix–xxxi. For the effects of this view on the semiotics of understanding and translating poetry, see Jakobson 1959; Steiner 1975, 261.

24 See also Chapter 5 of Hagberg 1995 for further criticism.

25 See Chapter 2.

as well as in related views about the communicative intention of art (Currie 2004, Chapter 6). However, 'getting' a musical form such as punk rock, jazz or blues (let alone any work that subverts recognizable boundaries) is not a matter of understanding communicable propositions about the work or its creators and their environment, no matter how much empathy one may be trying to employ. This is not to say that a song may not communicate any ideas to its listeners, including the one mentioned in the previous sentence, as hinted at by Dylan when he tells Mr Jones that he's 'been through all of F. Scott Fitzgerald's books' but doesn't know what is happening here (Dylan 1965).[26] However, if 'understanding a song' amounts to anything at all, it would not be a list of such ideas.

One could read everything there is to know about jazz and still not get it. The situation may seem analogous to that of Mary in Jackson's famous example of the expert on the neurophysiology of colour who has been confined to a black-and-white room (Jackson 1986). Factual knowledge is indeed not sufficient for understanding. However, this is not because what is missing is phenomenal knowledge, be it understood informationally or otherwise. 'Getting' jazz (or death metal, or whatever) is no simple matter of having a certain experience when it is played. It is about sharing an aesthetic sensibility with others. It may be described in words, but no words would help a person to get it who doesn't already.

There are ways in, of course. Greil Marcus' 1997 book *Invisible Republic: Bob Dylan's Basement Tapes* helps readers to *get* Bob Dylan and the Band's *The Basement Tapes* by pontificating on Americana. This is no experiential replacement for listening to the music, but what one gets by listening to *The Basement Tapes* is not phenomenal knowledge of what it is like to do so but all sorts of nods, tributes, allusions, subtleties, plays on words, aspirations and values: a whole world that cannot be reduced to either information or qualia. If there is anything (or any range of things) that it is like to listen to these songs, it will be the sort of thing captured by Marcus.[27] If anything is said in *The Basement Tapes*, if the work contains ideas of any kind, then they can be conveyed in books such as *Invisible Republic*. Rhees is committed to denying the very possibility of this. On his view, something is said in the Mona Lisa, but nobody can say what it is in either ordinary speech or another piece of art.

26 A possible joke here is that Fitzgerald published only half a dozen books or so. The chorus is most probably an echo of Mark Strand's 'something is happening that you can't figure out' (Strand 1964), itself a tribute to Albert Arnold Scholl (1957), although such trivia does not help one to understand Dylan's song.

27 For a Wittgensteinian understanding of experience reports, see Hacker 2012.

Rhees also denies that understanding amounts to factual knowledge (Rhees 1969, 166–8), but only because he maintains that while to understand art is to understand the ideas behind (what is said in) it, one cannot convey *what* is understood by any other means. Accordingly, when he talks of understanding the idea(s) in a work of art, he does not hold that this reduces to being able to repeat facts about what these ideas are. He remains committed, however, to there being such fixed ideas and to the claim that one's grasp of these amounts to understanding the work of art in question.

To be sure, experiencing jazz is necessary for 'getting' it, but it is not sufficient. Moreover, there is no one thing it is like to listen to some particular piece of blues, jazz or punk, let alone to listen to the genre in general. *A fortiori*, understanding jazz cannot be the same as knowing what it is like to listen to it, but nor is the understanding ineffable.[28] Two people can have a conversation about what is great about a new album and understand one another perfectly. However, they must both already be in the know. As with uncodifiable moral perception, no quantity of propositions can get you there; experience can make the difference, but there are no guarantees. K. W. Britton captures aesthetic attunement well:

> The understanding may not use words, there may not even be any conscious process: simply an appropriate response. To be able to interpret symbols in some way or other is to have some understanding of life. (Britton 1977, 221)[29]

Neither understanding nor communication is reducible to the acquisition of new facts. There is a difference between understanding the words a speaker has said and understanding the speaker – understanding the 'why' as well as the 'what'. Wittgenstein states that 'if a lion could talk, we could not understand it' (PPF, § 327), not because of any insurmountable language barrier, but because we would not know what it was aiming to do with its words. We need to free ourselves from approaching communication as something geared towards the transmission of information.

In the case of aesthetics, this involves rejecting the supposition that the meaning of a work of art is whatever the author intended to communicate

28 See Hagberg 1995, 8–22. Moore (1997) holds that certain kinds of understanding (e.g. religious) amount to practical knowledge of how to show things that cannot be said. By contrast, I have been emphasizing that we can say what we have understood and yet fail to communicate it.

29 Disappointingly, Britton thinks of works of art in terms of *symbols*.

with it and that to understand the work is to understand this meaning – an old chestnut in a new fire.

Hagberg rescues the innocuous view that a work of art may have been produced with certain intentions from the perilous theory that these must have at some (prior or concurrent) point been fully articulated in the artist's mind (Hagberg 1995, 79). He offers an analogy between jazz improvisation and Wittgenstein's account of the relation of understanding meaningful speech acts to utterer intention. Neither requires a mental image of any kind (ibid., 84). Indeed, artists, like all other agents, 'often learn things about their own works after completing them', which is not to say that they discover things about their own intentions but rather, as illustrated by the case of T. S. Eliot, that something about the 'content' of their own work may be revealed to them.[30] The observer is in a better place than the agent to see patterns and recurring motifs across the latter's behaviour and can, in this respect, understand them better. The same holds true of art (the critic as psychiatrist).

Elsewhere, I have argued that artistic intention is relevant only to the appreciation of the artistic process, not to that of its product.[31] At most, aesthetic appreciation of the artistic product requires that we see it as such,[32] although the postmodern embrace of Cecilia Giménez's infamous 'monkey mural' botching of Elias Garcia Martinez's fresco *Ecce Homo* suggests that the possibility of unintentional art is not to be dismissed too easily.

30 I discuss the latter in Sandis 2010c in relation to the debates between McDowell (2009) and Pippin (2010) on retrospective accounts of intention. For the parallel debate in relation to artistic intention and 'what is there' to be seen, see Cavell 1969, 230 ff. Cavell's radical conclusion is that '[t]he artist is responsible for everything that happens in his work – and not just in the sense that it is done, but in the sense that it is *meant*' (ibid., 237). The other side of this coin is that '[i]n the land he has made, the artist is entitled to everything he wants, if it's there' (ibid., 233).

31 Sandis 2017a, in which I tackle Livingstone (2005) and Uidhir (2013). My account may be contrasted with those of Gregory Currie (1989, 46–84; 2004, Chapter 6) and Dennis Dutton (2009, 47 ff.), both of whom view artworks as actions of some kind, whereas I view them as the products of action. (I share Currie's conviction that aesthetics should be informed by much more general questions concerning meaning, intention and action, but we do not agree in any of these areas.)

32 Cf. Ground 1989, 29 ff.

Ecce Homo by nineteenth-century painter Elias Garcia Martinez on the walls of Santuario de Misericordia church in Borja, Spain. The three photographs show the changing face of the artwork between 2010 and 2012. In the first photograph, slight speckling is apparent. In the second photograph, large patches of white dominate the picture. One theory is that Giménez had already begun her work on the painting at this point, and the white marks are the result of her scraping away the paint. The third photograph shows Cecilia Giménez's 2012 attempted restoration of the fresco. Handout photo by Centro de Estudios Borjanos/ ABACAPRESS.COM. Reprinted by permission from Alamy.

If the aesthetic relevance of the process/product distinction is as I maintain it to be, Hagberg's points will need to be translated into points about art *qua* doing rather than thing done. I do not wish to dwell on this distinction here but rather to push his proposal further in two additional directions. First, we must distinguish the artist's meaning from artistic meaning, just as we distinguish speaker meaning from expression and utterance meaning. Second, whatever the role of intention may be, there is the separate question of whether what is understood is an idea of some kind and, indeed, whether there is something it is to understand a work of art at all. I have been less ready to answer this question positively than Hagberg, although if I did, we would be in agreement that – as with people – such an understanding would not reduce to knowledge of any propositional content.[33]

You aim to draw a duck but inadvertently draw a duck–rabbit. Are we to deny that this is what you have drawn? Oedipus similarly loses control over

33 Hagberg (1994) answers this question by appealing to four stories by Henry James through the lens of Wittgenstein's language games.

what he does. His deeds break free from his intentions; he 'learns what he has done from the way things turn out'. This wedge between intention and action is always there; it is no different in the case of art.[34] Does that mean that an artist might not fully understand their own work? They certainly may have been blind to aspects of it that were *there* to be seen – to be gotten. As Jonathan Lear states:

> The point is neither to reveal the hidden secret of Oedipus nor to add one more interpretation to the good-enough pile, but to invite one to see something which is right there in the text. (Lear 1998, 39)[35]

Is understanding a work of art tantamount to understanding its meaning and being able to give an answer equivalent to that requested by the stereotypical British bobby who asks, 'What is the meaning of all this then?' For me, Borges' and Chekhov's stories are comedic to the core, but I have a friend who insists that they are deeply tragic. Must either one of us have failed to understand them? And what if I sometimes see them as funny and other times as tragic, depending on my mood?[36]

These and other problems in aesthetics cannot be divorced from questions central to the philosophy of action, of which speech act theory is ultimately a subdivision. Perhaps the most relevant subdivision is the theory of communication and understanding. The Lockean conception of understanding as the obtaining of relevant information has found new life in the empathy industry, information and communications technology,[37] neuro-aesthetics and more. However, just as new facts about people can render them more confusing, so too with art. Aesthetic understanding is not a matter of understanding any ideas that an artwork contains. *A fortiori*, information about the artist's life and intentions is as likely to lead to bafflement as it is to understanding, and any understanding it might manage to provide will be of the artistic process rather than the artwork itself.

I have attempted to show that Lockean approaches to understanding systematically neglect crucial aspects of our experience of art. To maintain that

34 See Sandis 2017b, 218.

35 The difference between seeing something that is right there and interpreting it is complicated by the related distinction between Wollheim's *Seeing-In* and Wittgenstein's *Seeing-As*, which, among other things, arguably contains an objective/subjective distinction (see essays in Kemp and Mras 2016).

36 This reading of exactly the same narrative in diametrically opposed ways is quite different from Woody Allen's *Melinda and Melinda*, which provides two different ways of fleshing out the same story outline.

37 See Chapter 10.

understanding art is a matter of learning facts about the artist and/or her milieu is to just not get it. To imagine that there must always be something to understand and that this involves knowledge of an idea is unhappily to reduce all art to conceptual art.

Epilogue

John Wisdom, writing about the meaning of life, asserts that 'when we ask "what is the meaning of all things?"', we 'cannot answer such a question in the form: "The meaning is this"', for 'what one calls answering such a question is not giving an answer' (Wisdom 1965, 41). Might the same be true of 'the meaning' of an artwork? Wisdom invites us to consider the following scenario:

> Imagine that we come into a theatre after a play has started and are obliged to leave before it ends. We may then be puzzled by the part of the play that we were able to see. We may ask 'What does it mean?'. In this case we want to know what went before and what came after in order to understand the part we saw. But sometimes even when we have seen and heard a play from the beginning to the end we are still puzzled and still ask what does the whole thing mean. In this case we are not asking what came before or what came after, we are not asking about anything outside the play itself. We are, if you like, asking a very different sort of question from that we usually put with the words 'What does this mean?' But we are still asking a real question, we are still asking a question which has sense and is not absurd. For our words express a wish to grasp the character, the significance of the whole play [...] Is the play a tragedy, a comedy or a tale told by an idiot? (Wisdom 1965, 40)[38]

Wisdom concludes that life has a meaning that cannot be reduced to an enumeration of points but is not ineffable either:

> When we ask what is the meaning of this play or this picture we cannot express the understanding which this question may lead to in the form of a list of just those things in the play or the picture which give it its meaning. No. The meaning eludes such a list. This does not mean that

38 Wisdom is, of course, making analogies between theatre and life, and the allusion is to Macbeth's words upon hearing from Seyton that Lady Macbeth has died: 'Life [...] is a tale told by an idiot, full of sound and fury, signifying nothing' (*Macbeth*, Act 5, Scene 5).

> words quite fail us. They may yet help us provided that we do not expect of them more than they can do. (ibid., 41)

One may 'get' or fail to 'get' a given work of art. This can only ever amount to understanding if it allows for a plurality of incommensurable – and at times contradictory – things to be understood. There is no such thing as understanding the meaning of an artwork. To the extent that we can talk of understanding art at all, this is not a matter of being able to list the ideas it contains or the topics it is ostensibly about, but nor is aesthetic understanding a matter of attuning oneself to the ineffable. If an artwork could speak, we could not understand it.

Chapter 10

WITTGENSTEIN AND COMMUNICATION TECHNOLOGY: IN CONVERSATION WITH RICHARD HARPER

Prologue

When Danièle Moyal-Sharrock had the idea that, for the British Wittgenstein Society's tenth anniversary conference, we should focus on Wittgenstein in the twenty-first century, we decided that we absolutely needed something on technology, and who better than Richard Harper on information communication technology? In what follows, we discuss the *in vivo* use of categories in the design of communications and artificial intelligence (AI) technologies, as well as how this use needs to evolve to allow creative design to flourish. The conversation will be of interest to anyone concerned with our ever-evolving uses of technology in everyday interaction.

Why People Communicate

CS: Professor Harper has led research groups at Xerox Europarc as well as Microsoft Research in Cambridge for many years. He founded and directed the Digital World Research Centre at the University of Surrey. He is now the co-director of the Institute for Social Futures at Lancaster University. So maybe he could talk about the twenty-second century as well! He is also a partner in Social Shaping Research, which he may tell you about a little later if you ask him. You are probably all asking what this has to do with Wittgenstein (or maybe not…), and so I thought I would begin by asking Richard how he ended up here. With this kind of background, what brings you to our Wittgenstein Society? Why are you here, Richard?

RH: As an undergraduate in the late seventies, I did sociology, amongst other courses, at Manchester University, and there we were introduced to Wittgenstein. His philosophy was viewed as an integral part of understanding social science. Winch in particular was our mode of introduction to his philosophy – in his *The Idea of a Social Science.* There was a main course for every social scientist which was called *Mind and Society,* taught by Professors Wes Sharrock and John Lee; some of you here will have met them. They are sociologists and were interested in Wittgenstein and Winch for two or three reasons, one to do with the possibility that one would need to be careful about the categories used to explain things in the social sciences. The danger in sociology particularly (as in all the social sciences) is to be hijacked by categories, and Wes and John taught us to be very sensitive to the need to be adroit in the use of categories – not just how you label social types but how you understand social actions, you know, the way you describe them, the categories that pertain. And they thought that particularly some of the arguments on the history of religion, which were very pertinent to sociology, and which Wittgenstein had explored in some of his work and which Winch also explored, suggest that we need to be especially careful about explanation of human conduct when the thing about that conduct is a rather precise, rather particular idea related to a bunch of ideas with particular shapes and relations to action. Going to a church is not just something done from habit; it fosters a feeling in the body that allows a willingness to touch God. That was one of the examples of the sort of careful, precise set of relations to actions and ideas in society we were warned to look out for. Wittgenstein's remarks on the mind, mindfulness and 'mind in action' were very encouraging to sociologists, we were taught, because they suggested that perhaps *mind* can be thought of as a socially organized phenomenon made relevant in action or made irrelevant in social organizations, in such a way that some things about the mind became private, some other things public in socially demonstrative ways. Essentially the phenomenon, 'the mind', was something society arranged and was manifested in language use, and that is social use. Language is society in this view, part of what makes it. Hence, mind could become a topic in sociology – *Mind and Society.*

We were also taught that Winch offered the most explosive argument of all about social explanation and theory in his claim that descriptions and explanations of human conduct could be – are – internal to one another. So, to properly describe an action is to describe it in terms which make sense to the parties involved (putting it simply), and this really begged the issue of what sociological explanation would become since hitherto – before Winch – sociological explanation had been governed by the principle that sociologists know better than those they study, the hoi polloi, the guys on the street. The people we were looking at were fools, on this traditional view, subject to ideological trappings and such. We sociologists were in ivory towers, on elegant seats and, through our judicious reading and our pre-Wittgensteinian philosophies, knew better than the hoi polloi. We could tell them how social structures governed their lives, what they thought, did. But then what we found with Winch was someone saying perhaps we need to understand the hoi polloi from their own perspective – that understanding how they do their world would be in terms relevant to them since it was those terms which gave that world *its sense*.

Now this contagion of possibilities – this new view – was wonderfully encapsulated by an extremely difficult person and an extremely difficult sociological writer called Harold Garfinkel. Garfinkel was not a Wittgenstein reader; in fact, there is no evidence to suggest he ever read Wittgenstein. But what he did have was a genius to realize, in his own research in the 1950s and 1960s, that talk seems to be integral to action and that to understand language categories in talk you needed to understand the action in question. This was emphatically what we were taught in *Mind and Society*. This is what we were taught Wittgenstein argued, though Wittgenstein was not too interested in empirical topics or sociological ones like Garfinkel. In any case, if you want to understand the action in question, according to Garfinkel, you need to understand the talk; the two went hand-in-hand. And what that meant was that if you are going to do sociology, if you are going to do field work, say, like an anthropologist, do not just go and look at the social structure, as it were; do not look at power, gender, organization processes (leaving aside how you might do that). Look at talk, look at talk in the workplace, say, and then see how those things, like power, are manifest through talk. And through the talk, in the things people do.

Now, that's not the only way you can do sociology. Because even after Garfinkel, it still makes sense, in sociology, to ignore talk; and you can, perfectly reasonably, treat the world as populated by agents who do not tell their stories and look at the world that way. You know, various forms of statistical approaches do not need talk to make interesting observations about social patterns – dynamics in income for example. Yes, you can actually produce very interesting research that way, but we were taught another view – and that is to say, No, do not do that, instead look at talk as part of the agency of those you are studying. And that led me to do my PhD. I looked at chartered accountancy, at the work of auditors in a company called Arthur Anderson, gone now, of course, and what people talked about in their work. How talk was part of their work with numbers. Shall I say more about that?

CS: Yes, why not. And maybe say something about doing things with Wittgenstein rather than commenting on Wittgenstein, which you alluded to with Garfinkel. And what that means.

RH: Oh, OK, so listen. I have heard two or three really great talks today. One of the things about Peter Hacker's talk this morning is that he showed what I noted in my PhD, and what I try to teach my PhDs and undergraduates about social organization, about people interacting: it is that when they talk, when they interact, they do it praxiologically – yes, in time, but they also do it collaboratively, they do it procedurally with each other, they learn about how to do 'talk things' together. What I mean is that talk is not just part of action, as Wittgenstein would say, but talk is done collaboratively. This sounds daft because it's so obvious, but what I mean is that language use is essentially a sociological phenomenon, not a cognitive one or even a philosophical one. Eh, what do I mean? So, even now, I can look in wonder at the still faces in front of me – here and now – and see that those still faces, the audience's faces, are showing a willingness to listen to me. It's very flattering. So my point is not that, the flattering; it's that we are doing this collaboratively, this lecture conversation thing, and that also happens when people do anything together, when they are talking, say, using language; they do it together, and if they are doing it together then one wants to go and look at how they do it together. One does not want to look at language use from one person's point of view, you need to look at action with words as joint action.

CS: Aren't there any exceptions?

RH: So let me get back to my thread. I was thinking, earlier, why is this being presented to a group of Wittgensteinians as a possibility – you know, that language is a joint enterprise? Surely they will have read Harold Garfinkel, surely they will have read ethnomethodological studies done in his name, which are all about the procedural arrangements of talk and language in action, about how the mind, for example, is made manifest in terms of talk, manifest in things people do together, in the dance of mums and babies and the way they sing to each other in their ums and ahs, in fathers and sons and how they challenge and mock, in those interactions which are praxiological though time. First this then that, in sequences of words.

In my research, that has often been the key topic I have been interested in, given that's how you should understand social action and how it's organized; given that it has a procedural form, a collaborative affair in language; given that you are disciplined by a desire not to be tempted by irrelevant categorization; given that you are also disciplined by a desire not to allow mysterious categories to help explain things other than the categories that are intrinsic, internal to the setting; namely, talk, turns, chat, being together in words.

So, then, what do you come up with? I mean, if this is your view? Now what you come up with are, often, fairly prosaic things. To run ahead, when I first went to work at Microsoft Research, they were really keen on me helping them explore why people communicate. Because part of my career has been exploring how people communicate, writing books about how people communicate, writing a whole book, imagine, on why teenagers text, so, absolutely I was excited at that prospect – can you imagine going to a company with billions of dollars and say this is why people text? So I did a big presentation on communication, and this is, oh, was 10–15 years ago, and this was the topic. What I was trying to explain to the engineers then, in that presentation, was that there are lots of reasons why people might communicate. Sometimes it's instructive communication. When you sit next to Constantine, for example, then you listen, you are going to be instructed by him. Sometimes, for another example, when you go out with a friend, for example my best friend Phil, he will talk at me and it's not instructing, he's just talking at me, and I just listen. I am a bucket for him to pour words into. He does not instruct me about anything. For me it is just a listening. But it's different from what I do with Constantine. A listening can have different purposes. And so I said to the Microsoft engineers, the Outlook team, 'What could the future of communication be? You could say that what you've done with Outlook is build a communications channel, which is like a vision of a cybernetic exchange, like Locke's vision of communication, telementation. Stuff is in here, in the head of the user, and the email is used to send it, that stuff, over there, to that person's head. An organizational actor over here has stuff that needs to go to an organizational actor over there'. And I said 'OK, if you have done that, is there some stuff you have missed? Other kinds of communications doings? And I suggested to them that one of the things you might say when you look at teenagers, when you look at them talking to each other, is: What do you see? 'All of you in the Outlook team', I said, 'presumably are old enough to possibly have had kids, to see kids and to wonder, when kids are standing at street corners, what it is they say to each other? And if they are not at street corners, they are sitting in the living room playing games, on-line games, say – what is it they say to each other?' I suggested to [the] Microsoft Outlook team they just pause and think 'What is it that teenage boys say to each other?' And I paused, and I said, 'Nothing, they are saying absolutely nothing'. Now the moral of that is not to be contemptuous of them and say what idiots we have produced! I was saying to the Outlook folks, perhaps you might think of a communication technology that might allow nothing to be said. After all, that's what these teenagers do, so why not support it?

So what on earth would that be?

Take the possibility that when you send a message, the whole purpose of the message is this [Richard slaps Constantine gently on his back]: it says 'Wake up, come on, look at me'. And then a reciprocation – Constantine does something back. Now the key property of that message – the one I have just sent – is not that it is content-free, but something else: another property of that message is that once it is sent it does not matter anymore; you do not need an audit trail of slaps on the back saying 'notice me', 'notice me'. Likewise with teenage boys' talk – what you need is a vehicle for them to prod each other and prod each other back, just like I prodded Constantine. What you want to do is get a little economy of prodding, which is what teenage boys do, and if they do not punch each other, as I just did with Constantine, they hit each other with words. The words have no meaning except the dance, which is 'notice me', 'notice me'. That's the category that conveys, describes that type of communication.

So I suggested to the Outlook folks that they might engineer a communications application for a mobile phone called *ephemeral messaging*. When you send a message, the message can be 'timed out' so that it would disappear after, oh, let's say 30 seconds. It might have other properties, like when it arrives on your mobile phone – this is the one that really upset them – the sender could choose the ring tone that announces its arrival. So instead of the receiver deciding how their phone rings, the sender chooses how it does and sends that ring tone as part of the message – so when I send one to Constantine, it would be 'Constantine, get off that book, get off that book, get off that book! Stop reading!' or 'Constantine, wake up! Wake up!' You could say really offensive things, and I suggested that part of the fun of being able to do that might be that teenagers, for example, and youngsters more generally, would know they could use this communications thing to be offensive. But not really offensive, because it's like the currency of their talk, it's what's playful to them, and they know what is an appropriate thing to do. So they might just send a message for the silly sound the ring tone makes, like 'whoop-whoop-whoop', because it will make them, the person they send it to, snigger and giggle. It might embarrass the recipient because Mum and Dad are around, say. My point is that this might be a property of [a] communication pattern, a dance, a turn taking when the turns did not do anything except make play. A turn at play. And I explained that this was pointless, in a sense, this kind of messaging. But that this was its character, how it needs to be understood, its value, what it was, the category of forms of communication relevant here.

I explained that engineering such an application might be quite a complex thing to do because you would have to make it so that your phone would have control over a remote phone. This is not what is normally inside the communications application, so here you would need to do something that is normally external to the communication application, namely, control the auditory function of the phone, and that kind of thing is normally handled in the operating system of the phone, of the remote phone, the one you are as it were calling with this messaging app. And the engineers laughed at me, and they said, 'Why would we want to do this? Surely we would want to teach teenagers to do Outlook to document their communication through purposeful communication. Why would you want them to mess about?'

And at that moment I wilted, and I thought, I'm not going anywhere at Microsoft. My attempt to convey what people do with communication with a subtle use of categories – where one use is to do playful, pointless messaging as a means of noticing each other and a category that is thus different from what you might call the category of functional messaging, the sort of thing done with an Outlook email – had not been understood. Or, if it had, had not persuaded the engineers. This was not a category they wanted to honour with code. Of course, maybe my example was not right, I should not have offered such an extreme contrast. But I thought they might see how teenagers do not do functional communication in their own families, and so this might make sense to them. But it did not.

That was my first big presentation. Five years later, Instagram messages are the commonplace that acknowledges this very category of being in touch. Be that as it may, what I'm trying to say here is what I learned, and the discipline I was taught 'by Wittgenstein' at Manchester, was to have the good grace to try and see what people are doing when they communicate, try and be in touch, and to learn what the perspicuous description of it would be. To understand, to look at boys with each other, and think, actually if you listen to them as a parent, what you see is just *boys being together*, and it does not matter if they are speaking Latin or whispering hoots or grunting like monkeys when they are there, what they are doing is *being together*. And then you can create opportunities – technological ones – for that form of being together – something like a playful, ephemeral messaging platform that would let them feel as if they are together even when they are apart.

CS: You basically described poking before, which later become a thing on Facebook. So I used to have a special ringtone for when my mother rang, but then she rang me accidentally when she was next to me, and that wasn't a good idea, so it can backfire.

Audience: Are you going to share that with us?

CS: I'm not going to tell you what it said. OK, we've had discussions earlier today about the empirical versus the conceptual and describing conceptual truths and making empirical observations. Do you have views on how these two come together in your line of work?

RH: When I was an undergraduate, like a lot of undergraduates, I was not really sure what I wanted to do. I was encouraged to do social science, and social science sort of appealed a bit more than philosophy because it seemed a bit more applied, but it really was not that applied, so when I had the chance to go to corporate life, to make, build, to engage with making things, that seemed appealing. So, when I had the chance, first of all, the first thing I did was phone my Dad because my Dad, who was an engineer, would say to me – and indeed he did – 'Oh, you will have a proper job then?' He meant, though he did not say it, a proper job rather than being an academic and sociologist who just wrote about things. Also, he was enchanted by the possibility of making things. Now what's this got to do with this question? Oh, what have I learnt, how the empirical and the conceptual come together? Well, what I learned in the business of spending 10–20 years in corporate life, when you are working with engineering, what happens is you come to learn that you can be really cack-handed with your account of the phenomena and your understanding of language – despite your training. And when I say cack-handed, I mean to say the following: one of the things you have to worry about when you are working with a team of engineers is what motivates them. Now when I did my big presentation which failed to persuade the engineers that they should build ephemeral messaging, I did not really take seriously that if you get up on a Monday morning and you are coming in to spend five days doing some software engineering, then you need to have something that makes you think 'this is not a really miserable job', and what motivates you is the aspiration that you are doing something good and powerful. If you say to a bunch of engineers who are earning hundreds of thousands of dollars a year, 'Hey guys, why don't you come in and make an application that teenage boys can use, and it's going to have no residue, no social benefit, it's just going to let them play endlessly?' they are going to look at you and think 'Oh yeah, great. Go and get a small start-up company to do that, but I'm not doing that, I'm going to do something important'. And it's not that they are pompous, it's that they are genuine, and they are decent people who want to make a difference. One of the things you have to think about is what are the kinds of motivations they have. They do not admire teenage boys and their giggling talk; they want boys to grow up. So that colours their motivations, the engineers' motivations.

Talking with Machines

RH: Let me give another example. One of the problems in the explorations of concepts and categories I have encountered has related to projects looking at memory and how you can replicate memory. Now the engineers in computer science who I have worked with on this have imagined that human memory is like a machine memory. Now, you might think of all the classic arguments of Wittgenstein, including arguments made famous by the homunculus argument, and the disdain that that philosopher has for the idea of memory as container, as a thing that is filled, which is pretty much what this computer science vision of memory is. But, OK, when you are working with engineers who are motivated to build something, if they have a vision that they can make a computational memory like a human memory, then justifying the thing they can build on their computer by saying it is like the 'computer mind' is what gets them going. It gets something built. And what do you end up with? You get a big, visual data processing database. That's the kind of thing they build, a data base with images. So, that seems a like a long way from the concept of mind, sure, but it is something. It is a functioning machine. And it is also incredibly fast, it's incredibly well indexed, you've got all kinds of relationships between these visual objects and ways you can string them together, and so it's fantastic in lots of ways. In your view, it's not 'the mind' or whatever that might be, not a thing, but what it is is a doing, yes? It is a really interesting machine they have built that *does interesting things.* They would not have built it if they did not think that what they were building was just like the human mind.

So what I have learned is if I had said to them beforehand: 'No, this is not how the mind works, you should not use that metaphor; you should think of the memory as a verb, as a place you visit, as a place that you assemble, a place that you make relevant in chit-chat and talk. And, further, that you judge people's powers of social competence by the way they invoke the past, not by their objective truth with which they go to the past', they will say (the engineers): 'I do not know what you are talking about, Richard'.

My point is that the engineers have concepts that let them act and those concepts that let them act are, I think, the *right concepts* for the work they are doing – the *work of engineering*. The problem for people like me is saying, 'OK, when is the moment when those right concepts are no longer right for the job at hand, which is the moment when they have built something and when we need to start thinking about interfaces for it'. So you then ask, 'How might you use these sorts of data stores?'

If you use such a system, let's take a thing called Sensecam – a wearable automatic camera device that could take thousands of pictures at various frequencies during the day like a visual memory prosthesis. A standard conception related to this device, one related version, is that you just need to remember a moment, say, when I first met Constantine this morning, and this device, this Sensecam, would have indexed that little moment and you could retrieve images for that moment. We suggested, and tried to persuade the engineers, that that was not quite the right way to treat Sensecam. It begged questions about what indexing would mean here. Surely a person would need to know what it is they are looking for if they were to find it on Sensecam, so it was like, we are not sure Sensecam can do anything for you except be a resource. A resource for what? It is not a memory. It's a data store. So what you needed to do was allow that database to be something that you might visit and use as a kind of resource to bring 'the past' – pictures of the past – into talk, or, let's say, when you are sending messages. You marshal it to make images available when you need them. Or perhaps, for another possibility, you could use Sensecam data to construct little 'days in your life', a series of pictures brought together like a cartoon or that you might send to your partner as artful renderings, as a kind of poetry made of visual lyrics, as it were, of your circumstances – a writing in pictures. And we proposed that you would have an interface for that creativeness, and we would need to devise that.

The point is that there would be a moment when you wanted the engineers to move towards thinking about these purposes and novel interface ideas; that it would be *at that point* that we needed to start persuading them that perhaps, then, at that moment, their psychologistic kind of Turing-theoretic notion of memory was no longer applicable.

So, what I am saying is that I have learned over the years that it is best to be careful about the applicability of categories and concepts. One needs to *let them do* various kinds of work. Rather than saying this concept is wrong here, one needs to accept that some concepts can be right in all sorts of strange and interesting places if you understand what right means there and then.

And I hate to say that one of the things I have noticed over the years is that those trained in philosophy can have a tendency to elevate their powers of control over categories, as if they have a kind of imperial role across everyday life so that they adjudicate the meaning of categories. In my view, this is not how Wittgenstein tried to encourage us to see categories as diverse and to be understood in use, but goes against it somehow – it seems to imply that categories should be systematic and tidy, imperial, and philosophers can adjudicate about this role.

Well, actually, lots of categories, when they get tied down to moments of action, to different places, do really particular things. From afar, philosophers can look at categories and complain that they should not be used in some way, but they do not know how that works, that use of a category, in that place; that if you understand them in action, in that place, you can see the credibility some uses might have. This does not mean you do not also need to show some finesse about when their moments of change might occur, when something's being built on a basis of a motivation related to one category turns into something else which you then need to redesign around a different category.

But my footing, as it were, in Wittgenstein, has given me the courage to say, *allow the action to speak*, that's what you should be thinking about, what are you trying to do next? – that's what you should ask. And once you can be clear about that, then you can appropriate the right set of categories to help you get there, to that next step. And this can mean you lose some battles on the way.

CS: I remember when I first came to visit you at Microsoft, thinking 'why on earth is this guy interested in me', and I walked into your office and saw Malcolm's *Memory and Mind* and some of Peter Hacker's books and then the penny dropped, but I want to ask you, did you convince Microsoft? So this kind of argument… look, if you think that communication is all about exchanging information for functional purposes, then you are going to sort of limit the kind of software or devices you build, and teenagers – or whoever – might want to communicate for all sorts of reasons that don't fit the Lockean model. Are they kind of getting convinced of this sort of thing now? You mentioned Instagram.

RH: Well, not always. I have got patents for key aspects of what Instagram does. So that is good, but no, we did not make that product. In the kind of research life I have had, you get used to – as do those of you who are sturdy academics – you get to know that it is not necessarily whether your arguments are right or whether the paper you have written is perfect, it is not necessarily always whether it gets published that matters, but you stick to your arguments, you keep putting them forward, you do not give up. You do things for faith, in faith that it is in the right direction even if it does not always get noticed.

I have singularly failed to influence Microsoft on its communications models, despite the fact that I go to a head office of a company which makes billions and offer them what I think are ways forward, ways that I think my research shows are opportunities. One of my best moments was when I went to the head office of Outlook, the engineering team, and in their brainstorming room, what they call (they had a fantastic Californian name for it) Skunk Works Room, that was it, they had pictures of a magazine I had written, all over the walls – a magazine on why people communicate. And every example of why they communicate taken from that magazine on their wall – pinned up there – was not about functional exchange of information; it was about every other thing you might do! And they had it up there as their blueprints for the future! Including my ephemeral messaging concepts! None of those ideas ever showed up on a product. But I was gratified they were thinking about them; well, I assumed they were. My ideas got to the reviewing table.

But there are other examples where I do think I might have influenced technologies more successfully. Some of which everyone in this room will have used, I would think. I can think of something that I helped evolve but in some of these cases I do not have any credit for. I am not complaining about this, this lack of credit, because good ideas – and I am not saying mine are always good ideas – but rather, many of the ideas I toy with are common currency. Good ideas are often common ideas. So, in the case I am thinking of now, we were trying to persuade Bing that the problem with the search engine user experience was that it is conceived on the basis of the human user as merely an information seeker, like a computer trying to find a piece of target data, and so the systems are optimized around getting an answer to a question, data for the question, as quickly as possible, and the experience of using a search engine reflects that, the user interface and such.

Indeed, that model was used for search engines at first; indeed, one might say that was actually what those early users were doing. It really was a mixture of FBI agents and engineers in Palo Alto trying to find key pieces of information as quickly as possible. So, the model of the information forager was right at that time. But we tried to persuade Bing that if you looked at people searching today, years after the first search engines were built, say when search engines are being used now, today, on a Saturday morning for example, at home, what you would find is that the users seem to be doing something else. Not the same thing as these early models assumed. People seem to be using a search engine to *pass the time of day*. So, as a measure of this, there does not seem to be much logical connection between one search and another search.

When we talked to people who were using search engines on Saturday mornings, one of the things that they said to us about this strange voyaging, is they were just *playing on a search engine* and having fantasies about holidays, fantasies about sports cars or, at my age, a fantasy about motorbikes I suppose. And then they said, 'I wish you could keep that somehow and make, you know, links.' So we came up with the idea that when you did a search, you would not just have the kind of URLs or SERPs (Search Enquiry Results Page) as they are called, but you might do something else, which is create what we called a card.

Some of you will be old enough to know what a cigarette card is; some of you, if you are North American, will know what a baseball card is. It is like Constantine's notebook with a picture at the top and some text. So, we came up with the idea that when you do a search, the search engine would find websites that seem most likely to provide what you are looking for, but also go through those websites, take what seems to be the most likely picture and the most likely text from them for your search query, and create a card and present that card on the right of the search, like a little Wikipedia entry for that particular search, as the answer to your search. And we suggested that you could consolidate that – those cards – bring them together and keep them, and people could drag them onto their desktop (from their browser), or they could send them as an attachment in an email.

So, to put this another way, a user would do a search and make a little content, a little card in their search, so it would be a picture of, say, Peter, and some text from a website that has been scraped about Peter, and the card they had produced would be unique, an output of their search. And if they quite like that card, they could say, 'Look, I want to send it to a friend'.

And we said, we can do this! I mean, we said to ourselves we could make this application.

So, we did a big presentation in San Francisco to the Bing team, and before we went there, we got lots of patents and working prototypes and things to make our ideas seem real and profound. Anyway, we did the presentation and there was absolutely total silence – it was very weird. I mean, absolute total silence. No one said anything. And we were rushed out of the meeting room 10 minutes after our slot. And this presentation was to the head executive of Bing, who is now the director of Microsoft Research. OK, we thought, they did not like the idea, he did not like the idea; that is why the silence. But three months later, Google came up with the same thing, as did Bing – exactly the same thing! Cards! So we came to think that maybe they had been thinking just as we had at just the same time. The silence was actually an affirmation of our idea, but they did not want to tell us.

At that time, we did not know that. That our idea was on the mark. One of the reasons we got silence, we thought – we thought at the time – is that when we proposed these cards, some of these cards would not select the best picture of Peter [Hacker] or the best text of his or Constantine's works. There would be errors. And we assumed that the search engine people do not do errors, they are in the business of one hundred per cent perfection, and so our error rates were not acceptable to them. And that was the reason for the silence, that was what we thought, since we were proposing something that was not on their path to the Holy Grail – perfect content, perfect answers to search queries. That is how we walked away from that presentation. But, obviously, we were wrong. The search people do not mind errors if they think the user does not mind or is doing something else, if the *category of doings* is not like the information forager model but is something else, like journeying or gathering – card collecting, in this case.

So, today, if you put in my name in any search engine you will get a slightly random picture of me and some text scrapings – lots of good examples one can find – but anyway, there will be a card on the right of your SERPs page. You might not know it is called a card, but that is what it gets called. That card is lightly lashed together, it is not perfect and might have some wrong text or the wrong picture, the wrong Richard, but people like cards. Mostly, they are good enough, they do the trick. Millions of them are produced every day!

So, you know, I have had success, and the trick about this was to try and suggest to engineers you might make them think differently about the uses and the grammar of action, the grammars related to categories of doings – searchings, say, time-usings, gatherings, things you can do with search. Is this what you wanted to hear?

CS: It's what everybody wanted to hear. Just before we open up to questions, we have a few more minutes; I wanted to hear some things about meaning and understanding as well. Possibly in relation to AI.

RH: My last big job, just when I met with Constantine, was working with the speech engine folks at Microsoft, working on smart systems like Cortana and things like that. And this is illustrative of a number of things I have already mentioned. The speech engineers were completely enchanted by the possibility that you could build a speech engine which is ninety-five per cent more accurate in terms of reasonable interpretation to an utterance of a user. And on that basis, they felt like saying we could change how people use machines, and their aspiration was to maximize the accuracy of utterance recognition and, on that basis, maximize the sort of response that machines provided. Having done that, they said, surely a person would then be understood by the machine, and then a person would be able to understand the machine, so then you could have a *conversation between a person and a machine.*

And we said to them no, no, no, no, we understand the motivation you have got, which is to be able to talk to machines; that is a simple motivation, a kind of categorical criterion that you can use to say how can we pass this. People can use any utterance, more or less, and the machine will come up with some sensible response. That is not the same as saying, it is a different category from, people *having a conversation with a machine.*

Firstly, we said, or rather we tried to persuade them, what would a machine say to a user that would make for conversation? If I had asked the machine to find Constantine, and where he is, if the machine were to say 'Here is Constantine', would one call that a conversation? Well, it is certainly a verbal command and response cycle, but a *conversation*? Is not conversation about something else, interiority, perhaps, sharings about inner thoughts? Is not that what one might say is a conversation?

In that case, if a machine entered into a conversation, and – sticking with the same example – would it say, conversationally, 'I used this probabilistic technique, combined with this proportion of your prior search query cache, combined with this geographical location, to identify the kind of information you want – namely, where Constantine is'? Is that the *interiority* of the machine that would make for conversation?

When we doubted that this would make for a very good conversation, the engineers got very vexed and said, 'No, no!' So, we responded and asked them to take seriously what would conversation with a machine be about? What is it you are trying to achieve when you are having a conversation? We asked whether they were misappropriating the term 'conversation' when really all you have, what you have got with things like Cortana, is a speech dialogue system. An input-output procedure. And if the speech dialogue system works, surely you would need to understand why people want to speak to a machine, what benefits them in doing so, why they prefer sometimes to speak to a machine and sometimes prefer that a machine speak back, so to say. What the input-output is for. We asked, what would be the situations of use in which that desire would be applicable? That dialogue? If they elevated their aspirations into something which sounds like the question of understanding, which is often what is being implied when the term 'conversation' is used (its grammar if you like), we said that it becomes a different sort of thing.

What we did try and persuade them to accept, and Constantine and I are working on a paper on this, was to look at how *understanding makes sense* in certain places, is a sensible purpose, whereas in other places, or doings if you like, understanding has a more profound sense. It is also sometimes a word that labels something that can be subtle. It is one of those wonderful categories where you can use it as a label to point towards the evanescent – somehow the opposite of understanding. So, for example, if I were to speak to my hoover [vacuum cleaner], I would hope it would understand what I mean when I say 'Can you hoover [vacuum] my carpet?' When I ask one of my teenage boys, 'Do you understand what it feels like to be a vexed father?', I do not expect him to say yes or no. I am saying something about the relationship, I am using the word 'understand' differently. But if that example is saying anything for the engineers using speech systems, it is saying they have a need to make a taxonomy of those tasks where the understanding which is produced between an interaction and a user and a machine is the kind of interaction where the understanding that is required is achievable by the machine and desirable on the part of the user. Does the user, do I, want to find that my hoover is like Oliver, my middle boy, who yesterday morning was so hungover that he did not know what house he was in? I do not want my machines to be giving me unnecessary interiority, I do not want to understand in that sense. I genuinely do not want to know my hoover is hungover.

So you need to come up with a set of criteria for distinguishing where the meaning of understanding is intelligible and applicable and those places where understanding is one of those phrases which label the fantastic, awesome, wonderful richness of human endeavour. When I say things like, 'Do I want to understand what my wife was thinking when I came down here on a Sunday morning to a Wittgenstein conference?' – probably not. My point is some words, some categories, are very powerful, very useful, but you need to be careful with them, and in my business, my career, navigating doings with words, conceptual analysis with words, and trying to get things done is – has been – like a handicap race [in] which I have fallen over lots of times but it has been a great pleasure to compete in. Understanding is one of the words I have tangled with, as is communication and the phrase 'being in touch'.

CS: Thanks so much Richard, that's really wonderful. We have time for some questions if anyone has anything they want to ask.

Artificial Minds

Q: Have you had any experience with engineers trying to produce intelligent machines, or anything like intelligent machines, like intelligent cars, and the problems that might pose?
RH: Yes, though one problem here is that there are many different types of what an intelligent machine could be, and many different forms of intelligence or intelligent roles. So one of the things you might say about intelligent cars is that what the car is doing is behaving like a train, and one of the things you might say about a train is that it is a wrought iron solution to intelligence because the tracks dictate where it goes. Now the problem with the car is that it has evolved in a situation where there is choice. We are now moving away from a situation where there is choice, to a situation where there is less choice. Traffic volume means that there are fewer choices to make. We have to drive in train-like caravans. So, when it comes to intelligent cars, it seems to me better to think of them like trains. So, in my mind, intelligent cars are not very intelligent. That they use a lot of AI to make probabilistic technique judgements about proximities, trajectories and routes, yes, OK, but to me that is not hugely interesting. It is a mere engineering problem.

There are lots of other ways to use intelligent systems where the meaning seems more appropriate, closer to the everyday meaning of intelligence. Let me give you an example of the kind of complexities though. For many years, search engineers thought that the problem their technologies solved would be, would come to be, solved by AI. That is, they would come to use AI to predict what the users wanted and to have targets available to respond to those wants. A user wants to search for this, and the search engine delivers it. The answer. Yet when mobile phones took off and, in particular, when mobile phones were internet enabled and searches on mobile phones started, it made a complete mockery of the role of AI in search because it turns out that where you are on your mobile phone is massively determinant of what you are searching for. So, if I am looking for a Katja [Behrens], say, where I am determines which Katja I am interested in. The one I am after is almost certainly the one who lives nearby, not one who lives in Alaska. Massively. My cache, my historical record of use, the history of my prior searches, other determinations of what I might be looking for, all of which might use probabilistic AI techniques to come up with an answer to which Katja I am after, might be relevant, but nearly always not as relevant as where I am. So, the hope that AI would help search engines better determine what answers I need is not as great as we thought. It turns out where you are is more important. And that does not sound like information that requires intelligence. It is just a geographic coordinate.

So how our AI unfolds is much more complicated than would seem. As it happens, this Wednesday I have a meeting with [a] Microsoft operating company that might have a big problem with AI. That is, they have clients who imagine that AI is going to solve lots of problems, and they have machine learners from the laboratories who say they have solved everything, and the two do not meet in any regard whatsoever because one of the problems the clients have is that they imagine you can make data of things – where there is no sensible way of making the phenomenon in question into the data types AI systems require. I will give an example. Some large retail companies want to know if you can use vision techniques to identify from a person's face what they want when they walk into a shop. You get machine learners that say we can read moods, so they put those two together. The big companies and the machine learners must be able to do this, and in the middle, you have people trying to make a business out of it, and they asked: 'Richard, can you come along and help us disentangle this terrible mess?' Because there is no way this is going to be solved, and part of the problem here is that expectations of people in AI are grotesque and have become hyperbolic and often turn around really detailed possibilities, and detailed possibilities which need to be thought through properly. A nice example is whether visual processing machines can identify intention from the shapes of faces and the movements we use in everyday language expressions. But in a shop, all the camera sees when it captures a signal of someone standing still is not a person but a still creature – it is not a lingering creature; to linger is an implication about purpose. Lingering is incarnate in action, in how we understand people, but it is not visible in what a camera sees. But this is what the shops are interested in – how do you recognize that some person's movement is a lingering? If so, why are they lingering, what is it saying about them? Can you recognize that the creature has stopped moving because they have seen something on the shelves? Or because a purchase has been brought to mind, to their mind, by the placement of goods in the entrance to the shop, and so they pause, they linger? And that is a big achievement for vision systems because, when the creature stops moving, it is not necessarily visible what they are about. Visible here means two things – as in things seen and things seen as actions in the Winchean sense, as purposeful, as understood in terms of a concept of action. A vision system cannot distil the difference between a lingering which is pointless and one that is purposive – a pause to prepare for a purchase.

Q: OK, I agree that there's a lot of fun in this area, there's a lot of natural and good fun in this area, but I cannot deny the fact that I am very troubled that this is sounding as if it's an ethics free zone. Technology is reaching a point where there's virtually no limit to what we can create to meet a demand or a requirement or wish or a desire of a market who will pay money for it. That leads to the question – and it seems to me to be a very genuine, real ethical and cultural question – where there are no such limits, how do we decide, should we simply make anything, everything, because we can? Should we make anything and everything because someone we've seen is willing to buy it? This seems to me to be a serious question which is having a cultural impact. Many of the things you have mentioned, I mean my first reaction when you said about the fact of what had happened, was at last I have found out whose fault it was.

RH: I wholly agree with that. What one learns from reading Wittgenstein, is how delicate and diverse are the issues that are articulated through different forms of expression, and likewise with technology: it is not to be thought of in terms of ethics in a carte blanche way. There are all sorts of different sets of possibilities and issues and different sets of ways of making ethical choices which are effectively bound up with the particularities of some kind of engineered, technologically enabled possibility.

So, with that as background, let me answer your question this way. When I first made this presentation about being able to control the remote phone, I said to them (the engineers), I can show you how interruption in talk is a recognizable phenomenon. And I can show you as well that people respond to an interruption by noting it is an interruption and deal with it accordingly. They manage that unethical conduct, if you like. Further, I can also show you that sometimes people will allow interruptions because some things deserve to be interrupted – sometimes interruptions are OK. Now, by the same token, given this, I suggested that an ethics of interaction would emerge with a communication channel in which one could manipulate my recipient's messaging device in a way that seemed unethical – through interruption, say. So, I would sometimes wind up a friend by calling at inappropriate times, by interrupting them, but I would, over time, come to settle into a pattern where most often the regime of behaviour would be subject to propriety – my friend would allow a little interruption, I would create some. It would not just be me, either: sometimes my friend would impose controls on me, like deleting my messaging rights if I interrupted too much, and this would affect me. I would have to renegotiate comms rights. We would eventually come to a settled pattern, if you like, an ethical way of handling the borders of communications ethics together. Of course, interruptions seem a long way from ethics, from, oh, let us say, trolleology and the kinds of examples – risible in my view – used in that form of thinking about ethics. My point is that there are ways in which propriety and ethics can show themselves, in all sorts of subtle ways, and if you wanted to tame the big technology companies, the way to do that is not to approach them in the general, not through trolleology reasoning, but approach them on specific sets of issues and specific solutions to do with, say, communications, and the way forward is to show how ethical operations could be done and managed by the users, and these operations could be an outcome of good design, design that allows users to act with propriety. Managing interruptions depends on allowing interruptions; technologies of communication might allow that.

Q: Just on a similar kind of vein, one of the things that technology and AI try to do is a lot of machine learning, trying to predict what I want, and I wondered whether that was a value you thought would shift. Will there be other values that will be more important later? It's actually a problem for me that it does that. Not only are the predictions sometimes quite incompetent, sometimes they are helpful, but sometimes they're not. But I don't want it to – especially Google – I don't want it to guess at what I'm looking for because that distorts my process, so I then have to take quite a lot of trouble to make sure it doesn't do that.

RH: No, exactly, and here's a good example of ethics, which is I think that ethical considerations sometimes need to be cut open and made a practical matter; something that a user, in my language, can act on and manage if you like, so that people can make different choices around what the technology can do. So, for example, sometimes I do not mind when the search engine uses my history and makes some predictions that can make my search quicker. But, you know, sometimes other considerations come into play. Let me illustrate. We had a big project with Bing on ethics and search. It turns out that on Saturday morning there is [a] very interesting user behaviour phenomenon that shows itself because search engines are often emptied on Saturday mornings; the cache is removed, people reboot search engines – well, not just the search engines, but the browsers too. And Bing was convinced this was because people were doing porn on Saturday mornings and trying to hide their activities. That is why they deleted their search history. (That is what I mean by emptying the search engine. It is putting it simply, but it is pretty much what happens.)

And we did studies which showed virtually no one was doing porn on Saturday mornings; they were shopping. And one of the things that they were doing was getting fed up with the predictive aspects of the systems leading them back to the same set of things to buy – boots, boots, boots! But we also found that sometimes they were genuinely wanting to hide what they were doing, their shopping; they wanted to hide it from their partner but not because it was porn. But because they were trying to buy a present for their partner!

So, are there ethics here? Yes. But they are prosaic, in a sense. It is not big ethics here, but the ethics of buying presents and not being found out, and, related to that, there is the practical desire to get the search engine to work for me, and not constrain me by overly predicting what I am doing. When I shop, when anyone shops, one shops for this and then gets bored. Then, one looks for something else. It is hard to predict when that happens. And so users end up having to show the search engine this by emptying its cache, so that a new session starts.

So, is there an ethical muddle? Who is doing what here? The technologists, the search folks or the user? There are lots of ways of figuring this out and moving forward, allowing a better dialogue between the user and the system, and so forth, allowing what I just called better management. I think the user should be heavily involved in this.

But there are also these big arguments about, for example, the ethics of keeping personal data. This seems to me a different set of questions. Now one of the things you might say about the ethics of personal data is that it is a great myth on the part of the search engine companies that they do anything with much of the data they collect. They genuinely cannot do anything with most of it because – well, what do you do with it? Aggregations of these data most often come up with pretty bland implications. Someone who has just looked at a car is probably just about to look at a car again. That is what you find. You do not need rocket science for that, you do not need state of the art AI to do that. Nor do you need cloud farms with billions of instances of the same; so it is bizarre that the search engine companies and browser companies seek to gather all these user data. It is just digital dirt.

Q: Well, this is possibly a question about those big data farms where they – as you point out – there is very little practical stuff that is got out of it, and so, going back to your question about concepts being right and wrong, and your suggestion was that concepts that motivate engineers are just sort of fine, so they just keep them turning over and producing this stuff, and then at the end of the process we come along and adapt it and make it useful to us by giving it – applying a new category. But then there is this issue that, well, maybe, the concepts that are motivating engineers have a kind of logic and destination and perhaps a religion of their own that are all heading in a certain direction and, as it were, trying to humanize the project [which] at the end of the process might be, might not be a failsafe project.

RH: Yes, I think that can be, but I also think you are doing a kind of sociology of reasoning.

Q: Well, you're a sociologist!

Epilogue

RH: Now, hold on – let me finish. There is a tendency in sociological treatments of 'reasoning' that exaggerates the structure and scope of reasons. It is a kind of craving, to put it in Wittgensteinian terms, this bigging-up reasons. For example, sociologists are particularly keen to give a kind of eschatological flavour to reasons, as if the reasons to do this here and now are related to the end of the world, as if reasons, ideas, are all a schema. Think of Jameson, a cultural theorist but basically a sociologist. But in contrast, when I have worked with engineers, very few link the ideas that motivate some product they are building with bigger, longer-term goals. Their reasons are, well, more piecemeal. You know, one of the things you might say about lots of scientists is that they have a philosophy of science, and they are very keen to explore and understand what science might be and what it leads to – its big-picture outcomes. The way these outcomes are described varies in different regimes of science, but the general tenor is common – think of the claims physics makes about the reality of the universe. You know the kind of scientism one comes across. But it is not likewise with most engineers. They have a very rough and ready view of reasons and the categorizations to do with those reasons. Occasionally, you will meet someone with a religious-like edifice wrapping up their work – I want to make the world a better place with the digital, you know that sort of thing – but they are rare. Mostly what motivates them is, really, things like it is a Monday, or it is a Friday, and it's crude, and it's simple. It is almost inane in its symbolism. But they abide by these reasons, however inane they might seem to be. I mean, their reasons are basically practical. Really, once they have done it, made whatever it is they are making, they have no reasons; they do not seem to be (I am saying this as a kind of anthropologist) wed to the reasons that persuaded them to make that thing. They are perfectly happy to be sold another set of accounts for that thing that makes sense for them, that would get them out of bed on a Monday morning. They would not take any old view, though, I am not saying that. The issue here is really to do with motivation, what provides it, ensures it. Software engineering is a really miserable job. It is incredibly difficult, and you can spend weeks on an algorithm, and if you are not totally convinced that algorithm is going to make a difference, you are not going to do it. It really is, it is not a simple problem, so having reasons for working on it is part of how you get work done.

But what I am saying is that this view, this view is always also somehow deeply practical. It is not pious; it is not part of some big system of ideas. I gave you an example of memory, how a notion of the mind having memory like a computer was part of the motivational fabric that produced that wearable camera device I spoke about, Sensecam. But the engineers did not think they were making claims about cognitive science or reflecting some unified idea of what the mind was. All they thought was, 'That is a good idea. I could build that'. And once they had done it, they were very happy to let other people come along and say, let us forget that memory thing and do this with Sensecam. But they needed that idea to enchant them, to make them want to do it, when doing it is, well, hard, a daily grind. Coding is work, after all, it is not art. So, you need vehicles to motivate you. Concepts. There you go. I would like to finish now. I have run out of words.

Epilogue

In her 1987 book *Plans and Situated Actions: The Problem of Human-Machine Communication*, Lucy A. Suchman anticipated that talk of computers' being able to *think* would be superseded by talk of machines that can *understand.* As with thinking, the industry didn't need to work hard to fashion a sense in which robots and artificial assistants could be said to understand (and be understood by) us.[1] The question that is left relatively unexplored, at least by philosophers, is how machines can both enable and impede inter-human understanding. I hope this conversation has at least helped to shed a little light on this.[2]

1 See Sandis and Harper 2017.

2 For a recent study of technology's use in human–animal interaction, see van der Linden 2022.

REFERENCES

Abelson, R. 1963. '*Free Action* by A. I. Melden'. *Philosophy and Phenomenological Research* 23, no. 4 (June 1963): 616.

Achinstein, P. 1975. 'The Object of Explanation'. In *Explanation*, edited by S. Körner, 1-45. Oxford: Blackwell.

Ackerman, R. 1987. *J. G. Frazer: His Life and Work.* Cambridge: Cambridge University Press.

Adamson, P. 2016. 'Rules for the History of Philosophy'. Published 31 December 2016. Accessed 2 June 2024. https://historyofphilosophy.net/all-20-rules-history-philosophy.

________. 2018. 'Comment on Lenz', in Lenz 2018a.

Addis, M. 1999. *Wittgenstein: Making Sense of Other Minds.* Farnham: Ashgate.

Alexander, P. 1963. *Sensationalism and Scientific Explanation.* London: Routledge and Kegan Paul.

Allen, W. 2004. *Melinda and Melinda.* Century City, LA: Fox Searchlight.

al-Tawhidi, A. H., and A. A. Miskawayh. 2021. *The Philosopher Responds: An Intellectual Correspondence from the Tenth Century.* Translated by Sophia Vasalou and James E. Montgomery. Library of Arabic Literature: 72. New York, NY: NYU Press.

Anscombe, G. E. M. (1957) 1963. *Intention.* 2nd ed. Oxford: Basil Blackwell.

________. (1974, 1989) 2005. 'Von Wright on Practical Inference'. In *The Philosophy of Georg Henrik von Wright*, edited by P. A. Schilpp and L. E. Hahn. La Salle, IL: Open Court. As Reprinted as 'Practical Inference' in *Human Life, Action and Ethics: Essays by G. E. M. Anscombe*, edited by M. Geach and L. Gormally. Exeter: Imprint Academic, 109–47.

________. (1975) 1981. 'The First Person'. In *Mind and Language: Wolfson College Lectures 1974*, edited by S. Guttenplan. Oxford: Oxford University Press. As Reprinted in *Metaphysics and the Philosophy of Mind.* Oxford: Blackwell, 21–36.

Appiah, K. A. 2008a. *Experiments in Ethics.* Cambridge, MA: Harvard University Press.

________. 2008b. 'Experimental Philosophy'. *Proceedings and Addresses of the American Philosophical Association* 82 (2): 7–22.

Armstrong, D. M. 1962. *Bodily Sensations.* London: Routledge and Kegan Paul.

Asad, T. 2012. 'Thinking about Religion, Belief, and Politics'. In *The Cambridge Companion to Religious Studies*, edited by R. A. Orsi, 36–57. Cambridge: Cambridge University Press.

Austen, J. 1813. *Pride and Prejudice.* London: T. Egerton.

Austin, J. L. 1966. 'Three Ways of Spilling Ink'. *The Philosophical Review* 75 (4): 427–40.

________. 1979. *Philosophical Papers.* Edited by J. O. Urmson and J. G. Warnock.

Avramides, A. 2000. *Other Minds.* London: Routledge.

________. (2019) 2023. 'Other Minds'. In *Stanford Encyclopedia of Philosophy*. Stanford University, 2023. Article first published 2 May 2019; last modified 19 December 2023. Accessed 31 May 2024. https://plato.stanford.edu/archives/win2023/entries/other-minds.

Avramides, A., and M. Parrott, eds. 2019. *Knowing and Understanding Other Minds*. Oxford: Oxford University Press.

Bagehot, W. 1867. *The English Constitution*. Reissue edition, 2009. Oxford: Oxford University Press.

Baier, A. C. 1985. *Postures of the Mind: Essays on Mind and Morals*. Minnesota, MN: University of Minnesota Press.

________. 2009. 'Acting in Character'. In Sandis 2009a, 241–56.

Baker, G. P., and P. M. S. Hacker. 1985. *Wittgenstein: Rules, Grammar and Necessity*. Vol. 2 of *An Analytical Commentary on the* Philosophical Investigations, *Essays and Exegesis of §§ 185–242*. Oxford: Blackwell.

________. 2009. *Wittgenstein: Rules, Grammar and Necessity*. Vol. 2 of *An Analytical Commentary on the* Philosophical Investigations, *Essays and Exegesis of §§ 185–242*. 2nd ed. Extensively revised by P. M. S. Hacker. Oxford: Wiley-Blackwell.

Baker, N. E. 2012. 'The Difficulty of Language: Wittgenstein on Animals and Humans'. In Forsberg et al. 2012, 45–64.

Bambrough, R. 1979. *Moral Scepticism and Moral Knowledge*. London: Routledge and Kegan Paul.

Barnes, J. 1987. 'Teachers of Moral Prudence', *The Cambridge Review* 108: 174–177.

Baron-Cohen, S. 2011. *Zero Degrees of Empathy: A New Theory of Human Cruelty*. London: Allen Lane.

Barr, D. 2016. 'Orlando Isn't about Gun Control or Terror: It's about Hate'. *The Big Issue*, no. 1210 (June 20–26): 13.

Barthes, R. 1964. *Elements of Semiology*. Translated by A. Lavers and C. Smith, 1967. London: Jonathan Cape.

Bassham, G., and J. L. Walls, eds. 2005. *The Chronicles of Narnia and Philosophy: The Lion, the Witch, and the Worldview*. Peru, IL: Open Court Press.

Baum, F. 1900. *The Wonderful Wizard of Oz*. Illustrated by W. W. Denslow. Chicago, IL: George M. Hill.

________. 1907. *Ozma of Oz*. Illustrated by J. R. Neill. Chicago, IL: Reilly and Britton.

Beardsmore, R. 1992. 'The Theory of Family Resemblances'. *Philosophical Investigations* 15 (2): 131–46.

________. 1996. 'If a Lion Could Talk…' In *Wittgenstein and the Philosophy of Culture*, edited by K. S. Johannessen and T. Nordenstam, 41–59. Vienna: Hölder-Pickler-Tempsky.

Behrens, K. 2018. *Click: Exploring Social Actions in the 21st Century*. Hatfield: University of Hertfordshire.

Bekoff, M. 2007. *Animals Matter: A Biologist Explains Why We Should Treat Animals with Compassion and Respect*. Boulder, CO: Shambhala Publications.

________. 2018. *Canine Confidential: Why Dogs Do What They Do*. Chicago, IL: University of Chicago Press.

Bennett, A. 2012. 'Cocktail Sticks'. In *Hymn and Cocktail Sticks: Two Recollections*. London: Faber and Faber, 77–120.

Bennett, J. 1964. *Rationality*. London: Routledge and Kegan Paul.

Berlin, I. 1974. 'The Divorce between the Sciences and the Humanities'. *Salmagundi* 27 (Summer–Fall): 9–39. As Reprinted in Berlin 1998, 326–58.

________. 1998. *The Proper Study of Mankind.* Edited by H. Hardy and R. Hauscheer. London: Pimlico.

Bevir, M. 1999. *The Logic of the History of Ideas.* Cambridge: Cambridge University Press.

________. 2009. 'Anglophone Historicism: From Modernist Method to Post-analytic Philosophy'. *Journal of the Philosophy of History* 3: 211–24.

Bevir, M., and N. Choi. 2015. 'Anglophone Historicism'. *Journal of the Philosophy of History* 9 (3): 327–46.

Bierce, A. (1911) 2000. *The Unabridged Devil's Dictionary.* Edited by D. E. Schultz and S. J. Joshi. Athens, GA: University of Georgia Press.

Blassime, A., C. Sandis and L. Bortolotti. 2012. 'Two Approaches to Animal Ethics and the Case of Great Apes'. In *Philosophical Perspectives on Animals: Mind, Ethics, Morals,* edited by K. Petrus and M. Wild, 269-94. New York, NY: Springer.

Bloom, P. 2016. *Against Empathy: The Case for Rational Compassion.* London: Bodley Head.

Boas, F. 1928. Foreword to Mead 1928, xiii–xv.

Boden, M. 2006. *Mind as Machine: A History of Cognitive Science,* Vol. 2. Oxford: Oxford University Press.

Borges, J. L. (1939) 2000. 'Pierre Menard, Author of the Quixote'. In *Fictions,* translated by A. Hurley, 33–43. London: Penguin Classics.

Boucher, S. 1995. 'The Life, Times, and Legacy of R. G. Collingwood'. In *Philosophy, History, and Civilization: Interdisciplinary Perspectives on R. G. Collingwood,* edited by D. Boucher, J. Connelly and T. Modood, 1–31. Cardiff: University of Wales Press.

Brecht, B. 1977. *The Measures Taken and Other Lehrstücke.* London: Methuen.

_________. 1998. *Die Maßnahme: Zwei Fassungen.* Frankfurt: Suhrkamp.

Britton, K. 1977. 'Symbols'. In Vesey 1977, 208–22.

Buckareff, A. 2011. 'How Does Agent-Causal Power Work?' *The Modern Schoolman* 88: 105–21.

Budiansky, S. 1998. *If a Lion Could Talk: How Animals Think.* London: Weidenfeld and Nicolson.

Burns, C. D. 1923. *The Contact between Minds.* London: Macmillan.

Burroughs, E. R. 1914. *Tarzan of the Apes.* Chicago, IL: A. C. McClurg.

Cahill, K. 2006. 'The Concept of Progress in Wittgenstein's Thought'. *The Review of Metaphysics* 60, no. 1 (September 2006): 71–100.

Carroll, L. 1865. *Alice in Wonderland.* Illustrated by J. Tenniel. London: Macmillan.

________. 1871. *Through the Looking Glass and What Alice Found There.* Illustrated by J. Tenniel. London: Macmillan.

________. 1895. 'What the Tortoise Said to Achilles'. *Mind* 4, no. 14 (April 1895): 278–80.

Carruthers, P. 2011. *The Opacity of Mind.* Oxford: Oxford University Press.

Carruthers, P., and P. K. Smith. 1996. *Theories of Theories of Mind.* Cambridge: Cambridge University Press.

Cassin, B. 2014. *Philosopher en langues: les intraduisibles en traduction.* Paris: Rue d'Ulm.

Cavell, M. 1996. *The Psychoanalytic Mind: From Freud to Philosophy.* Boston, MA: Harvard University Press.

Cavell, S. 1958. 'Must We Mean What We Say?' *Inquiry* 1 (1): 172–212. As Reprinted in Cavell 1969, 1–43.

________. (1969) 2002. *Must We Mean What We Say? A Book of Essays.* 2nd ed. Cambridge: Cambridge University Press.

Cerf, W. 1962. 'Studies in Philosophical Psychology'. *Philosophy and Phenomenological Research* 22, no. 4 (June 1962): 537–58.

Chapman, R. 2023. *Empire of Normality*. London: Pluto Press.

Charlemagne. 2004. 'I Understand, Up to a Point: Decoding a Euro-diplomat Takes More than a Dictionary'. *The Economist*, 2 September 2004.

Clark, S. R. L. 1991. *God's World and the Great Awakening*. Oxford: Clarendon Press.

Clark, S. R. L. 1997. *Animals and their Moral Standing*. London: Routledge.

Clastres, P. (1972) 2000. *Chronicle of the Guayaki Indians*. Translated by P. Auster. New York, NY: Zone Books.

Cockburn, D. 1990. *Other Human Beings*. London: Macmillan.

Collingwood, R. G. (1933) 2008. *An Essay on Philosophical Method*. New edition edited by J. Connelly and G. D'Oro. Oxford: Oxford University Press.

________. 1938. *The Principles of Art*. Oxford: Clarendon Press.

________. (1939) 2013. *An Autobiography*. 2nd ed., with other writings and essays on Collingwood's life and work. Edited by D. Boucher and T. Smith. Oxford: Oxford University Press.

________. (1940) 1998. *An Essay on Metaphysics*. Rev. ed. Oxford: Clarendon Press.

________. (1942) 1992. *The New Leviathan*. 2nd rev. ed. Oxford: Clarendon Press.

________. (1946) 2006. *The Idea of History* [IoH]. 2nd rev. ed. Oxford: Clarendon Press.

________. 2005. *The Philosophy of Enchantment: Studies in Folktale, Cultural Criticism, and Anthropology*. Edited by D. Boucher, W. James and P. Smallwood. Oxford: Clarendon Press.

Connelly, J. 2003. *Metaphysics, Method, and Politics*. Exeter: Imprint Academic.

________. 2009. 'R. G. Collingwood: From Anthropology to Metaphysics'. *Ethnographic Studies* 11 (Autumn): 3–23.

________. 2013. 'Collingwood's Controversies'. In *Collingwood* (1939) 2013, 399–425.

Cooke, D. 1959. *The Language of Music*. Oxford: Clarendon Press.

Coplan, A., and P. Goldie., eds. 2011. *Empathy: Philosophical and Psychological Perspectives*. Oxford: Oxford University Press.

Costello, B. 2019. *The Plural of Us: Poetry and Community in Auden and Others*. Princeton, NJ: Princeton University Press.

Cott, J., ed. 2006. *Dylan on Dylan: The Essential Interviews*. London: Hodder and Stoughton.

Crane, T. 2015. 'The Philosophy of Translation'. *Times Literary Supplement*, 28 January 2015.

Croce, B. (1938) 1941. *History as the Story of Liberty*. Translated by S. Sprigge. London: Allen and Unwin.

Currie, G. 1989. *An Ontology of Art*. New York, NY: St Martin's Press.

________. 2004. *Arts and Minds*. Oxford: Oxford University Press.

da Col, G., and S. Palmié, eds. 2018. *The Mythology in Our Language: Remarks on Frazer's Golden Bough*. Translated by S. Palmié. Chicago, IL: Hau Books.

d'Amico, R. 2011. 'Historicism'. In *A Companion to the Philosophy of History and Historiography*, edited by A. Tucker, 243–52. Oxford: Wiley-Blackwell.

Dancy, J. 2000. *Practical Reality*. Oxford: Clarendon Press.

Danto, A. C. 1965. *Analytical Philosophy of History*. Cambridge: Cambridge University Press.

________. 1966. 'The Problem of Other Periods'. *Journal of Philosophy* 63, no. 19 (October 1966): 566–76.

Das, K. L. 2006. *Philosophical Relevance of Language: A Methodological Reflection.* New Delhi: University of North Bengal.

Das, V. 2020. *Textures of the Ordinary: Doing Anthropology after Wittgenstein.* New York, NY: Fordham University Press.

Davidson, D. (1963) 2001. 'Actions, Reasons, and Causes'. *Journal of Philosophy* 60: 685–700. As Reprinted in Davidson 2001, 3–20.

________. (1967) 2001. 'Causal Relations'. *Journal of Philosophy*, 64 (21): 691–703. As Reprinted in Davidson 2001, 149–62.

________. (1970) 2001. 'Mental Events'. In *Experience and Theory*, edited by L. Foster and J. W. Swanson, 79–101. Amherst, MA: University of Massachusetts Press. As Reprinted in Davidson 2001, 202–25.

________. (1976) 2001. 'Hempel on Explaining Action'. *Erkenntnis* 10:239–53. As Reprinted in Davidson 2001, 261–76.

________. (1978) 2001. 'Intending', in *Philosophy of History and Action* 11: 41–60. As Reprinted in Davidson 2001, 83–102.

________. 1984. 'Thought and Talk'. In *Inquiries into Truth and Interpretation*, 155–70. Oxford: Clarendon Press.

________. 2001. *Essays on Actions and Events.* 2nd revised ed. Oxford: Clarendon Press.

Davisson, Z. 2017. *Kaibyō: The Supernatural Cats of Japan.* Seattle, WA: Chin Music Press.

________. 2020. *Yūrei: The Japanese Ghost.* 2nd ed. Seattle, WA: Chin Music Press.

de Gaynesford, M. 2006. *I: The Meaning of the First Person Term.* Oxford: Oxford University Press.

de la Colina, J., and T. P. Turrent. 1986. *Objects of Desire: Conversations with Luis Buñuel.* Edited and translated by Paul Lenti. New York, NY: Rizzoli International Publications.

Dennett, D. C. 1979. 'Intentional Systems'. In *Brainstorms: Philosophical Essays on Mind and Psychology*, 3–22. Montgomery, VT: Bradford Books.

________. 1991. *Consciousness Explained.* New York, NY: Little, Brown and Co.

________. 1995. 'Do Animals Have Beliefs?' In *Comparative Approaches to Cognitive Science*, edited by H. L. Roitblat and J.-A. Meyer, 111–18. Cambridge, MA: MIT Press.

________. 1996. *Kinds of Minds: Toward an Understanding of Consciousness.* New York, NY: Basic Books.

________. 1998. *Brainchildren: Essays on Designing Minds.* Boston, MA: MIT Press.

Descombes, V. 1992. *Proust: Philosophy of the Novel.* Translated by C. C. Macksey. Stanford, CA: Stanford University Press.

________. 2014. *The Institutions of Meaning: A Defence of Anthropological Holism.* Translated by S. A. Schwarz. Boston, MA: Harvard University Press.

Despret, V. 2008. 'The Becomings of Subjectivity in Animal Worlds'. *Subjectivity* 23: 123–39.

Deutscher, G. 2011. *Through the Language Glass: Why the World Looks Different in Other Languages.* London: Arrow.

Dilman, I. 2002. *Wittgenstein's Copernican Revolution: The Question of Linguistic Idealism.* London: Palgrave Macmillan.

Dilman, I., and D. Z. *Phillips. 1971. Sense and Delusion.* London: Routledge and Kegan Paul.

Dilthey, W. 1961. *Patterns and Meaning in History: Thoughts on History and Society.* Edited by H. P. Rickman. London: Harper Torchbooks.

Donagan, A. 1987. *Choice: The Essential Element in Human Action.* London: Routledge and Kegan Paul.

D'Oro, G. 2000. 'Collingwood on Re-enactment and the Identity of Thought', *Journal of the History of Philosophy* 38 (1): 87–101.

________. 2003. 'Collingwood and Ryle on the Concept of Mind'. *Philosophical Explorations* 6 (1): 18–30.

________. 2007. 'Two Dogmas of Contemporary Philosophy of Action'. *Journal of the Philosophy of History* 1: 11–26.

________. 2011.'Davidson and the Autonomy of Human Sciences'. In *Dialogues with Davidson: New Perspectives on his Philosophy*, edited by J. Malpas. Boston, MA: MIT Press.

________. 2012. 'Reasons and Causes: The Philosophical Battle and the Meta-Philosophical War'. *Australasian Journal of Philosophy* 90 (2): 207–21.

D'Oro, G., and C. Sandis. 2013a. 'From Anti-Causalism to Causalism and Back: A Century of the Reasons/Causes Debate'. In D'Oro and Sandis, eds, 2013b, 1–47.

________. 2013b. *Reasons and Causes: Causalism and Non-Causalism in the Philosophy of Action.* London: Palgrave Macmillan.

Dray, W. 1957. *Laws and Explanation in History.* Oxford: Clarendon Press.

________. (1963) 1974. 'Historical Explanation of Action Reconsidered'. In *Philosophy and History: A Symposium*, edited by S. Hook, 105–35. New York University Press. As Reprinted in *The Philosophy of History*, edited by P. Gardiner. Oxford University Press, 66–89.

________. 1980. *Perspectives on History.* London: Routledge and Kegan Paul.

Drury, M. O. C. 1973. *The Danger of Words.* London: Routledge and Kegan Paul.

Dumont, L. 1983. *Essais sur l'individualisme.* Paris: Seuil.

Dupré, J. 2002. *Humans and Other Animals.* Oxford: Oxford University Press.

Dutton, D. 2009. *The Art Instinct.* Oxford: Oxford University Press.

Dylan, B. 1965. 'Ballad of a Thin Man'. In *The Lyrics Since 1962.* New York, NY: Simon and Schuster, 2014.

Eco, U. 1975. *A Theory of Semiotics.* Bloomington, IN: Indiana University Press.

________. 1976. *A Theory of Semiotics.* London: Macmillan.

________. 1986. *Semiotics and the Philosophy of Language.* Bloomington, IN: Indiana University Press.

Eliot, T. S. (1923) 1961. 'The Function of Criticism'. *Criterion* 2, no. 5 (October 1923): 31–42. As Reprinted in *Selected Essays*, 23–34. London: Faber and Faber.

Engelmann, P. 1967. *Letters from Ludwig Wittgenstein, with a Memoir.* Edited by B. McGuinness, translated by L. Furtmüller. Oxford: Blackwell.

Epstein, R. A. 2005. 'Animals as Objects, or Subjects, of Rights'. In *Animal Ethics: Current Debates and New Directions*, edited by C. R. Sunstein and M. Nussbaum, 143–61. Oxford: Oxford University Press.

Evans-Pritchard, E. E. 1937. *Witchcraft, Oracles, and Magic Among the Azande.* Oxford: Oxford University Press.

Ewing, A. C. 1953. *Ethics.* London: The English Universities Press.

Fingarette, H. 1969. *Self-Deception.* London: Routledge and Kegan Paul.

Finnegan, R. 2011. *Why Do We Quote? The Culture and History of Quotation.* Cambridge: Open Book Publishers.

Flaubert, G. 1913. *Le dictionnaire des idées reçues.* Paris: L. Conard.

Forsberg, N., M. Burley and N. Hämäläinen, eds. 2012. *Language, Ethics and Animal Life: Wittgenstein and Beyond.* London: Bloomsbury.

Foster, Charles. 2016. *Being a Beast.* London: Profile Books.

Franz, P. 2018. 'We vs Them'. *Times Literary Supplement* 6029 (19 October 2018), 30.

Frazer, J. G. (1890) 1922. *The Golden Bough: A Study in Magic and Religion*. Abridged 1922 ed. London: Palgrave Macmillan.

Fried, E. 1964. *Warngedichte*. Munich: Carl Hauser Verlag.

Gablik, S. 1976. *Magritte*. Boston, MA: Little Brown and Company.

Gaita, R. 2002. *The Philosopher's Dog*. New York, NY: Routledge.

Gallese, V. 2001. The "Shared Manifold" Hypothesis: From Mirror Neurons to Empathy, In *Journal of Consciousness Studies*, 8 (5–6): 33–50.

Gallie, W. B. 1955. 'Essentially Contested Concepts'. *Proceedings of the Aristotelian Society*, n.s., 56: 167–98.

Geach, P. 1957. *Mental Acts*. London: Routledge and Kegan Paul.

Geertz, C. 1973. *The Interpretation of Cultures*. New York, NY: Basic Books.

Giambatista, R. C., and J. D. Hoover. 2009. 'An Empirical Test of "Behavioral Immersion"'. *Experiential Learning Developments in Business Simulation and Experiential Learning* 36: 124–31.

Ginsberg, A. (1958) 1984. 'The Lion for Real'. In *Collected Poems 1947–1980*, 174–5. New York, NY: Harper and Row.

Glendinning, S. 1998. *On Being with Others*. London: Routledge.

Glock, H.-J. 1996a. *A Wittgenstein Dictionary*, Oxford: Blackwell.

________. 1996b. 'On Safari with Wittgenstein, Quine and Davidson'. In *Wittgenstein and Quine*, edited by R. Arrington and H.-J. Glock. London: Routledge, 144–73.

________. 2000. 'Animals, Thoughts and Concepts'. *Synthese* 123: 35–64.

________. 2005. 'Wittgenstein and History'. In *Wittgenstein: The Philosopher and his Works*, edited by A. Pichler and S. Saatela, 236–62. Bergen: University of Bergen Press.

________. 2006. 'Thought, Language and Animals'. In *Deepening Our Understanding of Wittgenstein*, edited by M. Kobe. Special issue, *Grazer Philosophische Studien* 71: 139–60.

________. 2014. 'Reasons for Action: Wittgensteinian and Davidsonian Perspectives in Historical and Meta-Philosophical Context'. *Nordic Wittgenstein Review* 3 (1): 7–46.

________. 2023. 'Reflections and Replies'. In *Wittgenstein and Beyond: Essays in Honour of Hans-Johann Glock*, edited by C. C. Pfisterer, N. Rathgeb and E. Schmidt, 307–31. London: Routledge.

Glock, H.-J., and J. Hyman. 2017. *A Companion to Wittgenstein*. Oxford: Oxford University Press.

Glover, J. 2014. *Alien Landscapes: Interpreting Disordered Minds*. Cambridge, MA: Harvard University Press.

Godfrey-Smith, P. 2014. *Other Minds: The Octopus and the Evolution of Intelligent Life*. London: William Collins.

Goldie, P. 2012. *The Mess Inside: Narrative, Emotion, and the Mind*. Oxford: Oxford University Press.

Goodman, N. 1968. *Languages of Art*. Indianapolis, IN: Bobbs-Merrill.

Gray, J. 2002. *Straw Dogs*. London: Granta.

Grimm, S. R. 2016. 'How Understanding People Differs from Understanding the Natural World'. *Philosophical Issues* 26 (1): 209–25.

Ground, I. 1989. *Art or Bunk?* London: Bristol Classical Press.

Gudovitch, R. 2012. 'What's Wrong with a Bite of Dog?' In Forsberg et al. 2012, 139–51.

Gustafsson, Y., C. Kronqvist and M. McEachrane, eds. 2009. *Emotions and Understanding: Wittgenstein Perspectives*. London: Palgrave Macmillan.

Hacker, P. M. S. (1972) 1986. *Insight and Illusion*. 1st and 2nd ed. Oxford: Oxford University Press.

________. 1990. *Wittgenstein: Meaning and Mind: Volume 3 of an Analytical Commentary on the* Philosophical Investigations, *Part II: Exegesis §§ 243–427.* Oxford: Blackwell.

________. 1996a. *Wittgenstein's Place in Twentieth-Century Analytic Philosophy.* Oxford: Blackwell.

________. 1996b. *Wittgenstein: Mind and Will: Volume 4 of an Analytical Commentary of the* Philosophical Investigations, *Part II: Exegesis §§ 428–693.* Oxford: Blackwell.

________. 2012. 'The Sad and Sorry History of Consciousness: Being, among Other Things, a Challenge to the "Consciousness-studies Community"'. In *Human Nature, Royal Institute of Philosophy Supplement* 70, edited by C. Sandis and M. J. Cain, 149–68. Cambridge: Cambridge University Press.

________. 2015. 'Forms of Life'. Special issue on forms of life, *Nordic Wittgenstein Review* 4:1–20.

Hagberg, G. L. 1994. *Meaning and Interpretation: Wittgenstein, Henry James, and Literary Knowledge.* Ithaca, NY: Cornell University Press.

________. 1995. *Art as Language: Wittgenstein, Meaning and Aesthetic Theory.* Ithaca, NY: Cornell University Press.

Haidt, J. 2012. *The Righteous Mind: Why Good People are Divided by Politics and Religion.* London: Allen Lane.

Hamilton, A. 2014. *The Routledge Guidebook to Wittgenstein and On Certainty.* London: Routledge.

Hamlyn, D. W. 1957. *The Psychology of Perception.* London: Routledge and Kegan Paul.

Hampshire, S. 1959. *Thought and Action.* London: Chatto and Windus.

Hanson, A., and R. Martin. 1973. 'The Problem of Other Cultures'. *Philosophy of the Social Sciences* 3: 191–208.

Harding, C. 2018a. *Japan Story: In Search of a Nation, 1850 to the Present.* London: Allan Lane.

________. 2018b. 'Ghosts on the Shore'. *Aeon*, 6 August 2018.

________. 2019. 'Supernatural Japan'. *BBC Radio* 3, 15 August 2019.

Harman, G. 1973. *Thought.* Princeton, NJ: Princeton University Press.

Harrison, B. 1832. *The Study of Different Languages, As It Relates to the Philosophy of the Human Mind.* Oxford: Prize Essay Read in the Sheldonian Theatre.

Hartley, L. P. 1953. *The Go-Between.* London: Hamish Hamilton.

Hearn, L. (1896) 2022. *Kokoro: Hints and Echoes of Japanese Inner Life.* Lincoln, NE: Zea Books.

________. 1904. *Kwaidan: Stories and Studies of Strange Things.* New York, NY: Houghton Mifflin.

Hearne, V. 1994. *Animal Happiness.* Brooklyn, NY: Harper Collins.

Hendry, J. 1995. *Understanding Japanese Society.* 2nd ed. London: Routledge.

________. 2021. *An Affair with a Village.* Stirling: Extremis Publishing.

Hempel, C. G. 1942. 'The Function of General Laws in History'. *Journal of Philosophy* 39, no. 2 (January): 35–48.

________. 1962. 'Rational Action', in *Proceedings and Addresses of the American Philosophical Association* 35: 5–23.

________. 1974. 'Reasons and Covering Laws in Historical Explanation'. As Reprinted in *The Philosophy of History*, edited by P. Gardiner, 90–105. Oxford: Oxford University Press.

Hertzberg, L. 2005. 'The Limits of Understanding'. *SATS: Northern European Journal of Philosophy* 6 (1): 5–14.

Higginbotham, J. 1980. 'Pronouns and Bound Variables'. *Linguistic Inquiry* 11 (4): 679–708.
Hintikka, M. B., and J. Hintikka. 1986. *Investigating Wittgenstein.* Oxford: Blackwell.
Hofstadter, D. R. 1979. *Gödel, Escher, Bach: An Eternal Golden Braid.* New York, NY: Basic Books.
Hornsby, J. 1980. *Actions.* London: Routledge.
________. 1997. *Simple Mindedness: In Defense of Naive Naturalism in the Philosophy of Mind.* Cambridge, MA: Harvard University Press.
Hume, D. (1739–40, 1978) 2000. *A Treatise of Human Nature.* 2nd ed. Edited by L. A. Selby-Bigge, revised by P. H. Nidditch. Oxford: Clarendon Press. As Reprinted Oxford Philosophical Texts edition by D. F. Norton and M. J. Norton.
Hutto, D. D. 1996. 'Was the Later Wittgenstein a Transcendental Idealist?' In *Current Issues in Idealism*, edited by P. Coates and D. D. Hutto, 121–53. London: Continuum.
________. 2007. 'The Narrative Practice Hypothesis: Origins and Applications of Folk Psychology'. In *Narrative and Understanding Persons*, edited by D. D. Hutto, 43–68. Cambridge: Cambridge University Press.
Iacoboni, M. 2008. *Mirroring People: The Science of Empathy and How We Connect With Others.* New York, NY: Farrar Straus & Giroux.
Jackson, F. 1982. 'Epiphenomenal Qualia'. *Philosophical Quarterly* 32 (127): 127–36.
________. 1986. 'What Mary Didn't Know'. *Journal of Philosophy* 83: 291–5.
Jakobson, R. 1957. 'Shifters, Verbal Categories and the Russian Verb'. As Reprinted in Jakobson 1984, 41–59.
________. 1959. 'On Linguistic Aspects of Translation'. In *On Translation*, edited by R. A. Brower, 232–9. Cambridge, MA: Harvard University Press.
________. 1960. 'Closing Statement: Linguistics and Poetics'. In *Style in Language*, edited by T. A. Sebeok, 350–77. Cambridge, MA: MIT Press.
________. 1984. *Russian and Slavic Grammar: Studies 1931–1981.* Edited by L. R. Waugh and M. Halle. Berlin: De Gruyter.
James, W. (1939) 2013. 'A Philosopher's Journey: Collingwood in the East Indies'. In Collingwood (1939) 2013, 501–48.
Jung, C. G. 2009. *The Red Book: Liber Novus [1914–1930].* Edited by Sonu Shamdasani, translated by Mark Kyburz. New York, NY: John Peck and Sonu Shamdasani.
Kemp, G., and G. M. Mras, eds. 2016. *Wollheim, Wittgenstein, and Pictorial Representation: Seeing-As and Seeing-In.* London: Routledge.
Kenny, A. J. P. 1963. *Action, Emotion and Will.* London: Routledge and Kegan Paul.
________. 1993. *Aquinas on Mind.* London: Routledge.
________. 2002. *The Unknown God: Agnostic Essays.* London: Continuum.
Kim, J. 2010. *Essays in the Metaphysics of Mind.* Oxford: Oxford University Press.
Kinghorn, K. 2005. 'Virtue Epistemology: Why Uncle Andrew Couldn't Hear the Animals Speak'. In Bassham and Walls 2005, 15–26.
Kipling, R. 1894. *The Jungle Book.* London: Macmillan.
Klages, L. 1929–32. *Der Geist als Widersacher der Seele*, vols. I–III. Leipzig: Johann Ambrosius Barth.
Klagge, J. C., ed. 2001. *Wittgenstein: Philosophy and Biography.* Cambridge: Cambridge University Press.
________. 2011. *Wittgenstein in Exile.* Cambridge, MA: MIT Press.
Klagge, J., and A. Nordmann, eds. 1993. *Ludwig Wittgenstein: Philosophical Occasions 1912–1951.* Indianapolis, IN: Hackett Publishing Co.

Knobe, J., and Nichols, S., eds. 2008. *Experimental Philosophy*. Oxford: Oxford University Press.

Knowles, D. 2010. 'Hegel on Action, Reasons, and Causes'. In Laitinen and Sandis 2010a, 42–58.

Koestler, A. 1940. *Darkness at Noon*. London: Macmillan.

________. 2018. *Sonnenfinsternis: Nach dem deutschen Originalmanuskript*. Coesfeld: Elsinor Verlag.

Kovessi, J. 1967. *Moral Notions*. London: Routledge and Kegan Paul.

Krishnamurti, J. 1992. *On Relationship*. San Francisco, CA: Harper Collins.

________. 2010. *Freedom from the Known*. San Francisco, CA: Harper Collins.

Kristeva, J. 1984. *Revolution in Poetic Language*. New York, NY: Columbia University Press.

Krznaric, R. 2014. *Empathy: A Handbook for Revolution*. London: Random House.

Kursell, J. 2010. 'First Person Plural: Roman Jakobson's Grammatical Fictions'. *Studies in East European Thought* 62, no. 2 (June): 217–36.

Kuusela, Oskari, and Marie McGinn, eds. 2011. *The Oxford Handbook of Wittgenstein*. Oxford: Oxford University Press.

Kwon, H. 2018. 'Wittgenstein's Spirit, Frazer's Ghost.' In da Col and Palmié 2018, 87–96.

Laitinen, A., and C. Sandis, eds. 2010a. *Hegel on Action*. Palgrave Macmillan.

________. 2010b. 'Hegel and Contemporary Philosophy of Action'. In Laitinen and Sandis 2010a, 1–21.

Landau, J. 1968. 'John Wesley Harding'. *Crawdaddy!*, 15 May 1968, 16.

Lange, E. M. 2017. 'Wittgenstein on Solipsism'. In Glock and Hyman 2017, 159–74.

Lear, J. 1998. *Open Minded: Working Out the Logic of the Soul*. Cambridge, MA: Harvard University Press.

________. 2006. *Radical Hope: Ethics in the Face of Cultural Devastation*. Boston, MA: Harvard University Press.

Leavis, F. R. 1936. *Revaluation: Tradition and Development in English Poetry*. London: Chatto and Windus.

________. 1952. *The Common Pursuit*. London: Chatto and Windus.

________. 1969. *English Literature in Our Time and for the University*. London: Chatto and Windus.

________. 1974. *Essays in Criticism*. Edited by J. Tasker. London: Chatto and Windus.

________. 1978. *Myth and Meaning: Cracking the Code of Culture*. Toronto, ON: University of Toronto Press.

Le Carré, J. 1996. *The Tailor of Panama*. London: Hodder and Stoughton.

Lenz, M. 2018a. 'Who Are We? Myths in the History of Philosophy (Part I)'. *Handling Ideas* (blog). 9 August 2018. https://handlingideas.blog/2018/08/09/who-are-we-myths-in-the-history-of-philosophy-part-i/. As Reprinted on the APA blog, 24 August 2018. https://blog.apaonline.org/2018/08/24/who-are-we-myths-in-the-history-of-philosophy-part-i/.

________. 2018b. 'On Saying "We" Again', *Handling Ideas* (blog). 28 August 2018. https://handlingideas.blog/2018/08/28/on-saying-we-again-a-response-to-peter-adamson/.

Lévi-Strauss, C. (1958) 1963. *Anthropologie structural*. Translated as *Structural Anthropology* by C. Jacobson and B. G. Schoepf. New York, NY: Basic Books.

________. 1962. *La Pensée sauvage*. Paris: Librairie Plon.

Levy, N. n.d. 'Experimental Philosophy: A Critique'. Unpublished manuscript.

Lewis, C. S. 1950. *The Lion, the Witch and the Wardrobe.* Illustrated by P. Baynes. London: Geoffrey Bles.

________. 1955. *The Magician's Nephew.* Illustrated by P. Baynes. London: The Bodley Head.

Livingstone, P. 2005. *Art and Intention: A Philosophical Study.* Oxford: Oxford University Press.

Lloyd, G. E. R. 2012. *Being, Humanity, and Understanding: Studies in Ancient and Modern Societies.* Oxford: Oxford University Press.

Locke, J. (1689) 1975. *An Essay Concerning Human Understanding.* 4th ed. Edited by P. H. Nidditch. Oxford: Clarendon Press.

Lugg, A. 2017. 'Impossible Colours: Wittgenstein and the Naturalist's Challenge'. In *How Colours Matter to Philosophy*, edited by M. Silva, 107–24. London: Springer.

Lyons, J. 1968. *Introduction to Theoretical Linguistics.* Cambridge: Cambridge University Press.

MacIntyre, A. C. 1958. *The Unconscious.* London: Routledge and Kegan Paul

________. 1964a. 'A Mistake About Causality in Science'. In *Philosophy, Politics and Society*, 2nd series, edited by P. Laslett and W. G. Runciman, 48–70. Oxford: Basil Blackwell.

________. 1964b. 'Is Understanding Religion Compatible With Believing?' In *Faith and the Philosophers*, edited by J. Hick, 119–24. London: Macmillan.

________. 1972. 'Hegel on Faces and Skulls'. As Reprinted in *The Tasks of Philosophy*, 74–85. Cambridge: Cambridge University Press.

Malcolm, N. 1959. *Dreaming.* London: Routledge and Kegan Paul.

________. 1982. 'Wittgenstein and Idealism'. In *Idealism: Past and Present,* edited by G. Vesey, 249–68. Cambridge: Cambridge University Press.

________. 1986. *Nothing is Hidden: Wittgenstein's Criticism of His Early Thought.* Oxford: Basil Blackwell.

Ma, L., and J. Van Brakel. 2016. *Fundamentals of Comparative and Intercultural Philosophy.* Albany, NY: SUNY Press.

Malle, B. 2004. *How the Mind Explains Behavior.* Boston, MA: MIT Press.

Marcus, G. 1997. *Invisible Republic: Bob Dylan's Basement Tapes.* New York, NY: Henry Holt and Company.

Margolis, J. 1980. *Art and Philosophy.* London: Harvester Wheatsheaf.

________. 2001. *Selves and Other Texts: The Case for Cultural Realism.* Pennsylvania State University Press.

Martin, R. 1977. *Historical Explanation: Re-Enactment and Practical Inference.* Ithaca, NY: Cornell University Press.

________. 2013. 'From Method to Metaphysics'. In Collingwood (1939) 2013, 353–75.

Matthews, G. B. 1977. 'Consciousness and Life'. *Philosophy* 52 (199): 13–26.

McDowell, J. 1996. *Mind and World.* 2nd ed. Cambridge, MA: Harvard University Press.

________. 2009. 'Towards a Reading of Hegel on Action in the "Reason" chapter of the Phenomenology'. In *Having the World in View: Essays on Kant, Hegel, and Sellars*, 166–84. Boston, MA: Harvard University Press.

McGinn, M. 2022. *Wittgenstein, Scepticism and Naturalism: Essays on the Later Wittgenstein.* London: Anthem Press.

McGuinness, B. 1988. *Young Ludwig: Wittgenstein's Life, 1889–1921.* Oxford: Oxford University Press.

________. 2001. 'Wittgenstein and the Idea of Jewishness'. In *Wittgenstein: Philosophy and Biography*, edited by J. Klagge, 221–36. Cambridge: Cambridge University Press.

________. 2002. *Approaches to Wittgenstein: Collected Papers*. London: Routledge.

________, ed. (2008) 2012. *Wittgenstein in Cambridge: Letters and Documents 1911–1951* [WC]. Oxford: Wiley-Blackwell.

McLaughlin, B. P. 2013. 'Why Rationalization is Not a Species of Causal Explanation'. In D'Oro and Sandis (eds), 97–123.

McMyler, M. 2011. Believing What the Man Says About His Own Feeling. In *The Philosophy of J. L. Austin*, edited by M. Gustafsson and R. Sørli, 114–45. Oxford: Oxford University Press.

Mead, M. 1928. *Coming of Age in Samoa: A Psychological Study of Primitive Youth for Western Civilisation*. New York, NY: William Morrow and Company.

________. 1964. 'Vicissitudes of the Study of the Total Communication Process'. In Sebeok 1964, 277–87.

Melden, A. I. 1961. *Free Action*. London: Routledge and Kegan Paul.

Meshaum-Muir, K. 2014. 'Three Simple Steps to Understand Art: Look, See, Think'. *The Conversation*, 22 October 2014.

Millikan, R. G. 1994. 'On Unclear and Indistinct Ideas'. *Philosophical Perspectives* 8 (Logic and Language):75–100.

________. 2005. *Language: A Biological Model*. Oxford: Oxford University Press.

Miyazaki, H. 2001. *Spirited Away*. Japan: Studio Ghibli.

Monk, R. 1990. *Wittgenstein: The Duty of a Genius*. London: Jonathan Cape.

Monk, R. 1991. *Wittgenstein: The Duty of Genius*. London: Vintage.

Moore, A. 1997. *Points of View*. Oxford: Oxford University Press.

________. (1985) 2010. 'Transcendental Idealism in Wittgenstein, and Theories of Meaning'. *Philosophical Quarterly* 35, no. 139 (April): 134–55. As Reprinted, with corrections and an appendix, in *The Later Wittgenstein on Language*, edited by D. Whiting, 191–212. Basingstoke: Palgrave Macmillan.

Moore, G. E. 1903. *Principia Ethica*. Cambridge: Cambridge University Press.

Moran, R., and M. J. Stone. 2009. 'Anscombe on the Expression of Intention'. In Sandis 2009a, 132–68.

Morrick, H., ed. 1967. *Wittgenstein and the Problem of Other Minds*. New York, NY: McGraw-Hill.

Morton, A. 2003. *The Importance of Being Understood: Folk Psychology as Ethics*. London: Routledge.

Mounce, H. O. 1989. 'The Aroma of Coffee'. *Philosophy* 64:159–73.

Moyal-Sharrock, D. 2004. *Understanding Wittgenstein's* On Certainty. Basingstoke: Palgrave Macmillan.

________. 2016a. 'The Animal in Epistemology: Wittgenstein's Enactivist Solution to the Problem of Regress'. *Hinge Epistemology*. Special issue, *International Journal for the Study of Skepticism* 6: 97–119.

________. 2016b. 'Wittgenstein and Leavis: Literature and the Enactment of the Ethical'. *Philosophy and Literature* 40 (1): 240–64.

Moyal-Sharrock, D., and C. Sandis, eds. 2022. *Extending Hinge Epistemology*. London: Anthem Press.

Mulhall, S. 2007. *Wittgenstein's Private Language: Grammar, Nonsense, and Imagination in* Philosophical Investigations, *§§243–315*. Oxford: Clarendon Press.

________. 2009. '"Hopelessly Strange": Bernard Williams' Portrait of Wittgenstein as a Transcendental Idealist'. *European Journal of Philosophy* 17 (3): 386–404.

Murdoch, I. 1992. *Metaphysics As a Guide to Morals.* London: Chatto and Windus.

Nadelhoffer, T., and Nahmias, E. 2007. The Past and Future of Experimental Philosophy. *Philosophical Explorations* 10 (2): 123–49.

Nagel, T. 1974. 'What Is It Like To Be a Bat?' *The Philosophical Review* 83, no. 4 (October): 435–50.

________. 1986. *The View from Nowhere.* Oxford: Oxford University Press.

Nakata, H., dir. 1998. *Ring.* Japan: Ringu/Rasen Production Committee.

Nawroth, C., Z. M. Martin and A. G. McElligott. 2020. 'Goats Follow Human Pointing Gestures in an Object Choice Task'. *Frontiers in Psychology* 11: 535850.

Newell, R. W. *Objectivity, Empiricism and Truth.* 1986. London: Routledge and Kegan Paul.

Nichols, S., and S. P. Stich. 2003. *Mindreading: An Integrated Account of Pretence, Self-Awareness, and Understanding Other Minds.* Oxford: Oxford University Press.

Nietzsche, Friedrich. (1878) 1996. *Human, All Too Human: A Book for Free Spirits* [HATH]. 2nd ed. Translated by R. J. Hollingdale. Cambridge: Cambridge University Press.

________. (1881) 1997. *Daybreak: Thoughts on the Prejudices of Morality* [D]. Translated by R. J. Hollingdale, edited by M. Clark and B. Leiter. Cambridge: Cambridge University Press.

________. (1883–1891) 1997. *Thus Spoke Zarathustra* [TSZ]. Translated by A. Del Caro, edited by A. Del Caro and R. B. Pippin. Cambridge: Cambridge University Press.

________. (1885–89) 2003. *Writings from the Late Notebooks* [WLN]. Translated by K. Sturge, edited by R. Bittner. Cambridge: Cambridge University Press.

________. (1886) 2001. *Beyond Good and Evil* [BGE]. Translated by J. Norman, edited by R.-P. Horstman and J. Norman. Cambridge: Cambridge University Press.

________. (1887a) 2001. *The Gay Science* [GS]. Translated by J. Nauckhoff and A. Del Caro, edited by B. Williams. Cambridge: Cambridge University Press.

________. (1887b) 1994. *The Genealogy of Morality* [GM]. Translated by C. Diethe, edited by K. Ansell-Pearson. Cambridge: Cambridge University Press.

________. (1889) 2005. *Ecce Homo: How One Becomes What One Is* (with *Other Writings*). Translated by J. Norman, edited by A. Ridley. Cambridge: Cambridge University Press.

________. (1889b) 2005. *The Anti-Christ, Ecce Homo, Twilight of the Idols, and Other Writings.* Translated by Judith Norman, edited by Aaron Ridley. Cambridge: Cambridge University Press.

________. (1901) 1967. *The Will to Power* [WTP]. Translated by W. Kaufmann and R. J. Hollingdale. New York, NY: Vintage Books.

Oakeshott, M. 1933. *Experience and its Modes.* Cambridge: Cambridge University Press.

O'Brien, L. n.d. 'Understanding Alien Psychologies', unpublished manuscript.

Osborne, C. 2007. *Dumb Beasts and Dead Philosophers: Humanity and the Humane in Ancient Philosophy and Literature.* Oxford: Oxford University Press.

Orvell, A., E. Korss, and S. A. Gelman. 2018. 'That's How "You" Do It: Generic You Expresses Norms During Early Childhood'. *Journal of Experimental Child Psychology* 165: 183–95.

Orwell, G. 1945. *Animal Farm.* London: Secker and Warburg.

Palmié, S. 2018. 'Translation is Not Explanation: Remarks on the Intellectual History and Context of Wittgenstein's *Remarks on Frazer*'. In da Col and Palmié 2018, 1–28.

Parkinson, G. H. 1977. 'The Translation Theory of Understanding'. In Vesey 1974, 1–19.

Parry, R. L. 2014. 'Ghosts of the Tsunami.' *London Review of Books* 36, no. 3 (February): 13–6.

________. 2016. 'Ghosts of the Tsunami.' *BBC Radio* 4, 11 March 2016.

________. 2017. *Ghosts of the Tsunami: Death and Life in Japan's Disaster Zone.* London: Jonathan Cape.

Parsons, C. 1974. 'The Liar Paradox'. *Journal of Philosophical Logic* 3 (4): 381–412.

Pascal, B. (1670) 2005. *Pensées.* Translated by R. Ariew. Indianapolis, IN: Hackett.

Pears, D. 2006. *Paradox and Platitude in Wittgenstein's Philosophy.* Oxford: Clarendon Press.

Penelhum, T. 1970. *Survival and Disembodied Existence.* London: Routledge and Kegan Paul.

Peters, J. D. 1999. *Speaking Into the Air: A History of the Idea of Communication.* Chicago, IL: University of Chicago Press.

Peters, R. S. 1958. *The Concept of Motivation.* London: Routledge and Kegan Paul.

Philips, D. Z. 2004. *Religion and Friendly Fire: Examining Assumptions in Contemporary Philosophy of Religion.* London: Ashgate.

Pihlström, S. 2015. 'Subjectivity as Negativity and as Limit'. In *Pragmatism, Kant, and Transcendental Philosophy*, edited by G. Gava and R. Stern, 217–38. London: Routledge.

Pinker, S. 2007. *The Stuff of Thought: Language as a Window into Human Nature.* London: Allen Lane.

Pippin, R. 2010. 'Hegel's Social Theory of Agency: The "Inner-Outer" Problem'. In Laitinen and Sandis 2010a, 59–78.

Pitcher, G. 1964. *The Philosophy of Wittgenstein.* Englewood Cliffs, NJ: Prentice-Hall.

Pole, D. 1972. 'Presentational Objects and their Interpretation'. In *Royal Institute of Philosophy Lectures* 6 (March 1972: *Philosophy and the Arts*), 147–64. London: Macmillan.

Popper, K. (1945) 2002. *The Open Society and Its Enemies.* Centenary Edition. London: Routledge.

________. 1957. *The Poverty of Historicism.* London: Routledge and Kegan Paul.

Potts, T. 1977. 'The Place of Structure in Communication'. In Vesey 1977, 91–115.

Prinz, J. 2012. *Beyond Human Nature.* London: Allen Lane.

Pritchard, D. 2011. 'Wittgensteinian Pyrrhonism'. In *Pyrrhonism in Ancient, Modern, and Contemporary Philosophy*, edited by D. E. Machuca, 193–202. Dordrecht: Springer Science and Business Media.

________. 2016. *Epistemic Angst: Radical Skepticism and the Groundlessness of Our Believing.* Princeton, NJ: Princeton University Press.

________. 2017. 'Wittgenstein on Scepticism'. In Glock and Hyman 2017, 563–75.

Quante, M. 2004. *Hegel's Concept of Action.* Translated by D. Moyer. Cambridge: Cambridge University Press.

Reppert, V. 2005. 'The Green Witch and the Great Debate: Freeing Narnia from the Spell of the Lewis-Anscombe Legend'. In Bassham and Walls 2005, 260–73.

Rhees, R. 1969. *Without Answers.* London: Routledge.

________. 2006. *Wittgenstein and the Philosophy of Discourse.* 2nd ed. Edited by D. Z. Phillips. Oxford: Blackwell.

Richter, D. J. 2004. 'Ludwig Wittgenstein'. *Internet Encyclopedia of Philosophy*, 30 August 2004.

Ricœur, P. 2004. *Memory, History, Forgetting.* Translated by K. Blamey and D. Pellauer. Chicago, IL: University of Chicago Press.

Rizzolatti, G., and Craighero, L. 2004. 'The Mirror-Neuron System'. *Annual Review of Neuroscience* 27 (1): 169–92.

Russell, B. 1940. *An Inquiry into Meaning and Truth.* Edinburgh: Bishop and Sons.

Ryle, G. 1949. *The Concept of Mind.* London: Hutchinson.
Saari, H. 1989. 'R. G. Collingwood on the Identity of Thought'. *Dialogue: Canadian Philosophical Review* 28: 77–89.
Sagan, C. et al., eds. 1978. *Murmurs of Earth: The Voyager Interstellar Record.* New York, NY: Ballentine Books.
Sandis, C. 2006a. 'The Explanation of Action in History'. *Essays in Philosophy* 7 (2): 200–11.
________. 2006b. 'Animals'. In *Essentials of Philosophy and Ethics*, edited by M. Cohen, 11–14. London and New York, NY: Hodder Education/Oxford University Press.
________. 2009a. *New Essays on the Explanation of Action.* London: Palgrave Macmillan.
________. (2009b) 2024. 'Gods and Mental States: The Causation of Action in Ancient Tragedy and Modern Philosophy of Mind.' In Sandis 2009a, 358–85. As Reprinted in Sandis 2024, 127–45.
________. 2009c. 'Hume and "Motivating Reasons"'. In *Hume on Motivation and Virtue: New Essays*, edited by C. Pigden. Basingstoke: Palgrave Macmillan.
________. 2010a. 'The Experimental Turn and Ordinary Language'. *Essays in Philosophy* 11 (2): 181–96.
________. 2010b. 'Animal Ethics'. In *Ethics: A University Guide*, edited by R. H. Corrigan and M. E. Farrell, 21–39. Gloucester: Progressive Frontiers Press.
________. (2010c) 2024. 'The Man Who Mistook his Handlung for a Tat: Hegel on Oedipus and Other Tragic Thebans'. *Bulletin of the Hegel Society of Great Britain* 62:35–60. As Reprinted in Sandis 2024, 158–74.
________. 2011a. 'A Just Medium: Empathy and Detachment in Historical Understanding'. *Journal of the Philosophy of History* 5 (2): 179–200.
________. 2011b. 'Action, Reason, and the Passions'. In *The Bloomsbury Companion to Hume*, edited by A. Bailey and D. O'Brien, 199–213. London: Bloomsbury.
________. 2011c. 'Pouring New Wine into Old Skin: Hume's Necessary Connexions'. In *Causation and Modern Philosophy*, edited by K. Allen and T. Stoneham, 166–87. London: Routledge.
________. 2012a. *The Things We Do and Why We Do Them.* London: Palgrave Macmillan.
________. (2012b) 2024. 'The Objects of Action Explanation'. *Ratio* 25, no. 3 (September): 326–44. As Reprinted in Sandis 2024, 78–86.
________. 2012c. Review of *The Righteous Mind*, by J. Haidt. *Times Higher Education*, 10 May 2012.
________. 2014. 'Memento Mori Ring'. In *People Are Strange: Museum Guide to Understanding Others.* Edited by D. O'Brien. Produced for Understanding Others, Ashmolean Museum, Being Human Festival, 15 November 2014.
________. 2015a. 'Towards a Philosophy of Understanding'. *The Socrates Almanac*, 67–68.
________. (2015b) 2024. 'Motivated by the Gods: Compartmentalized Agency and Responsibility'. In *Agency and Responsibility*, edited by A. Buckareff, C. Moya and S. Rosell, 209–25. Basingstoke: Palgrave Macmillan. As Reprinted in Sandis 2024, 146–57.
________. 2016. 'Philosophy's Influence on Technology Design – and Why It Needs to Change'. *The Conversation*, 12 February 2016.
________. 2017a. 'An Honest Display of Fakery: Replicas and the Role of Museums'. In *Philosophy and Museums: Ethics, Aesthetics, and Ontology*, edited by V. Harrison, G. Kemp and A. Bergqvist, 1-9. Cambridge: Cambridge University Press.
________. (2017b) 2024. 'The Doing and the Deed: Action in Normative Ethics'. *Royal Institute of Philosophy Supplements* 80:105–26. As Reprinted in Sandis 2024, 175–86.

________. 2017c 'Robot Reasons'. *The Philosophers' Magazine* 79, 4th Quarter, 22–3.

________. 2018. 'Enchanted Action'. *The Philosophers' Magazine* 80, 1st Quarter (20th anniversary issue), 18–19.

________. 2019a. *Character and Causation: Hume's Philosophy of Action*. New York, NY: Routledge.

________. (2019b) 2024. 'Are Reasons Like Shampoo?'. In *Explanation in Action Theory and Historiography*, edited by G. Schumann, 146–64. London: Routledge. As Reprinted in Sandis 2024, 113–24.

________. 2019c. 'We Philosophers', *The Philosophers' Magazine* 84, 1st Quarter, 14–16.

________. 2022. 'Consider the Squirrel: Hume as Hinge Epistemologist'. In Moyal-Sharrock and Sandis 2022, 193–214.

________. 2023. 'No Theory in Marienbad'. In *Film Without Theory*, edited by C. Fox and B. Harrison, 67–81. London: Palgrave Macmillan.

________. 2024. *From Action to Ethics: A Pluralistic Approach to Reasons and Responsibility*. London: Bloomsbury.

Sandis, C., and R. Harper. 2017. 'We Don't Want AI That Can Understand Us – We'd Only End up Arguing'. *The Conversation*, 21 August 2017.

Sandis, C., and C. Tejedor. 2017. 'Wittgenstein on Causation and Induction'. In Glock and Hyman 2017, 576–86.

Saul, J. M. 2012. *Lying, Misleading, and What is Said: An Exploration in the Philosophy of Language and Ethics*. Oxford: Oxford University Press.

Scammell, M. 2016. 'A Different Darkness at Noon'. *The New York Review of Books*, 7 April 2016.

Schama, S. 2006. *The Power of Art*. London: BBC Books.

Scheman, N. (1990) 1996. 'The Unavoidability of Gender'. *Journal of Social Philosophy* 2 (2–3): 34–39. As Reprinted in *Women, Knowledge, and Reality*, 2nd ed., edited by A. Garry and M. Pearsall. London: Routledge, 26–33.

Scholl, A. A. (1957) 1962. 'Something Makes Itself Known'. As translated by M. Hamburger in *Modern German Poetry, 1910–1960: An Anthology with Verse Translations*, 357–8. London: MacGibbon and Kee.

Schroeder, S. 2019. 'God, Lions, and Englishwomen: Wittgenstein on Understanding People'. In *Human Understanding as a Problem*, edited by J. P. Galvez and M. Gaffal, 171–84. Berlin: De Gruyter. As Reprinted in Schroeder 2024, 75–86.

———. 2024. *Language, Mind, and Value: Essays on Wittgenstein*. London: Anthem Press.

Schuessler, J. 2014. 'Book Portrays Eichmann as Evil, but Not Banal.' *The New York Times*, 2 September 2014.

Schulte, J. 2018. 'Body and Soul'. In *The Cambridge Companion to Wittgenstein*, 2nd ed., edited by H. Sluga and D. G. Stern, 305–31. Cambridge: Cambridge University Press.

Scruton, R. 1976. 'Self-Knowledge and Intention'. *Proceedings of the Aristotelian Society*, n.s., 77: 87–106.

Sebeok, T. A., ed. 1964. *Approaches to Semiotics*. The Hague: Mouton and Co.

________. 1976. *Contributions to the Doctrine of Signs*. Bloomington, IN: Indiana University Press.

Segal, E. A. 2018. *Social Empathy: The Art of Understanding Others*. New York, NY: Columbia University Press.

Shakespeare, W. n.d., ca. 1600. *Macbeth*. In *Folio* of 1623. London: Edward Blount and William and Isaac Jaggard.

Sharpe, L. 2005. *Creatures Like Us?* Exeter: Imprint Academic.

Shuji, O. 2017. 魂でもいいから, そばにいて: 3・11後の霊体験を聞 [Stay With Me, Even as a Spirit: Listening to Spiritual Experiences after 3/11]. Tōkyō: Shinchōsha.

Shweder, R. A. 1991. *Thinking Through Cultures: Expeditions in Cultural Psychology.* Boston, MA: Harvard University Press.

Smet, A. F., and Byrne, R. W. 2013. 'African Elephants Can Use Human Pointing Cues to Find Hidden Food'. *Current Biology* 23, no. 20 (October): 2033–37.

________. 2020. 'African Elephants Interpret a Trunk Gesture as a Clue to Direction of Interest'. *Current Biology* 30, no. 16 (August): R926–R927.

Smith, M., and P. Pettit. 1997. 'Parfit's "P"'. In *Reading Parfit*, edited by J. Dancy, 71–95. Oxford: Blackwell.

Soames, S. 2005. *Philosophical Analysis in the Twentieth Century*, vol. 2. Princeton, NJ: Princeton University Press.

Spaulding, S. 2018. *How We Understand Others: Philosophy as Social Cognition.* London: Routledge.

Spranger, E. (1914) 1928. *Lebensformen. Halle: Niemeyer. Translated as Types of Men by P. J. W. Pigors.* New York, NY: G. E. Stechert Company.

St Clair, W. 2014. 'Looking at the Acropolis of Athens from Modern Times to Antiquity'. In *Cultural Heritage Ethics: Between Theory and Practice*, edited by C. Sandis, 57–102. Cambridge: Open Book Publishers.

Steiner, S. 1975. *After Babel: Aspects of Language and Translation.* Oxford: Oxford University Press.

Stekeler-Weithofer, P. 2019. 'A Hegelian Logic of "Us": Implicit Forms and Explicit Representations of Actions and Practices'. *Hegel Bulletin* 40 (3): 374–97.

Stern, D. 2001. 'Was Wittgenstein a Jew?' In *Wittgenstein: Philosophy and Biography*, edited by J. Klagge. Cambridge: Cambridge University Press, 237–72.

Stevenson, R. L. 1887. *Memories and Portraits.* London: Chatto and Windus.

Stewart, M. A. 1977. 'Locke, Steiner and Understanding'. In Vesey 1977, 20–45.

Stoop, A. 1962. Review of *Free Action*, by A. I. Melden. *Australasian Journal of Philosophy* 40 (2): 247–49.

Stoutland, F. 1970. 'The Logical Connection Argument'. *American Philosophical Quarterly* 7: 117–29.

________. 1999. 'Intentionalists and Davidson on Rational Explanation'. In *Actions, Norms, Values*, edited by G. Meggle, 191–208. Berlin: Walter de Gruyter.

Strand, M. 1964. 'Something Is in the Air'. As Reprinted in *Collected Poems.* New York, NY: Knopf Doubleday, 2014.

Strawson, G. 2010. *Mental Reality*, 2nd revised ed. Boston, MA: MIT Press.

Strawson, P. F. 1959a. *Individuals: An Essay in Descriptive Metaphysics.* London: Methuen.

________. 1959b. Review of *Laws and Explanation in History*, by William Dray. Mind 68 (270): 265–68.

________. 1966. 'Aesthetic Appraisal and Works of Art'. *The Oxford Review* 3. As Reprinted in *Freedom and Resentment and Other Essays*, 2nd ed. London: Routledge.

Stueber, K. R. 2006. *Rediscovering Empathy: Agency, Folk Psychology, and the Human Sciences.* Cambridge, MA: MIT Press.

Stump, E. 2010. *Wandering in Darkness: Narrative and the Problem of Suffering.* Oxford: Oxford University Press.

Suchman, L. A. 1987. *Plans and Situated Actions: The Problem of Human-Machine Communication.* Cambridge: Cambridge University Press.

Sullivan, H. 2018. 'Never Nice? Love, Loneliness and Poetry in the Correspondence of Sylvia Plath'. *Times Literary Supplement* 6031, 2 November 2018, 3–4.

Tanney, J. 2009a. 'Gilbert Ryle'. *The Stanford Encyclopedia of Philosophy* (Winter 2009 edition), edited by Edward N. Zalta.

________. 2009b. 'Reasons as Non-causal, Context-placing Explanations'. In Sandis 2009a, 94–111.

Taylor, C. 1979. 'Action as Expression'. In *Intention and Intentionality: Essays for G.E.M. Anscombe*, edited by C. Diamond and J. Teichman, 73–90. Hassocks: Harvester Press.

________. 2010. 'Hegel and the Philosophy of Action'. As Reprinted in Laitinen and Sandis 2010a, 22–41.

Taylor, R. 1970. *Good and Evil*. London: Macmillan.

Teichman, J. 1974. *The Mind and the Soul*. London: Routledge and Kegan Paul.

Tejedor, C. 2014. *The Early Wittgenstein on Metaphysics, Natural Science, Language and Value*. London: Routledge.

________. 2023. 'Intercultural Understanding, Epistemic Interaction and Polyphonic Cultures'. In *Intercultural Understanding After Wittgenstein*, edited by C. Carmona, D. Perez-Chico and C. Tejedor, 21–36. London: Anthem Press.

Thomson, R. 1959. Review of *The Concept of Motivation*, by R. S. Peters. Philosophy 34, no. 128 (January): 72–3.

Tilghman, B. R. 1983. 'Understanding People and Understanding Art'. *Akten des 8. Internationalen Wittgenstein Symposiums*, 15–21 August 1983, 153–92. Wien: Verlag Hölder-Pichler-Tempsky.

Tor, S. 2014. 'Sextus and Wittgenstein on the End of Justification'. *International Journal for the Study of Skepticism* 4 (2): 81–108.

Tyler, T. n.d. 'Becoming What We Are'. Unpublished manuscript.

Uidhir, C. M. 2013. *Art and Art Attempts*. Oxford: Oxford University Press.

Vallée, R. 1996. 'Who Are We?' *Canadian Journal of Philosophy* 26 (2): 211–30.

Van der Dussen, J. W. 1995. 'The Philosophical Context of Collingwood's Re-enactment Theory'. *International Studies in Philosophy* 27 (2): 81–99.

Van der Linden, D., B. I. Davidson, O. Hirsch-Matsioulas and A. Zamansky. 2022. 'On the Role of Technology in Human–Dog Relationships: A Future of Nightmares or Dreams'. *IEEE Transactions on Technology and Society*. In press.

Verbinski, G., dir. 2002. *The Ring*. USA: MacDonald/Parkes Productions.

Vesey, G., ed. 1977. *Communication and Understanding*. Royal Institute of Philosophy Lectures, vol. X. Hassocks: The Harvester Press Limited.

Vico, G. (1725, 1744) 1999. *New Science: Principles of the New Science Concerning the Common Nature of Nations*. 3rd revised ed. Translated by D. Marsh. London: Penguin.

Vittorio, G. 2001. 'The "Shared Manifold" Hypothesis: From Mirror Neurons to Empathy'. *Journal of Consciousness Studies* 8 (5–6): 33–50.

von Savigny, E. 1991. 'Common Behaviour of Many a Kind: Philosophical Investigations section 206'. In *Wittgenstein's Philosophical Investigations*, edited by R. Arrington and H.-J. Glock, 105–19. London: Routledge.

von Wright, G. H. 1955. 'Ludwig Wittgenstein: A Biographical Sketch'. *The Philosophical Review* 64, no. 4 (October): 527–45.

________. 1971. *Explanation and Understanding*. London: Routledge and Kegan Paul.

Webb, S. J. 2005. 'Aslan's Voice: C. S. Lewis and the Magic of Sound'. In Bassham and Walls 2005, 3–14.

Weberman, A. J. 2005. *Dylan to English Dictionary*. North Charleston, SC BookSurge Publishing.

Weil, S. (1959) 1978. *Lectures on Philosophy*. Translated by H. Price. Cambridge: Cambridge University Press.

White, A. R. 1967. *The Philosophy of Mind*. New York, NY: A. A. Knopf.

________. 1972. 'What We Believe'. In *Studies in the Philosophy of Mind, American Philosophical Quarterly* monograph series, no. 6, edited by N. Rescher, 69–84. Oxford: Blackwell.

Whitman, W. 1856. *Leaves of Grass*, 2nd ed. Brooklyn, NY: Fowler and Wells.

Wilkes, C. V. 1978. *Physicalism*. London: Routledge and Kegan Paul.

Williams, B. (1974). 'Wittgenstein and Idealism'. In *Understanding Wittgenstein*, edited by G. Vesey (Royal Institute of Philosophy Lectures 7, 1972–73). London: Palgrave Macmillan. As Reprinted in *Moral Luck*. Cambridge: Cambridge University Press, 144–63.

________. 1981. *Moral Luck*. Cambridge: Cambridge University Press.

________. 2006. 'An Essay on Collingwood'. In *The Sense of the Past: Essays in the History of Philosophy*, edited by M. Burnyeat, 341-60. Princeton, NJ: Princeton University Press.

Williams, P. 2019. 'Trembling with Thought: Immersed in the World of the Former First Lady'. *Times Literary Supplement* 6045, 8 February 2019, 9–11.

Wilson, A. N. 2004. *My Name is Legion*. London: Hutchinson.

Winch, P. 1958. *The Idea of a Social Science*. London: Routledge and Kegan Paul.

________. (1964) 1972. 'Understanding a Primitive Society'. *American Philosophical Quarterly* 1 (4): 307–24. As Reprinted in Winch 1972, 8–49.

________. 1972. *Ethics and Action*. London: Routledge and Kegan Paul.

________. 1987. *Trying to Make Sense*. Oxford: Basil Blackwell.

Wisdom, J. (1952) 1965. *Other Minds*. 2nd ed. Oxford: Oxford University Press.

________. 1965. *Paradox and Discovery*. Oxford: Basil Blackwell.

Wittgenstein, L. (1921). *Tractatus Logico-Philosophicus* [TLP]. Translated by C.K. Ogden.

________. 1953. *Philosophical Investigations* [PI]. Translated by G. E. M. Anscombe. Oxford: Blackwell. This translation is only used where explicitly mentioned.

________. (1953) 2009. *Philosophical Investigations* [PI]. Translated by G. E. M. Anscombe. Revised 4th edition by P. M. S. Hacker and J. Schulte, including 'Philosophy of Psychology: A Fragment' [PPF]. Oxford: Wiley Blackwell.

________. 1959. *On Certainty* [OC]. Translated by G. E. M. Anscombe. Oxford: Blackwell.

________. 1961a. *Notebooks 1914–1916* [NB]. Translated by G. E. M. Anscombe. Oxford: Blackwell.

________. 1961b. *Tractatus Logico-Philosophicus* - Revised translation by D. F. Pears and B. F. McGuinness [TLP-R]. London: Routledge.

________. 1967. *Zettel* [Z]. Translated by G. E. M. Anscombe. Oxford: Blackwell.

________. 1977. *Remarks on Colour* [ROC]. Oxford: Blackwell.

________. (1979) 2018. *Remarks on Frazer's Golden Bough* [RFGB]. Translated by A. C. Milnes, revised by R. Rhees. Herefordshire: Brynmill. As Reprinted in da Col and Palmié 2018, 29–75.

________. 1982. *Last Writings on the Philosophy of Psychology*, vol. 1 [LW]. Edited by G. H. von Wright and H. Nyman. Translated by C. G. Luckhardt and M. A. E. Aue. Oxford: Blackwell.

________. 1988. *Remarks on the Philosophy of Psychology*, vol. 2 [RPP II]. Edited by G. H. von Wright and H. Nyman. Translated by G. G. Luckhardt and M. A. E. Aue. Oxford: Blackwell.

________. 1998. *Culture and Value* [CV]. Revised 2nd ed. Edited by H. Nyman and G. H. von Wright. Revised by A. Pichler. Translated by P. Winch. Oxford: Blackwell.

________. 2000. *Nachlass: The Bergen Electronic Edition* [BEE], inc. MSS 124, 135-7, 160, 165, 167; TS 232. Oxford: Oxford University Press.

________. 2005. *Big Typescript: TS 213*. Edited and translated by C. G. Luckhardt & M. A. E. Aue. Oxford: Blackwell

Wolfe, J., ed. 2011. *Journal of Inklings Studies* 1, no. 2 (October): Special Issue on C. S. Lewis and G. E. M. Anscombe.

Wollheim, R. 1968. *Art and Its Objects*. Cambridge: Cambridge University Press.

________. 1983. *On Art and the Mind*. Cambridge, MA: Harvard University Press.

Wood, J. 2005. *Nick Broomfield: Documenting Icons*. London: Faber and Faber.

Wrede, W. (1901) 1971. *The Messianic Secret*. Translated by J. C. G. Grieg. Cambridge: James Clarke and Co.

Wyatt, R. 1997. 'Free Will and Testament'. Genius. Accessed 18 July 2024. https://genius.com/Robert-wyatt-free-will-and-testament-lyrics.

Yanagita, K. (1910) 2010. *The Legends of Tōno*. 100th anniversary ed. Translated by R. A. Morse. Lanham, MD: Lexington Books.

Zahavi, D. 2014. *Self and Other: Exploring Subjectivity, Empathy, and Shame*. Oxford: Oxford University Press.

INDEX

www.ingramcontent.com/pod-product-compliance
Lightning Source LLC
LaVergne TN
LVHW090617090826
845264LV00022B/112

* 9 7 8 1 8 0 1 3 6 0 5 3 1 *